J

Date Dr

BIPt
9/22/93
2u

RENAISSANCE THEORY OF LOVE

THE CONTEXT OF GIORDANO BRUNO'S *Eroici furori*

JOHN CHARLES NELSON

Renaissance Theory of Love

THE CONTEXT OF
GIORDANO BRUNO'S *Eroici furori*

NEW YORK 1958
COLUMBIA UNIVERSITY PRESS

Preface

THE desirability of studying Bruno's *Eroici furori* in the light of
two traditional literary forms—prose commentaries on verses and
Platonic love treatises—was suggested to me by Professor Paul
Oskar Kristeller. My interest in Platonism began with the reading
of *The Republic* in his Humanities A class in Columbia College in
1942. In the course of my writing he made valuable suggestions
on numerous points. My gratitude to him is very deep.

I wish to thank Professor Enrico de' Negri, a number of whose
ideas—particularly about Dante's love theories and Bruno's relation
to the poetry of the *seicento*—I have utilized.

I wish also to thank Miss Elisabeth L. Shoemaker of Columbia
University Press for her careful editing of the manuscript and
Professor Louis F. Solano for helping me with proofreading. Final
responsibility for errors is mine.

A word about the translations of quotations from Italian and
Latin which are included for the convenience of some readers: I
have tried to make them as literal as possible, so that the original
quotations, which are also given, may be understood with their
aid. With minor exceptions, I have not re-edited the selections from
early editions: hence the antiquated spelling and punctuation in
some of them.

JOHN CHARLES NELSON

March 13, 1958

Contents

To BRUNA

Introduction

It is surprising that the Italian Renaissance produced no philosopher comparable in importance to the writers and artists of the period. Although there is perhaps no objective criterion for comparison in the arts between cultures so different as that of ancient Greece and Renaissance Italy, critics do not hesitate to point to a new Homer and a new Phidias in Florence. But one searches in vain for an Aristotle or a Plato. The dynamic force in this field seems to have been lacking. At first the respect for ancient authority was too great to permit more than a reworking and reconciliation of classical and Christian doctrines. The polemical struggle against these two bonds seems to have sapped the creative energy of the most daring and acute minds, leaving but little verve for the creation and systemization of new philosophies.

In the fifteenth century there was an enthusiastic and pervasive spirit of classical research. The discovery of ancient texts was the order of the day. The works of Plato and the extant works of Aristotle were translated or retranslated together with those of Greek poets and playwrights, historians and orators, while many writings of Cicero and other Latin authors—Lucretius, Tacitus, Plautus— were found and edited and republished. The world of letters was engaged in a gigantic mining enterprise, with the classical world as its mine. Grammar, rhetoric, history, poetry, and moral philosophy—the five *studia humanitatis* enumerated by Pope Nicholas V —meant primarily the discovery and assimilation and perhaps the emulation of Roman and Greek letters. Only a few men in the fifteenth century—Lorenzo Valla, Marsilio Ficino, and Giovanni Pico della Mirandola—transcend the primarily literary and scholarly objectives of Renaissance humanism. However, their originality and creativity is disciplined and limited by their respect for the Christian-classical heritage.

Giordano Bruno did not, like Ficino in the preceding century and Francesco Patrizzi in his own times, call himself a Platonist. His writings, especially the *Figuratio Aristotelici physici auditus* (1586), show that his knowledge of Aristotle's works was comparable to that of Aristotelian philosophers of the Renaissance. His approach is similar to that of the natural philosophers—Cardano, Telesio, and Campanella—who upheld independent investigation against Aristotelian authority. His thought derives a great deal from the humanists of the preceding century and a half: a belief in the primacy and power of the intellect, in the idea that true wisdom is rooted in the doctrines of the ancients, and in the naturalness of religion in man, who himself is a microcosm in which divine and earthly elements are conjoined, and the desire to revise and systematize ancient wisdom. His philosophy extends the anthropocentrism of Marsilio Ficino and Giovanni Pico della Mirandola. His viewpoint, however, is more comprehensive, more cosmic than that of the humanist editors and translators, and even among fifteenth and early sixteenth century humanists it is difficult to find anyone with his audacity and spirit of independence. Marsilio Ficino had realized Petrarch's dream of replacing Aristotle's authority with that of Plato. Bruno not only rejected the authority of Aristotle, but tended far more than Ficino and Pico to reject authority in general. His acknowledgment of the authority of dogma and discipline in the Roman Catholic Church was severely conditioned by two reservations: first, that Church control, doctrinal and moral, was appropriate and necessary to the mass of "vulgar" persons incapable of self-direction; and second, that the hierarchy should give him a free hand to pursue his speculations, so long as he acknowledged the valadity of Christian dogma and discipline within the realm—far short of cosmic—which he considered proper to it.

Bruno's attitude toward the Christian-classical synthesis of his predecessors, both theologians and humanists, is acutely critical.

He wished to replace adherence to authority by free speculative inquiry. His many quotations from classical and pre-classical thought are not adduced to confute or support accepted beliefs, but to support or direct his own investigations. His speculations are fertile with ideas and points of departure for later generations.

The primary purpose of this study is to further the understanding of Giordano Bruno's writings by an analysis of one of his most important works, the dialogue *De gli eroici furori,* in its relation to the genres of *trattati d'amore,* or Platonic love treatises of the late fifteenth and sixteenth centuries; and of prose commentaries upon sonnets or other verses, to both of which categories the *Eroici furori* belongs. Consequently this dialogue is also examined in its relation to the other philosophical writings of Bruno. The examination of love treatises, however, in the conviction that they have not been adequately analyzed heretofore in their doctrinal detail and inter-relation, is carried beyond the bare minimum of description necessary for the understanding of the *Eroici furori.* Their analysis, therefore, constitutes a secondary goal of this study. It will be seen that the strong influence of the tradition of love treatises upon the *Eroici furori* accounts for the marked Neoplatonism of this dialogue, which is stronger than in most of Bruno's works and is in contrast to some of them. The literary importance of the *Eroici furori* for the poetry of the seventeenth century, quite neglected by Bruno scholars, will also be demonstrated.

Critics of Bruno have not had an easy task. In their zeal to counteract the Church's condemnation of the man and his works, which all but obliterated his memory for the better part of three centuries, some scholars attributed to him a greater perspicacity than he had. Others, like Olschki, deceived by the disorganization and frequent inconsistency of his writings, failed to detect the authentic flame of genius. He has been hailed as a developer of such diverse and comprehensive systems as monadology, pantheism, evolution, and relativity; he has been portrayed as the forerunner of Galileo, of Descartes, of Spinoza, of Leibnitz. Frequently the scholars have been motivated either by an anti-clerical bias or by a zeal to justify the Church's condemnation and execution of Bruno. In the mid-twentieth century he continues to provoke fierce polemics regarding both his condemnation by the Church and his efficacy as a thinker. Gradually, however, scholars have defined his contribution and discovered his inadequacies with increasing insight and thoroughness.

Bruno's writings cover a wide range of subjects and do not constitute a system. In addition to his philosophical works, he wrote treatises on the logical system of Raymond Lully, mnemonics, mathematics, and magic; commentaries on Aristotle's physics; and the satirical comedy, *Il candelaio* (1582). His most important works are the Italian dialogues published in London: *De la causa, principio e uno* (1584), which discusses the fundamental divine nature and phenomena of matter and form, the constituent elements of the universe; the cosmological treatises, *La cena de le ceneri* (1584) and *De l'infinito, universo e mondi* (1584); the moral dialogue, *Spaccio de la bestia trionfante* (1584); *De gli eroici furori* (1585); and the trilogy in Latin verse and prose, published in Frankfurt in 1591, *De Triplici minimo et mensura; De monade numero et figura;* and *De immenso et innumerabilibus.*

Bruno is not a less interesting writer because of his lack of system. Some apparently contradictory aspects of his thought— e.g., immanence and transcendence—are in the last analysis complementary. In any case self-contradiction does not necessarily imply poverty of thought—as witness Plato and Aristotle, among others. Bruno is a fascinating figure to study: his cultural importance is many-sided. Anti-academic if not anti-literary, he is immensely erudite. Possessed of a phenomenal memory, he incorporates this ability in a mnemonic system too cumbersome to be of advantage to any disciple. Although he is a philosopher by vocation, the literary ramifications of his work sometimes seem to overshadow its philosophical importance. An enthusiast of the physical cosmos, he seizes upon the Copernican theory to further his attack upon the finite, geocentric system of Aristotle, whom he sees as a trifling man of letters, a pedant. He identifies himself with the pristine energy of pre-Socratic natural philosophers, whose mutual contradictions he often overlooks, and he takes it upon himself to vindicate their teachings against the falsification and subversion of a petty, jealous, unintuitive Aristotle, whom generations of pedants and vulgar minds have sanctioned as the ultimate formulator of truth. Inebriated with his concept of God in nature or nature deified, he yet postulates a divinity far, far removed from the world of human knowledge. In institutionalized Christian religion he sees merely the necessary regulation of the masses incapable of thought. Constitutionally a heretic, he is ready to acknowledge the Church in its historical functions; he shows great respect for St. Thomas Aquinas; some of his severest diatribes are reserved for the reformers, especially Calvin. But he wishes to preserve his own spiritual and intellectual freedom from external restraint of any kind. He is an *accademico di nulla accademia*. Severely intolerant of many viewpoints different from his own in philosophy and religion, he is in turn, and sometimes simultaneously, anticlerical, anti-Protestant, and anti-Jewish.

Clearly such a man should not be made a symbol of tolerance. What is dynamic and courageous in his attitude and conduct is the fierce determination with which he pursued his goal of unfettered philosophical investigation of nature. That undertaking indeed has made him a symbol of academic and intellectual freedom worthy of our gratitude and admiration to this day.

His life, like his writings, is consumed by his attempt at self-assertion in the face of institutionalized authoritarian discipline, religious, civil, and academic. In 1921 Vincenzo Spampanato published a definitive account of his life, as exhaustive as documents then available allowed. Further information about his trial was published by the Vatican in 1942 in Angelo Mercati's book, *Il sommario del processo di Giordano Bruno*.

Bruno was born at Nola, near Naples, in January or February 1548.[1] He studied at the *studium generale* of Naples; however, he attributed his principal instruction in philosophy to the Augustinian Fra Teofilo da Vairano, under whom he also studied in that city. On June 16, 1566, Bruno took his vows in the Dominican order at the Convent of Saint Domenic, which housed the *studium generale*. In 1572, at the prescribed age of twenty-four, he was promoted to the priesthood. Four years later, his penchant for classical

---

[1] The biographical facts here presented are based primarily upon Spampanato's research.

and heretical authors having come to the attention of his superiors, he was brought to trial for heterodoxy and fled to Rome, where he left the order. From that point onward his life is marked by intermittent travel, the external expression of inward dissatisfaction and intellectual agitation. A comparison to Dante's exile is not amiss. Bruno is successively at Noli, near Genoa, Savona, Venice, and Bergamo, briefly, before going to Geneva via France. Then we see him in Toulouse, in Paris, at Oxford, again in Paris, at Wittenberg, Prague, Helmstedt, and Frankfurt, before returning to Venice in 1592, after some fifteen years.

Everywhere he seems to have won both friends and enemies, the latter frequently having the last word; his bold and defiant manner constantly brought him into conflict with church and university authorities. In Geneva he was tried and disciplined, to his bitter disappointment, for having written a pamphlet which charged the professor De la Faye with committing twenty errors in a single lesson. Years later in Helmstedt in 1589 he was "excommunicated" by the Lutheran Church superintendent. Thus he seems to have achieved the unique distinction—dubious or commendable according to one's point of view—of being excommunicated or severely disciplined by all three of the major western Churches, Roman Catholic, Calvinist, and Lutheran.

At the *studium* in Toulouse he won a position as lecturer in philosophy after graduating as Master of Arts. At the Sorbonne in Paris he acquired an enthusiastic following by his rich and imaginative extemporaneous lectures illustrating the art of memory. He debated briefly at Oxford. The furor provoked in England by the publication of the *Cena de le ceneri,* mocking English learning and manners somewhat in the style of the *Candelaio,* is well known. He left the country in 1585, two years after his arrival there, with the French ambassador Mauvissiere, in whose employ he had been. In Paris in May 1586 he provoked the ire of professors whose Aristotelian doctrines he challenged. He found a more liberal atmosphere for a while at the University of Wittenberg, where he taught philosophy from 1586 to 1588. His "Valedictory Oration" delivered in March 1588 praises the spirit of academic freedom there. At Frankfurt in 1592 he inadvisedly accepted the invitation of Giovanni Mocenigo to come to Venice and teach that young nobleman his art of memory. Mocenigo in 1593 betrayed him to the Venetian inquisition. His trial, begun in Venice and soon transferred to Rome, was protracted for a period of over six years. Convicted on numerous charges of heresy, apostasy, blasphemy, and misconduct, he repeatedly refused to recant and was burned at the stake on February 17, 1600, in the Campo de' Fiori, Rome. Until the last he seems to have hoped that he could win the Pope to his way of thinking. In 1889, on the place of his execution, a monument was erected in his honor. He is a more controversial figure today than he was at the time of his trial and execution.

The most thorough survey and study of Bruno's writings undertaken to date is that by Felice Tocco in *Le opere latine di Giordano Bruno esposte e confrontate con le italiane;* and in the supplementary work, *Le fonti più recenti della filosofia del Bruno* (in *Rendiconti della Reale Accademia dei Lincei, Classe di Scienze Morali, Storiche e Filologiche, Serie Quinta,* I, 503–38; 585–622), which, despite the author's intention to remedy the lack of attention to Bruno's Renaissance sources imputed to his first work, fails to discover the important contribution of Marsilio Ficino to Bruno's thought (*ibid.,* p. 535). These studies and subsequent works by Spampanato, Gentile, and others largely supersede the previous scholarship of such authors as Bartholmess, Clemens, and Berti. Tocco in his major work on Bruno divides the Nolan's writings into five groups and examines each work in its turn: Lullian works; mnemonic works; expository and critical works; constructive works; and the philosophy of Bruno. In the fifth part he analyzes Bruno's philosophy in relation to his professed pre-Socratic sources. He distinguishes three phases in Bruno's writings: an original Neoplatonic mysticism, clearly apparent in *De umbris idearum;* Eleatic, pantheistic monism in *De la causa* and other Italian dialogues; and a final atomism, in *De minimo* and *De monade.*

Of the final development which he posits, he writes as follows:

Accettando l'atomismo, spoglio del suo carattere materialistico, il Bruno non credeva di contraddire al monismo eleatico, a quel modo che nessuna sostanziale differenza poneva tra il monismo eleatico e l'eracliteo; ma certo si allontanava di molto dal platonismo e più ancora dal neoplatonismo delle prime opere. E però nell'ultimo dei suoi poemi, che è pure l'ultima delle opere filosofiche da lui pubblicate, combatte con maggiore acredine che non nella *Causa* la teorica delle idee, e della subordinazione e della scala degli esseri non vuol più sentire parlare; perchè a tutti attribuisce lo stesso valore, essendo tutti della stessa qualità al pari degli atomi democritei.[2]

Accepting atomism devoid of its materialistic character, Bruno did not think he was contradicting Eleatic monism; similarly he posited no substantial difference between Eleatic monism and that of Heraclitus. But certainly he strayed a long way from the Platonism and still farther from the Neoplatonism of his early works. Consequently in the last of his poems, which is also the last of the philosophical works that he published, he combats the theory of ideas more acrimoniously than in the *Causa*, and will hear no more of the subordination and scale of beings. To all he attributes the same value, for all, like the Democritan atoms, are of the same quality.

The thesis of development in Bruno's writings, later taken up and reworked by Antonio Corsano, is a challenging, but hazardous theme. If the Latin trilogy is taken as Bruno's final statement and as a total rejection of Neoplatonism, how does one account for the return to Neoplatonic themes such as negative theology and the ontological hierarchy *Deus seu mens, intellectus seu idea, amor seu anima mundi* in the *Summa terminorum metaphysicorum*, written in 1591 and published in 1595, after the Latin poems, which, despite its title, is not purely expository? (Indeed, Corsano himself calls it *la estrema formulazione del pensiero del Bruno, Il pensiero di Giordano Bruno . . .* , p. 274.)

Furthermore, in the intermediate stage attributed by Tocco to the Italian dialogues, when Bruno allegedly was disavowing the earlier Neoplatonism of the *De umbris,* we find, a year after the "monistic," "materialistic," "pantheistic" *De la Causa* (1584), the thorough, undisputed Neoplatonism of the *Eroici furori* (1585). On the other hand, we find explicitly anti-Platonic passages in the *Cabala del cavallo pegaseo* (1585)[3] and a pervasive indifference to divine madness and ascetic ideals in the *Spaccio della Bestia Trionfante* (1584).

[2] Tocco, *Le opere latine di Giordano Bruno . . .* , p. 361.
[3] Bruno, *Opere italiane*, II, 270.

Tocco's examination of the individual works of Bruno is indeed sound and fruitful. The trend of Bruno's thoughts which he discovers is valid, if taken only in a general way, for all the internal divergencies in Bruno's writings cannot be explained by reference to the historical development of his thought. What seems in Bruno to be repudiation of one doctrine in favor of another is often merely a variation of emphasis or even of the author's mood.

Erminio Troilo, in *La filosofia di Giordano Bruno,* sustains the thesis of Bruno's development from Neoplatonic "mysticism" to Pre-Socratic materialism. He emphasizes the naturalistic side of Bruno's thought—*Deus sive Natura*—exclusively, and makes him out to be an anti-metaphysicist. Troilo takes scarcely any notice of the *Eroici furori.*

Giovanni Gentile's approach to Bruno departs from the meticulous philological method of Tocco to appraise Bruno's importance in the history of culture. His exception to the work of Tocco, whose individual analyses of Bruno's works he values highly, is that in his attempt to identify Bruno's myriad sources and the line of development of his speculation, Tocco misses the inherent spiritual unity of Bruno's message and its historical significance. Tocco is "more intent upon looking at the trees than at the forest" (Gentile, *Il pensiero italiano del rinascimento,* p. 313). Gentile pays particular attention to Bruno's ideas on the relation of philosophy to religion. His *Giordano Bruno e il pensiero del rinascimento,* published in 1920, was successively expanded in scope until the third edition was entitled *Il pensiero italiano del rinascimento.* The three chapters on Bruno in this work are a major contribution to the establishment of Bruno's true and proper role in the unfolding of the Renaissance. To Gentile Bruno is the hero of the Renaissance, who initiated the modern era with his proclamation of freedom of thought, an ideal consecrated by his martyrdom, which Gentile sees as a "necessary consequence of the progress of the human spirit" (*ibid.,* p. 293).

In altri termini, la nuova filosofia e la nuova scienza si distinguono dalla fede, non per mettere questa al di sopra di sè ed attribuirle il privilegio della verità ad esse irragiungibile, e a cui pur esse mirano; anzi per negarle ogni valore rispetto ai fini a cui la filosofia e la scienza s'indirizzano (*ibid.*).

In other words, the new philosophy and the new science are distinguished from faith not by putting the latter above themselves and attributing to it the privilege of truth unattainable by them, although they too aim at it; but rather by denying it any value in regard to the ends sought by philosophy and science.

Bruno, as does Galileo shortly afterward, chooses to believe in his own intelligence rather than in "a revelation which is the act of someone else" (*ibid.*).

Questa la nuova coscienza scientifica, che si accinge a guardare il reale con occhio puro d'ogni nebbia. Questo l'inizio dell'età moderna per il pensiero filosofico (*ibid.*).

This is the new scientific consciousness, which prepares to look at reality with clearest gaze. This is the beginning of the modern age for philosophic thought.

Gentile sees in Bruno a precursor of Spinoza's pantheism. He declares that Bruno's real object is the contemplation of the unity of nature; not the *mens super omnia,* but nature, the *Deus in rebus* of Spinoza (*ibid.,* p. 292). Bruno's real God is immanent rather than transcendent, although he does not deny the existence of the latter (p. 319).

Gentile recognizes the importance of Florentine Platonism in the formation of Bruno's thought (p. 164). He sees in the "natural or cosmic point of view" of Bruno and the "Renaissance man" the amplification of the "human point of view" of fourteenth- and fifteenth-century humanists (pp. 17–18).

Despite his caution to students of Bruno in the prefatory Bibliographical Note (p. xii) that Bruno is above the profaning strife of parties, politics, and particular and practical ends, Gentile himself seems to draw Bruno into the political arena in the very section of the book where he again asserts that Bruno is above mundane political and clerical skirmishes. In Chapter VIII, "Giordano Bruno," he derives support for the non-separation of state and religion in twentieth century society from Bruno's declaration that religion is necessary for the government of common people (pp. 266–268). Gentile's own views of the relation of religion to philosophy are markedly similar to those of Bruno.

Leonardo Olschki, in *Giordano Bruno,* sees in the mass of

Bruno's writings neither the historical development that Tocco and other scholars sought to reveal nor the spiritual unity discerned by Gentile, but a chaos too confused to express any consistent doctrine or message. This judgment is surely exaggerated and unjust. However, many of his particular observations on Bruno's work are keen and stimulating. He does not deny to Bruno an extraordinary genius, but sees him wasting it through lack of self-discipline and self-knowledge (p. 104). He finds Bruno erudite but unoriginal, his life and works a conglomeration of insoluble contradictions, his life more tragic than his death. Bruno has no doctrine of knowledge, but only an extraordinarily confused and discordant mixture of aphorisms (p. 21). He combines his various sources arbitrarily, without critical historical consciousness (p. 40).

Nel suo oscillare tra teismo e panteismo, tra mistica emanatistica e naturalismo, quell'Uno, quell'Assoluto gli rimase un mistero . . . (pp. 47–48: In his wavering between theism and pantheism, between emanative mysticism and naturalism, that One, that Absolute remained a mystery to him . . .).

He fails to recognize the antinomy of transcendence and immanence, or to see that his deification of matter renders superfluous the concept of a world soul (p. 52). He misunderstands Aristotle. His mathematics is an aberration (*ibid.*, p. 59). His phantasy is never creative, but only receptive, interpretive, combinative. He lacks not only a system, but the organic coherence of an intuition of the world (p. 91).

Con questo garbuglio di intuizioni e concetti non si può ricomporre una concezione del mondo coerente . . . (p. 69: With this hodgepodge of intuitions and concepts one cannot reconstruct a coherent concept of the world . . .).

In short, Olschki sees in Bruno not the inauguration of a new age in philosophy which Gentile hailed—with good reason—but the crisis and dissolution of humanism (p. 106). Equally unjust is his evaluation of Bruno's death: that he died not for a philosophic faith, but for aspirations which no one could understand; and that his work would have been a simple episode in the history of thought had not the sentence of his judges consecrated him and elevated him to a symbol. Olschki entirely overlooks the significance of the fact that Bruno himself chose to die rather than forsake his goal of freeing philosophy from the judgment and control of the Church.[4]

Antonio Corsano in his study, *Il pensiero di Giordano Bruno nel suo svolgimento storico*, sees Bruno as predominantly anti-Platonic and anti-humanist. He speaks of Bruno's *infaticabile polemica contro il dualismo platonico* (*Il pensiero di Giordano Bruno . . .* , p. 271: untiring polemic against platonic dualism), of *il monismo bruniano sovvertitore implacabile di gerarchie violentatrici della natura* (*ibid.*, p. 192: Brunian monism, the implacable subverter of hierarchies which violate nature). Even in Bruno's early works, such as *De umbris idearum*, Corsano discerns a stronger motive than Neoplatonism in an Averroistic orientation. He writes, for example, as follows:

Ma più che la remota illuminazione della mente plotiniana, o del Dio-mente del platonismo cristiano, vale pel Bruno la più vicina e operosa fonte d'illuminazione che è l'intelletto agente. Così non è plotiniana ma averroista la stessa dottrina dell'elezione al risveglio dell'umanità immersa in torpore semianimale . . . (pp. 82–83).

But more important for Bruno than the remote illumination of the Plotinian mind, or the God-mind of Christian Platonism, is that more immediate and efficacious source of illumination, the active intellect. Thus the very doctrine of mankind's choice to awaken from its semi-animal torpor is not Plotinian but Averroistic . . .

Si è potuto conchiudere sulla prima fase del pensiero del Bruno che il prevalente affermarsi dell'interesse pedagogico-illuministico si equilibria senza difficoltà con l'accettazione della disciplina logico-razionale dell'aristotelismo averroistico, accolto come il miglior retaggio della fede pedagogica e speculativa classica e medievale, e pertanto difeso contro le presunte innovazioni del ramismo (p. 105).

One may conclude about the first phase of Bruno's thought that the prevalent affirmation of his pedagogical, enlightening interest is easily balanced with the logical and rational discipline of Averroistic Aristotelianism, accepted as the best heritage of the classical and medieval pedagogical and speculative faith, and therefore defended against the presumed innovations of Ramism.

[4] Those who attribute Bruno's celebrity primarily to the Church's "mistake" in condemning and executing him should remember that, on the contrary, his condemnation by the Papacy greatly curtailed the circulation of his works.

Corsano sees in the *De l'infinito* Bruno's intention to "infrangere quell'ultimo schermo esemplaristico frapposto dal platonismo ficiniano fra cosmo intelligibile e cosmo fisico, cui la venerazione umanistica dava sugli spiriti presa forse maggiore che il più rigoroso e nudo ragionamento aristotelico" (p. 168: shatter that last exemplaristic screen interposed by Ficinian Platonism between the intelligible cosmos and the physical cosmos, to which humanistic veneration gave perhaps a greater hold on men's minds than the most vigorous and naked Aristotelian reasoning).

To one who sees as fundamental goals in the writings of Bruno a polemic against Platonic dualism and the Neoplatonic hierarchy, the *Eroici furori* must needs give pause. Corsano recognizes a conflict between this dialogue and other writings of Bruno, but does not admit the continuing influence of Platonism in his later writings. He declares that in the *Eroici furori* the Averroistic concept of the active intellect is replaced by that of the Neoplatonic intelligential light. He also notes the contrast in attitudes toward matter between the *Eroici furori* and the *Causa* (p. 204). However, he sees the *Eroici furori* as merely a contrasting episode in Bruno's progressive denial of transcendentalism. Of Bruno's Latin trilogy he writes as follows:

Sicchè resta ben confermato che la ricostruzione bruniana nei poemi non si allontana dalla originaria ispirazione antimetafisica dei dialoghi, non cerca nè consegue fondamenti ontologici, anzi rovescia ed elimina qualche tratto che nella precedente speculazione dei dialoghi (*Eroici furori*) avrebbe offerto il destro a una restaurazione delle vecchie distinzioni gerarchiche fra mondo intelligibile e mondo naturale (p. 231).

Thus it is clearly confirmed that the Brunian reconstruction in the poems does not deviate from the original anti-metaphysical inspiration of the dialogues. It neither seeks nor attains ontological foundations; on the contrary it overturns and eliminates some passages which in the preceding speculation of the dialogues (*Eroici furori*) would have opened the way to a restoration of the old hierarchical distinctions between the intelligible world and the natural world.

He has little to say about the atomism of Bruno's later works, which for Tocco is the culmination of Bruno's thought.

Sidney Greenberg in *The Infinite in Giordano Bruno* gives a thorough analysis of Bruno's concept of the infinite as expressed in his Italian dialogues. He traces the historical development of the concept of infinity from Aristotle through St. Thomas and Nicholas of Cusa to Bruno's formulation, and emphasizes the originality of Bruno in attributing an actual infinity to the universe by virtue of the immanence in it of the first cause, operating from within as "principle." The introductory pages contain an excellent brief historical review of Bruno criticism. Many of the concepts analyzed because of their relation to Bruno's theory of infinity, such as substance, cause and principle, matter and form, are discussed in detail in Bruno's dialogue *De la causa, principio e uno*. Hence Greenberg appropriately includes in his book his English translation of that dialogue.[5]

Giordano Bruno, His Life and Thought, by Dorothea Waley Singer, utilizes material from the files of the Warburg Institute in London in recounting Bruno's life and expounding his major works. The scope of the book is very broad; the approach is expository and descriptive, rather than analytical and critical. Included in the book is a translation into "the English of Bruno's own day" of *De l'infinito, universo e mondi*. The first appendix lists chronologically with appropriate bibliographical data all of Bruno's writings.

After the work of Spampanato in writing an exhaustive biography of Bruno from the meager sources available; of Tocco in his careful examination of all Bruno's extant writings; and of Gentile in his critique of our philosopher's pivotal significance in the evolution of European thought; there yet remain for the investigations of contemporary and future critics of Bruno important facets of his thought and historical importance. It is hoped that the present study will elucidate one of these key areas, previously little explored, sufficiently to bring into sharper focus the entire philosophy of Bruno.

[5] There is an earlier partial translation of it: Giordano Bruno, *Concerning the Cause, the Principle, and the One*. Translated by Josiah and Katherine Royce for the series, "Modern Classical Philosophers," edited by Benjamin Rand. Boston, 1908.

CHAPTER I

Prose Commentaries on Verses

WHEN Giordano Bruno in the *Eroici furori* expounded his[1] sonnets in a prose commentary he was following a well established tradition. The first Italian works in which a poet explained his own sonnets and *canzoni* were the *Vita Nuova* and the *Convivio* of Dante. The earliest formal vernacular commentary upon vernacular verse is that attributed to Egidio Colonna in the early years of the *trecento* upon the *canzone* of Guido Cavalcanti, *Donna mi prega*. About the same time or shortly prior, there appeared a Latin commentary by Dino del Garbo upon the same *canzone*, which has continued to elicit commentaries until the present day. Late in the fifteenth century Lorenzo de' Medici and Girolamo Benivieni commented on their own sonnets, and Giovanni Pico della Mirandola wrote a commentary on Benivieni's *Canzone d'amore*. In 1548 Pompeo della Barba read to the Florentine Academy an *Exposition of a Platonic sonnet*. These commentaries are only the more important examples of what was a definite literary genre in the Renaissance, with origins and precedents in the Middle Ages and in late antiquity.[2] In the middle ages expositions of classical texts—not only Cicero's rhetoric and Priscian's grammar, but also such poets

[1] Bruno does not comment upon the four sonnets which he borrows from Luigi Tansillo.

[2] Dante and Cavalcanti's commentators transferred to the realm of vernacular literature the pre-existing school form of commentary. Dante's letter to Can Grande della Scala, the earliest specimen of commentary upon the *Divine Comedy*, also belongs to this genre.

as Vergil, Ovid, and Lucan—were one of the main methods of teaching.[3]

THE *Vita Nuova* AND THE *Convivio* OF DANTE

In our consideration of Dante's *Vita Nuova* and *Convivio* we shall pay special attention to their formal aspect of prose commentaries upon poetry. Properly speaking, this description fits only the *Vita Nuova*, for the three *canzoni*, or at least the first two, of the *Convivio* are rather in the nature of ornaments affording a pretense for the "commentary," which expounds doctrines that could just as well stand independent of the *canzoni*. Formally, however, the *canzoni* are the *vivanda* (main course), and the commentary *pane* (bread).

Superficially the *Vita Nuova* appears to be a simple record of events factual or imagined, naively told. But to each event of Beatrice's life which he relates—a "new" life because extraordinary and previously unheard of[4]—the author attributes a "marvelous"

[3] See Richard William Hunt, "The introductions to the 'Artes' in the Twelfth Century," in *Studia mediaevalia in honorem admodum reverendi patris Raymundi Josephi Martin*. See also Edwin A. Quain, "The medieval accessus ad auctores," in *Traditio*, III, 215–64.

[4] Such was the Augustinian and medieval connotation of the adjective *novus*, which in classical Latin as well sometimes has such a meaning. Prof. Enrico de' Negri pointed out to me that paragraphs I and XXVIII of the *Vita Nuova*, read in conjunction, indicate that the title refers to the life of Beatrice rather than of Dante. They read as follows:

I. In quella parte del libro de la mia memoria dinanzi a la quale poco si potrebbe leggere, si trova una rubrica la quale dice: *Incipit vita nova.* Sotto la quale rubrica io trovo scritte le parole le quali è mio intendimento d'assemplare in questo libello; e se non tutte, almeno la loro sentenzia.

XXVIII. . . . E avvegna che forse piacerebbe a presente trattare alquanto de la sua partita da noi, non è lo mio intendimento di trattarne qui per tre ragioni: la prima è che ciò non è del presente proposito, se volemo guardare nel proemio che precede questo libello; la seconda si è che, posto che fosse del presente proposito, ancora non sarebbe sufficiente la mia lingua a trattare come si converrebbe di ciò; la terza si è che, posto che fosse l'uno e l'altro, non è convenevole a me trattare di ciò, per quello che, trattando, converrebbe essere me laudatore di me medesimo, la qual cosa è al postutto biasimevole a chi lo fae; e però lascio cotale trattato ad altro chiosatore. . . .

I. In that part of the book of my memory prior to which little could be read there is found a rubric that says, "A new life begins." Below that rubric I find quality replete with theological symbolism. Ostensibly, the function of the commentary is first, before each poem, to narrate the events which caused the poet to compose the verses, and second, after each poem until Chapter 31 and immediately before each poem thereafter, to divide the verses into parts and to briefly elucidate obscure points. Its real function, however, is to reveal more clearly than the verses themselves the supernatural quality of Beatrice's life, which is seen in the commentary in retrospect. The metaphor which controls the form of the book is that of the *libro de la mia memoria* to which Dante refers in the first line. Indeed, it is apparent from elements lacking in the sonnets themselves, but insinuated into the commentary (e.g., Chap. IX), that some of the sonnets were actually written at an earlier date than the prose passages. Thus Dante in the *Vita Nuova* plays the dual role of poet-protagonist and scribe-glossator.

In the *saluto* (greeting) of Beatrice is Dante's *salute* (salvation). Love, personified, counsels Dante according to reason (*Vita Nuova,* Chap. IV) and masters him by virtue of the *gentilissima* Beatrice (*ibid.,* Chap. IX). When Dante, counseled by Love (*ibid.*), seeks his second "screen lady" to hide his true love for Beatrice, many people talk about it "beyond the bounds of courtesy," with the result that Beatrice denies him "her sweetest salutation" in which was his "beatitude" (*ibid.,* Chap. X). Dante's description of the effects of Beatrice's "wondrous" salute shows a complete identification of his love with Christian charity. Beatrice's salute denied him, Dante, still guided by Love, finds his beatitude "in that which cannot fail"

written the words which it is my intention to reproduce in this little book, and if not all, at least their import.

XXVIII. . . . Although it might be pleasing at present to treat somewhat of her departure from us, it is not my intention to treat of it here, for three reasons. The first is that it does not belong to the present undertaking, if we wish to regard the introduction that precedes this little book. The second is that even if it belonged within the present undertaking, my tongue would still not be sufficient to treat fittingly of that. The third is that, if one and the other were true, it would not be proper for me to treat of that because it would be necessary in so doing for me to become the praiser of myself—a thing most blameworthy of him who does it. And therefore I leave such treatise to another glossator. . . .

In the first tractate of the *Convivio,* Chapter 2, Dante says, "Parlare alcuno di se medesimo pare non licito" (To speak of oneself appears not to be permissible). There is the further consideration that in the Middle Ages a "Life" of someone meant a completed life written when that person was no longer living.

him—*in quelle parole che lodano la donna mia* (*Ibid.*, Chap. XVIII: in those words which praise my lady).

These verses, beginning with the *canzone, Donne ch'avete intelletto d'amore* (*ibid.*, Chap. XIX), are *matera nuova e più nobile che la passata* (new and more noble matter than the preceding). Beatrice is praised as a *maraviglia* (marvel) desired in heaven, a "new thing" of God; the exemplar by whom beauty itself is judged, producing in noble hearts the prime Christian virtue of humility. The *stilnuovo* psychology of enamoring by spirits of love which pass through the eyes is repeated after Guinizelli. These points are evident in the following excerpts from the *canzone*:

> Angelo clama in divino intelletto
>   e dice: "Sire, nel mondo si vede
>   maraviglia ne l'atto che procede
>   d'un'anima che 'nfin qua su risplende." . . .
> Dico, qual vuol gentil donna parere
>   vada con lei, che quando va per via,
>   gitta nei cor villani Amore un gelo,
>   per che onne lor pensero agghiaccia e pere;
>   e qual soffrisse di starla a vedere
>   diverria nobil cosa, o si morria.
> E quando trova alcun che degno sia
>   di veder lei, quei prova sua vertute,
>   chè li avvien, ciò che li dona, in salute,
>   e sì l'umilia, ch'ogni offesa oblia.
> Ancor l'ha Dio per maggior grazia dato
>   che non pò mal finir chi l'ha parlato.
> Dice di lei Amor: "Cosa mortale
>   come esser pò sì adorna e sì pura?"
> Poi la reguarda, e fra se stesso giura
>   che Dio ne 'ntenda di far cosa nova.
> Color di perle ha quasi, in forma quale
>   convene a donna aver, non for misura:
>   ella è quanto de ben pò far natura;
>   per essemplo di lei bieltà si prova.
> De li occhi suoi, come ch'ella li mova,
>   escono spiriti d'amore inflammati,
>   che feron li occhi a qual che allor la guati,
>   e passan sì che 'l cor ciascun retrova:
>   voi le vedete Amor pinto nel viso,
>   la 've non pote alcun mirarla fiso.

An angel calls in the divine intellect and says, "Sire, in the world is seen a marvel in the act that proceeds from a soul which shines as far as this height. . . ."

I say, let whosoever would seem a gentle lady go with her, for when she goes along the way Love casts a chill into base hearts whereby their every thought freezes and perishes. And whosoever risked to remain and behold her would become something noble or would die. And when she finds anyone that is worthy of seeing her, that one experiences her virtue, for that which she gives him in salvation occurs to him and makes him so humble that he forgets every offense. God has granted her besides as a greater grace that he who has spoken to her cannot end ill.

Love says of her, "How can a mortal be so lovely and so pure?" Then he looks at her and swears within himself that God intends in her to make something new. She has a color as of pearls, in form such as becomes a lady to have, not beyond measure. She is as much of goodness as nature can create; by her model is love tested. From her eyes, however she turns them, issue flaming spirits of love that strike the eyes of him who then looks on her, and penetrate so that each one finds his heart. You see Love pictured in her face where no one can hold his steadfast gaze.

In the *congedo* the *canzone* is directed only to noble[5] hearts:

> ingegnati, se puoi, d'esser palese
> solo con donne o con omo cortese.
> (*Vita Nuova,* Chap. XIX)

try, if you can, to be clear only with ladies or a courteous man.

Not only this *canzone,* but the entire book, like *stilnuovo* poetry generally, is directed to a select audience of intelligent readers. For this reason, Dante declares, he limits the subdivisions of this *canzone* in his prose commentary.

Dico bene che, a più aprire lo intendimento di questa canzone, si converrebbe usare di più minute divisioni; ma tuttavia chi non è di tanto ingegno che per queste che sono fatte la possa intendere, a me non dispiace se la mi lascia stare, chè certo io temo d'avere a troppi comunicato lo suo intendimento pur per queste divisioni che fatte sono, s'elli avvenisse che molti le potessero audire (*ibid.*).

I confess indeed that to unfold the meaning of this *canzone* further it would be needful to employ smaller divisions. But he, however, who

[5] Noble is intended in Dante's sense of moral rather than hereditary nobility.

has not sufficient wit that he can understand it by these that have been made will not displease me by letting it be; I fear indeed that I have communicated its meaning to too many even by these divisions that have been made, if it were to happen that many should hear them.

The following sonnets, *Amore e 'l cor gentil sono una cosa* and *Ne li occhi porta la mia donna Amore,* proceed to express *stilnuovo* motives, as their respective first lines indicate.

The prose passages after Dante's vision of Beatrice's death, centrally placed in the twenty-third of the forty-two chapters which comprise the *Vita Nuova,* bring out more strongly than ever the miraculous and symbolic character of Beatrice's life. When Dante saw Beatrice preceded by Giovanna, the lady of his "first friend" Guido Cavalcanti, Love told him that Giovanna was so called from the John "who preceded the true light, saying: *'Ego vox clamantis in deserto: parate viam Domini.'* " [6]

The number nine appears in the time of Beatrice's death according to three calendars, having been first foreshadowed by the third vision of her death, which appears to Dante in the ninth day of his illness. Indeed, the number nine occurs in each of the three visions which foretell her death. Chapter XXIX explains the significance of the insistent recurrence of the number nine in the life and death of Beatrice: nine is the square of three, which signifies the trinity, and is therefore a miraculous number; Beatrice herself is "by similitude" a number nine—in short, a miracle.

. . . Questo numero fue ella medesima; per similitudine dico, e ciò intendo così. Lo numero del tre è la radice del nove, però che, sanza numero altro alcuno, per se medesimo fa nove, sì come vedemo manifestamente che tre via tre fa nove. Dunque se lo tre è fattore per se medesimo del nove, e lo fattore per se medesimo de li miracoli è tre, cioè Padre e Figlio e Spirito Santo, li quali sono tre e uno, questa donna fue accompagnata da questo numero del nove a dare ad intendere ch' ella era uno nove, cioè uno miracolo, la cui radice, cioè del miracolo, è solamente la mirabile Trinitade (*Vita Nuova,* Chap. XXIX).

. . . This number was she herself, by similitude, I say, and thus I understand it. The number three is the root of nine since without any

---

[6] Beatrice's striking resemblance to Christ—analogical, not equivalent—in this and other passages is discussed at length in Charles S. Singleton, *An Essay on the "Vita Nuova."* The exposition of the *Vita Nuova* presented in this chapter is frequently influenced by Professor Singleton's essay.

other number whatever, by itself it makes nine, as we see manifestly that three times three makes nine. If therefore three is by itself the factor [producer] of nine and the sole factor of the miracles is three, that is, Father and Son and Holy Spirit, who are three and one, this lady was accompanied by this number nine to give to understand that she was a nine, that is, a miracle whose root—of the miracle, that is— is solely the wondrous Trinity.

In the thirty-fifth chapter Dante describes the *donna gentile* who looked upon him with pity. Five sonnets are devoted to her.

Finally the poet had a remarkable vision which determined him to say no more of the blessed Beatrice until he "were able to more worthily treat of her." He affirms his hope "to say of her that which was never said of any lady" (*ibid.,* Chap. XLII).

Dante's love poetry inherited much from Guido Guinizelli: the lover's praise of his lady, the severe effects on the poet of his love, the entrance of love into the heart by way of the eyes are themes present in Guinizelli's poetry, though not originated by him. The identification of love with the *cor gentile* is original in Guinizelli and is derived from him, with the other themes mentioned above, by Dante.

Both Guinizelli and Cavalcanti had compared their ladies to angels. However, the connotations of theological symbolism which Dante's metaphors carry do not appear in their poems, and only Dante adds a "reasoned prose" commentary to affirm the seriousness of his assertion that his lady is a miracle. In the school of the *dolce stil nuovo,* as in the poetry of Petrarch, the poet praises his lady and strives to be worthy of her by assuming many virtues. But in the *donna angelicata* of Tuscan lyrical poets other than Dante there is yet the conflict between the chivalric idea of love of woman, and Christian charity. It took the poetic verve and uncompromising character of Dante to combine these two concepts of love without destroying either. The theme of praise remains in Dante's poetry, but love continues in an upward path toward God somewhat as in the Platonic concept of love. In loving Beatrice, Dante loves God.

Dante's *Convivio* is a banquet of knowledge (*scienza*) which he, as one who has sat at the foot of those who sit at the *beata mensa,* prepares in the vulgar tongue for those who, because of family cares or laziness, have not been able to satisfy their hunger for knowledge. He takes the liberty of speaking of himself for the two allowable "necessary reasons" of "fear of infamy and . . . desire to impart doctrine" (*Convivio*, Tractate I, Chap. ii). His fear of infamy results from the possible misinterpretation of some *canzoni* which he formerly wrote, in which he seems to have been ruled by passion. A commentary, purposely composed in a grave style, is therefore necessary "to show their true meaning . . . because it is hidden under a figure of allegory" (*ibid.*).

E con ciò sia cosa che la vera intenzione mia fosse altra che quella che di fuori mostrano le canzoni predette, per allegorica esposizione quelle intendo mostrare, appresso la litterale istoria ragionata; si che l'una ragione e l'altra darà sapore a coloro che a questa cena sono convitati (*ibid.*, I, i).

And since my true intention was other than that which the aforesaid *canzoni* outwardly show, by allegorical exposition I intend to show their meaning alongside the literal, reasoned story, so that the one reason and the other will afford savor to those who are invited to this supper.

The literal sense is "fictitious" (*ibid.*, II, xv); the allegorical sense is "true" (*ibid.*, II, xii). Then he will endeavor to write in "temperate and virile" style, whereas in the *Vita Nuova* he was "fervid and passionate" (*ibid.*, I, i).

The commentary will show that "not passion but virtue" was the motivating force of the poems; thereby it will give delight and instruction (*ibid.*, I, ii). The commentary of each *canzone*—there were to be fourteen—will clarify respectively the literal, allegorical, moral, and anagogic senses, and will impart knowledge and virtue to its readers.

Lo dono veramente di questo comento è la sentenza de le canzoni a le quali fatto è, la qual massimamente intende inducere li uomini a scienza e a vertù, sicome si vedrà per lo pelago del loro trattato (*ibid.*, I, ix).

The contribution of this commentary, really, is the sense of the *canzoni* to which it is addressed, which means above all to induce men to knowledge and to virtue, as will be seen by the mass of their treatment.

In the case of the first two *canzoni* the allegory consists mainly in the identification of the *donna gentile* with Philosophy. Only in the third *canzone* is allegory abandoned, as the subject matter of love is replaced by that of nobility; the subsequent prose commentary consequently is limited to an exposition *secondo la lettera*.

The first tractate, which is introductory in nature, after justifying the composition of a commentary in which the author speaks of himself, proceeds to excuse the "substantial stain" (*ibid.*, I, v) of writing in Italian instead of the "more beautiful, more virtuous, and more noble Latin." He adduces three reasons—the wish to avoid the inappropriate relation which would result from a Latin commentary upon vulgar verses;[7] "promptness of liberality," Italian being useful to more persons than Latin as the language for commenting on Italian verses; and "the natural love for one's own language" (*Convivo*, I, v). In the Biblical phraseology of the concluding paragraph of the first tractate there is the strong implication that Dante was motivated by an attitude of Christian charity to adopt the language understood by the multitude in the "bread" or prose commentary of the *Convivio*:

> Questo sarà quello pane orzato del quale si satolleranno migliaia, e a me ne soperchieranno le sporte piene. Questo sarà luce nuova, sole nuovo, lo quale surgerà là dove l'usato tramonterà, e darà lume a coloro che sono in tenebre e in oscuritade, per lo usato sole che a loro non luce.

> This will be that barley bread with which thousands will be filled, and full baskets will be left over for me. This will be a new light, a new sun, that will rise where the used one will set, and will give light to those who are in shadows and darkness, since the used sun does not shine for them.

The *Convivio* is one of the first instances of the use of Italian for scientific prose. Dante himself was aware of the importance of this fact.

> Chè per questo comento la gran bontade del volgare di sì [si vedrà]; però che si vedrà la sua vertù, sì com'è per esso altissimi e novissimi

---

[7] Latin, a naturally "sovereign" language, cannot be the "servant" of Italian.

concetti convenevolmente, sufficientemente e acconciamente, quasi come per esso latino, manifestare (*ibid.*, I, x).

For by this commentary the great goodness of the Italian vernacular [will be seen]; since its virtue will be seen, as the highest and newest concepts are set forth through it fittingly, adequately, and worthily, as though it were in Latin itself.

Both Beatrice and the *donna gentile* are depicted as real persons in the *Vita Nuova*. It is not very important whether or not the plot in which Dante involves them corresponds to events that actually occurred in the poet's life; for that matter the biographical facts which we know do not enable us to ascertain the truth. Dante himself declares in the *Convivio* (*ibid.*, II, i) that the poetical narration is "fables" (*favole*) and that the literal sense is a "fine falsehood" (*bella menzogna*) under which the "truth" of allegory is hidden. The important aspect of these two persons is the poetic and philosophical-theological use which Dante made of them. Beatrice has her full symbolic development in the *Divine Comedy,* the *donna gentile* in the *Convivio*.

Dante's allegorical identification of the "gentle lady" with philosophy is explicit only in the *Convivio*. It is reasonable to conjecture that the lack of this identification in the *Vita Nuova* determines the triumph at the end of that work of the poet's love for Beatrice and the rejection of his second love as an unworthy vacillation on his part. In the *Vita Nuova* the *donna gentile* appears simply as a beautiful and merciful young woman.

Allora vidi una gentile donna giovane e bella molto, la quale da una finestra mi riguardava sì pietosamente, quanto a la vista, che tutta la pietà parea in lei accolta (*Vita Nuova*, Chap. XXXV).

Then I saw a gentle lady, young and very beautiful, who from a window looked on me so compassionately, as it appeared, that all compassion seemed gathered in her.

In the *Convivio* her first appearance to Dante is described in solemn words which relate her coming to the death of Beatrice:

Cominciando adunque, dico che la stella di Venere due fiate rivolta era in quello suo cerchio che la fa parere serotina e matutina, secondo diversi tempi, appresso lo trapassamento di quella Beatrice beata che vive in cielo con li angeli e in terra con la mia anima, quando quella gentile donna, cui feci menzione ne la fine de la Vita Nuova, parve primamente, accompagnata d'Amore, a li occhi miei e prese luogo alcuno ne la mia mente (*Convivio*, II, ii).

Beginning, then, I say that the star of Venus two times had revolved in that circle of hers that causes her to appear evening and morning according to the different seasons, after the passing of that blessed Beatrice who lives in Heaven with the angels and on earth with my soul, when that gentle lady of whom I made mention in the end of the *Vita Nuova* first appeared, accompanied by Love, before my eyes and took a certain place within my mind.

When in the *Convivio* the *donna gentile* is conceived as the figure of Philosophy, there is no longer any obstacle to loving her. In the *canzone, Voi che 'ntendendo il terzo ciel movete,* the second part, which consists of the second, third and fourth stanzas, describes the struggle in Dante's soul between the two ladies for the poet's love, and prepares the triumph of the gentle lady, Philosophy. The mechanical reason for this transfer of the poet's love is given in Chapter VIII of the second tractate: love is the effect of the intelligences who move the planet Venus, who can operate only in "subjects who are placed under their circulation." After her death Beatrice is "outside of their power." Hence they transfer their virtue to the *donna gentile.* A more profound explanation for the poet's new love may, perhaps, be discovered in the words quoted above (*ibid.*) which describe the appearance of the *donna gentile* "accompanied by Love." If love is understood in the sense that it is given in the second tractate of the *Convivio,* and that it has generally in Dante's writings—a spiritual emotion identifiable with Christian charity—the conflict of this love with the love of Beatrice is resolvable, in the way that reason can be reconciled with revelation.

> Voi che 'ntendendo il terzo ciel movete,
> udite il ragionar ch'è nel mio core. . . .
> (*ibid.*, II, first *canzone*)

You that by understanding move the third heaven, hear the reasoning that is in my heart . . .

The second tractate, ostensibly the explanation of this *canzone*, explains the angelic orders in such a way as to ascribe to the third heaven, Venus, a special relationship to the Holy Spirit.

Per che ragionevole è credere che li movitori del cielo de la Luna siano de l'ordine de li Angeli, e quelli di Mercurio siano li Arcangeli, e quelli di Venere siano li Troni; li quali, naturati de l'amore del Santo Spirito, fanno la loro operazione, connaturale ad essi, cioè lo movimento di quello cielo, pieno d'amore, dal quale prende la forma del detto cielo uno ardore virtuoso, per lo quale le anime di qua giuso s'accendono ad amore, secondo la loro disposizione (*ibid.*, II, v).

For it is reasonable to believe that the movers of the heaven of the Moon are of the order of Angels, those of Mercury Archangels, and those of Venus the Thrones, who, their nature formed by the love of the Holy Spirit, carry on their operation consonant with their nature, that is, the movement of that heaven full of love, from which there takes the form of the said heaven a virtuous ardor, because of which the souls here below are kindled to love, according to their disposition.

The second verse, *udite il ragionar ch'è nel mio core,* ties the concept of love here expressed to that of the *dolce stil nuovo* as Dante explains it to Bonagiunta da Lucca in the twenty-fourth canto of the *Purgatorio*—Love which "dictates within" (*ditta dentro*). The prose commentary in Chapter VI of the second tractate confirms this interpretation:

Dico: *Udite il ragionar* lo quale *è nel mio core*: cioè dentro da me, chè ancora non è di fuori apparito. E da sapere è che in tutta questa canzone, secondo l'uno senso e l'altro, lo "core" si prende per lo secreto dentro, e non per altra spezial parte de l'anima e del corpo.

I say, hear the reasoning that is in my heart; that is, within me, because it has not yet appeared outwardly, and it is to be known that in this whole *canzone,* according to the one sense and the other, the heart stands for the secret within and not for any other special part of the soul and the body.

The first stanza of the second *canzone* again takes up the theme of Love's internal dictation and blames the deficiencies of the poem on the poet's inability to transcribe all that he hears or even all that he understands of the world of Love.

> Amor che ne la mente mi ragiona
> de la mia donna disiosamente,
> move cose di lei meco sovente,
> che lo 'ntelletto sovr' esse disvia.
> Lo suo parlar sì dolcemente sona,
> che l'anima ch' ascolta e che lo sente

dice: "Oh me lassa! ch' io non son possente
di dir quel ch' odo de la donna mia!"
E certo e' mi convien lasciare in pria,
s'io vo' trattar di quel ch' odo di lei,
ciò che lo mio intelletto non comprende;
e di quel che s' intende
gran parte, perchè dirlo non savrei.
Però, se le mie rime avran difetto
ch' entreran ne la loda di costei,
di ciò si biasmi il debole intelletto
e 'l parlar nostro, che non ha valore
di ritrar tutto ciò che dice Amore.

Love that in the mind talks to me affectionately of my lady often tells me such things of her that the intellect loses its way over them. His speech so sweetly sounds that the soul that listens and hears him says, "Alas! for I am not able to speak that which I hear of my lady!" And certainly if I wish to treat of what I hear of her, it is better for me to leave from the first that which my intellect does not comprehend, and great part of what is understood, because I should not be able to say it. And so if my verses that enter upon the praise of her shall have defect, one must blame my feeble intellect and our speech, which has not the power to reproduce all that Love says.

Having identified the *donna gentile* with Philosophy, Dante proceeds to treat various problems and topics of medieval culture, giving his work the flavor of a popular encyclopedia. Love, philosophy, the soul, cosmology, imperial authority, and nobility are discussed in the third and fourth tractates.

The theme of the second *canzone*, which begins the third tractate, is the praise of the *donna gentile*, somewhat after the fashion of the verses which praise Beatrice in the *Vita Nuova*:

Non vede il sol, che tutto 'l mondo gira,
cosa tanto gentil, quanto in quell' ora
che luce ne la parte ove dimora
la donna, di cui dire Amor mi face. . . .
Suo esser tanto a Quei che lel dà piace,
che 'nfonde sempre in lei la sua vertute,
oltre 'l dimando di nostra natura. . . .
In lei discende la virtù divina
sì come face in angelo che 'l vede . . .
gentile è in donna ciò che in lei si trova,
e bello è tanto quanto lei simiglia. . . .

Sua bieltà piove fiammelle di foco,
animate d'un spirito gentile
ch' è creatore d'ogni pensier bono;
e rompon come trono
l'innati vizii che fanno altrui vile.
Però qual donna sente sua bieltate
biasmar per non parer queta e umile,
miri costei ch' è essemplo d'umiltate!
Questa è colei ch' umilia ogni perverso:
costei pensò chi mosse l'universo.

The sun that circles the whole world sees nothing so gentle as in that hour that it shines in the part where lives the lady of whom Love makes me speak. . . .

Her being is so pleasing to Him who gives it to her that He ever infuses in her His virtue, beyond the demand of our nature. . . .

In her descends the divine virtue as it does in an angel who sees Him. . . .

In woman that is gentle which is found in her, and whatever resembles her is beautiful. . . .

Her beauty rains little flames of fire animated by a gentle spirit that is creator of every good thought; they destroy like thunder the innate vices that make others vile. Let any woman, therefore, who hears her beauty blamed for not appearing quiet and humble look upon her who is the model of humility. She is the one who humbles every perverse person: He who moved the universe thought her [i.e., created her].

By allegory love in the second and third tractates of the *Convivio* becomes a philosophical "study" (*ibid.*, II, xv).

Onde è da sapere che per amore, in questa allegoria, sempre s'intende esso studio, lo quale è applicazione de l'animo innamorato de la cosa a quella cosa (*ibid.*).

Hence it is to be known that by love in this allegory is always meant the zeal which is the application of the soul enamored of the thing to that thing.

Philosophy is not only Dante's lady, but was the lady of the authors—Boethius and Cicero in particular—who guided Dante into the philosophic studies. Philosophy is a merciful woman, the daughter of God, queen of all, most noble and beautiful. In philosophy is salvation.

. . . Boezio e Tullio . . . con la dolcezza di loro sermone inviarono me, come detto è di sopra, ne lo amore, cioè ne lo studio, di questa donna gentilissima Filosofia . . . (*ibid.*).

Boethius and Cicero . . . with the sweetness of their discourse dispatched me, as is related above, into love, that is, to the study of this most gentle lady, Philosophy . . .

. . . Io, che cercava di consolarme, . . . giudicava bene che la filosofia, che era donna di questi autori, di queste scienze e di questi libri, fosse somma cosa. E imaginava lei fatta come una donna gentile, e non la poteva immaginare in atto alcuno, se non misericordioso . . . (*ibid.,* II, xii).

. . . I, who sought to console myself . . . was well convinced that philosophy, which was the lady of these authors, this knowledge, and these books, was a very great thing. And I imagined her made like a gentle lady and could not imagine her in any act if not merciful . . .

. . . Questa donna fu figlia di Dio, regina di tutto, nobilissima e bellissima Filosofia . . . (*ibid.*).

This lady was the daughter of God, queen of all, most noble and most beautiful Philosophy . . .

Veramente in voi è la salute, per la quale si fa beato chi vi guarda, e salvo da la morte de la ignoranza e da li vizii (*ibid.,* II, xv).

Truly in you is salvation, whereby he who looks at you is made blessed, and safe from the death of ignorance and from vices.

The *Convivio* justifies Dante's love in the *Vita Nuova* of the *donna gentile* by attributing to her the character of Philosophy; it in a sense authorizes the *Divine Comedy,* in which the poet's journey unfolds because of the intercession in his behalf of love. The doctrinal bases of the *Comedy* are laid in the *Convivio*. Virgil is motivated by the compassion of three ladies to guide Dante to the Earthly Paradise, where Beatrice awaits him. The virtuous man before Christ's Passion lived according to the four cardinal virtues of prudence, fortitude, justice, and temperance, represented by Dante in the figure of Vergil, who is able to guide Dante only as far as Eden. The new guide, Beatrice, must lead Dante heavenward by the theological virtues of faith, hope, and charity which God in His grace revealed to sinful man in the coming of Christ.

Thus the story of Beatrice in the *Divine Comedy,* because of her allegorical role, becomes generically a legend. Medieval Christian legends combine a real element, such as a well-known person or event, with a symbolic element. In so doing the author strives to the utmost to lend credence to the miraculous by realism in detail. Dante's challenge to the reader of his journey through the other world is, "Believe me; I have been there."

One of Dante's most powerful legends, poetically and emotionally, is the story of Paolo and Francesca in the fifth canto of the *Inferno,* which reveals Dante as the brilliant portrayer of the passionate, all too human lovers who typify but one of the many varieties of love about which Dante subtly theorizes in the *Comedy.* To the reader of such unsurpassed poetry it seems that an abyss separates Dante from previous and contemporary Tuscan poets of love. Only in Guido Cavalcanti's hints of tragedy do we find an intimation of the passion described by Dante. It is indeed possible that Dante had in mind the *canzone* on love of his "first friend" when he depicted the *mal perverso* (*Inferno,* V, 93) which led the passionate couple to their death: "Amor condusse noi ad una morte" (l. 106: Love led us to one death). The dark and stormy atmosphere of their infernal location is reminiscent of the *oscuritade* which characterizes the passion described by Cavalcanti.

> Io venni in luogo d'ogni luce muto,
>   che mugghia come fa mar per tempesta,
>   se da contrari venti è combattuto.
> La bufera infernal, che mai non resta,
>   mena li spirti con la sua rapina;
>   voltando e percotendo li molesta.
>   (*ibid.,* ll. 28–33)

I came upon a place deprived of every light, that roars as does the sea in tempest if it is beaten by contrary winds.

The infernal storm that never rests leads on the spirits with its rapine; turning and buffeting, it molests them.

The love of Paolo and Francesca, again like the love described in Cavalcanti's *canzone,* is altogether hopeless:

> nulla speranza li conforta mai,
> non che di posa, ma di minor pena.
>   (ll. 44–45)

no hope ever comforts them, let alone of surcease, not even of lesser punishment.

Here is the "black air" ("l'aura nera") where the "vice of luxury" (l. 55) is punished, which identified *libito* with *licito* (l. 56).[8]

> . . . "Oh lasso,
> quanti dolci pensier, quanto disio
> menò costoro al doloroso passo!"
> (*ibid.*, ll. 112–114)

. . . Alas, how many sweet thoughts, what desire led them to the sorrowful step!

The tale of these *anime affannate* (*ibid.*, l. 80) illustrates after Cavalcanti the futility of sensual love. For Dante, but not for Cavalcanti, such illicit love, following blind passion in opposition to divine law, is a perversion of man's native motivation toward his Creator. A man's love must either partake of the cosmic force which created and unites the universe or destroy the man.

In the twenty-fourth canto of the *Purgatorio* Dante returns to the *canzone, Donne ch' avete intelletto d'amore*. It is especially significant that he dates from this poem the "new rhymes" of the *dolce stil nuovo*. His dialogue there with Bonagiunta da Lucca is as follows:

> "Ma dì s' i' veggio qui colui che fore
> trasse le nuove rime, cominciando
> 'Donne ch' avete intelletto d'amore.' "
> E io a lui: "I' mi son un, che quando
> Amor mi spira, noto, e a quel modo
> ch' e' ditta dentro vo' significando."
> "O frate, issa vegg' io" diss'elli "il nodo
> che 'l Notaro e Guittone e me ritenne
> di qua dal dolce stil nuovo ch' i' odo!
> Io veggio ben come le vostre penne
> di retro al dittator sen vanno strette,
> che delle nostre certo non avvenne;
> e qual più a riguardare oltre si mette,
> non vede più dall' uno all' altro stilo";
> e, quasi contentato, si tacette.
> (*Purgatorio*, XXIV, ll. 49–63)

[8] Cf. Torquato Tasso's formula in the *Aminta*: "S'ei piace, ei lice" (If it is pleasing, it is permissible).

"But say if I see here him who brought forth the new rhymes, beginning 'Ladies who have intelligence of love.' "

And I to him: "I am one who when Love inspires me takes note and signifies according to the manner in which he dictates within me."

"O brother, now I see," said he, "the bond that restrained the Notary and Guittone and me short of the sweet new style that I hear.

"I well see how your pens follow close behind the dictator, which assuredly did not happen with ours;

"and he who sets himself to look further sees no further difference between the one style and the other." And as though satisfied, he was silent.

The innovation of the *dolce stil nuovo* in Dante's eyes is the immediacy with which the poet in his writing follows the dictates of Love. The key to the interpretation of this famous passage is the meaning intended in the word "Love." Bonagiunta and the Notary, Iacopo da Lentini, and Guittone d'Arezzo, like other poets of the Sicilian and Tuscan schools, had written primarily love poetry. It is consequently not unreasonable to see as Dante's innovation the infusion into Italian love lyrics of the theological concept of *caritas*. Such indeed is the connotation of love in the *Vita Nuova,* in which occurs the *canzone* which Dante identifies with the "new rhymes," *Donne ch' avete intelletto d'amore.* In the trilogy—if one may use this term—constituted by the *Vita Nuova,* the *Convivio,* and the *Divine Comedy,* love is repeatedly identified with *caritas.* Following the definition of love as *virtus unificativa et concretiva* Dante defines love in the *Convivio* as "spiritual union of the soul and the thing loved."

Amore, veramente pigliando e sottilmente considerando, non è altro che unimento spirituale de l'anima e de la cosa amata; nel quale unimento di propia sua natura l'anima corre tosto e tardi, secondo che è libera o impedita (*Convivio,* III, ii).

Love, rightly choosing and subtly considering, is none other than the spiritual uniting of the soul and the thing beloved; in that uniting the soul of its own proper nature runs fast and slow according as it is free or hindered.

Love is not only the unifying theme of Dante's poetry, but, as explained by Vergil in the seventeenth canto of the *Purgatorio,* is the sole unifying force in the universe.

"Nè creator nè creatura mai"
 cominciò el, "figliuol, fu sanza amore,
 o naturale o d'animo; e tu 'l sai.
Lo naturale è sempre sanza errore,
 ma l'altro puote errar per malo obietto
 o per troppo o per poco di vigore.
Mentre ch'elli è nel primo ben diretto,
 e ne' secondi sè stesso misura,
 esser non può cagion di mal diletto;
ma quando al mal si torce, o con più cura
 o con men che non dee corre nel bene,
 contra 'l fattore adovra sua fattura.
Quinci comprender puoi ch' esser convene
 amor sementa in voi d'ogni virtute
 e d'ogne operazion che merta pene.
   (*Purgatorio,* XVII, ll. 91–105)

"Neither Creator nor creature ever, my son," he began, "was without love, either natural or of the soul; and you know it.

"Natural love is always without error, but the other may err by a bad object or by too much or too little vigor.

"While it is directed toward the first good and in the secondary ones measures itself, it cannot be the cause of evil delight;

"but when it is twisted toward evil or runs toward goodness with more or less care than it ought, against the Creator his creature works.

"Hence you can understand that love must be the seed of every virtue in you and of every deed that deserves punishment"

There are not two principles or two gods in the universe, good and evil, but one only—love. The moral ordering of the universe in the *Divine Comedy,* which Dante illustrates by appropriate legends from sacred and secular history, depends upon the degrees of love, which either draw the soul toward God or separate it from him. Around this single theme are drawn the particular plots of the three *cantiche* of the *Divine Comedy,* and that of the *Vita Nuova.* In the *Convivio* the association of love with philosophy permits the treatment of a variety of popular cultural topics.

In Dante's concept love is all-embracing. Not only is love the root of good and evil and even of their intermediates in the moral realm, but it is the controlling principle, unerring, in the realm of physics. This concept illustrates the need of unity which Dante shared especially with the Middle Ages and which philosophers of all ages have earnestly sought.

COMMENTARIES ON GUIDO CAVALCANTI'S *canzone*, "DONNA MI PREGA"

In the first quarter of the *trecento* the learned physician Dino del Garbo and an anonymous glossator called "Egidio Colonna" wrote interpretations of Guido Cavalcanti's *canzone* about love, *Donna mi prega.* Before the end of the sixteenth century at least nine writers commented on the poem.[9] The need for a commentary, as well as the very difficulties experienced by the commentators, is a result of the ode's extreme conciseness in stating an involved and abstract theory of love. After the manner of troubadour *tenzoni*, Cavalcanti replies with *Donna mi prega* to a sonnet addressed to him by Guido Orlandi, which posed several questions about the origin, nature and characteristics of love. Cavalcanti's answers are strikingly original, and are dramatic and even tragic in their resolution. Like a medieval prose *summa*, the *canzone* begins with an enumeration of the *didascalica*, or aspects under which the subject is to be considered. The questions to be discussed in the stanzas of the *Canzone d'amore*, as this work of consummate technical skill came to be called, are stated in the opening stanza, lines 10–14:[10]

là dove posa, e chi lo fa creare,	(stanza II)
e qual sia sua vertute e sua potenza:	(stanza III)
l'essenza poi e ciascun suo movimento,	(stanza IV)
e 'l piacimento che 'l fa dire amare,	(stanza V)
e s'omo per veder lo po' mostrare.	(stanza V)

where it resides, who causes its creation,
what its virtue and power may be;
then its essence and each of its motions,

[9] Dino del Garbo, Pseudo-Egidio Colonna, Ugo dal Corno, Marsilio Ficino, Mario Equicola, Jacopo Mini, Francesco de' Vieri, Paolo del Rosso, and Girolamo Franchetta. The commentary of Ugo dal Corno is considered lost, while those of Ficino and Equicola are relatively brief passages occurring in larger treatises.

[10] The text quoted is that given by James Eustace Shaw in *Guido Cavalcanti's Theory of Love*, pp. 3–8.

and the pleasure which causes it to be named love,
and whether man can demonstrate its nature.

This *canzone* is a "scientific" treatise based on scholastic psychology and doctrine and on the poet's personal experience; it is expressly addressed to *conoscenti* only. The dramatic conflict arises from the sensual-intellectual contradiction in man. Love is an *accidente che sovente è fero, ed è sì altero* (accident that is often fierce, and is so haughty); not rational or moral. The lover at first thinks he sees in his lady the fulfillment of the ideal of feminine beauty lodged in his fantasy; her eyes seem to express understanding. But when she is aware of the fierce sensuality awakened in her lover, she is frightened and becomes hostile. The illusion of love is shattered and the lover is left in a dejected condition called "death."

Cavalcanti's ode stands apart from the main body of *dolce stil nuovo* poetry by the rigorously scientific approach, which is reflected in its severity of style and its technical skill, by the minimization of spiritual and contemplative elements, and by the lack of any religious expression. Yet we find in it a few motives common to the poetry of Guinizelli, Dante, and other *stilnuovo* poets: love enters through the eyes; it renders the lover incapable of action, "dead";[11] it occurs mainly in "people of worth." The melancholy introspection characteristic of the school is intensified. But Cavalcanti does not here compare his lady to an angel, nor attempt to harmonize his love with a philosophical or religious system, Platonic or Christian. He remains closer to the senses than other poets of his school, and prides himself on the basis of experience which underlies the poem. His images are dark as those of Dante's hell; and love leads not to the lover's moral improvement but to his destruction.

The early commentators on the poem recognized that Cavalcanti's love is sensual. Cavalcanti and his first two commentators did not know the *Symposium*, as did later commentators, some of

---

[11] This love-death is mentioned specifically by Guinizelli, and the paralyzing disconcertion of the young Dante in the *Vita Nuova* is accompanied by the same symptoms.

whom read Platonic notions into the ode. Cavalcanti's love is
somewhat refined sexual love without courtly characteristics, which
rejects the declarations of Provençal and Italian poets—later repeated by writers of prose love treatises—that love is sweet even
in its pain, and that love is a source of knowledge and of moral
betterment.

We shall examine briefly the two extant commentaries of the
fourteenth century and the most interesting commentary of the
sixteenth century. Dino del Garbo's commentary, probably the first,
on Cavalcanti's *Canzone d'amore* is that of a learned physician
familiar with Aristotle's works, which he frequently quotes to show
the philosophical derivation of specific concepts adopted by the
poet. He does not deal with the text as poetry, nor does he consider
the poetic traditions which it continued and challenged. He treats
Cavalcanti's love as an exclusively sensual phenomenon, devoid of
any idealism; he consequently minimizes as much as possible the
intellectual element of ideal beauty which is posited in the second
stanza.

> Ven da veduta forma che s'intende,
> Che prende nel possible intelletto,
> Come in subietto, loco e dimoranza.

It comes from a form beheld that one understands, which takes its
place and residence in the possible intellect, as in its subject.

The poet's love, he says, is vehement and intemperate sexual
appetite.

. . . Amor accipitur dupliciter: . . . quedam passio per quam in-
clinatur et movetur appetitus in aliquam rem que uidetur sibi bona
propter complacentiam eius, ratione cuiuscumque actus illius rei: et isto
modo non accipitur hic. . . . Sed alio modo accipitur amor specialiter
et proprie pro passione quadam, que iam adeo est in appetitu uehementer
impressa, ut difficulter remoueatur ab ipso: que passio est proprie circa
actus uenereos, in quibus actibus est furiositas et intemperantia, cum in
illos actus homo inclinetur ex appetitu naturali. Et hoc modo intelligitur
hic de ista passione que dicitur amor: que passio, propter uehementem
eius impressionem iam alterat corpus alteratione non naturali: unde,
iam quod in ipso dicatur egrotare potiot[12] et auctores medicine, qui de

---

[12] A word of uncertain meaning. Professor Paul Oskar Kristeller suggests the
emendation *pateat*, canceling the comma after *unde*.

egritudinibus et de eorum curis determinant, tractant de hac passione et modum etiam curationis suae. Et vocatur talis passio "ereos" ab auctoribus medicine.[13]

. . . Love is taken in two ways. . . . A certain passion by which the appetite is inclined and motivated toward something which appears good to it because of its pleasing condition, by reason of whatever act of that thing. Here it is not taken in this way . . . But in another way love is taken specially and characteristically as a certain passion which is stamped in the appetite so far that only with difficulty can it be removed from it. This passion expressly concerns venereal acts, in which there is violent agitation and intemperance, whereas in the former acts man is inclined by natural appetite. And so this passion which is called love is understood here: this passion alters the body because of its vehement impact with an unnatural alteration; whence it appears indeed that in this condition love may be called a sickness, and medical authors who fix the limits of sicknesses and of their cures treat of this passion and even of its cure. Such passion is called *ereos* by medical writers.

This passage states Dino's fundamental attitude toward the *Canzone d'amore.* He proceeds as a medical doctor, as later does the physician Ficino, to examine Cavalcanti's fierce passion as an illness—*ereos*—accompanied by alterations of temperature, color, tears and laughter, joy and desperation, fears and hope. These *alterationes* continued to receive ample poetic and literary expression in the sonnets of Petrarch, as in the literature of courtly love, and in Bruno's portrayal of "heroic" love. The cause of the alterations, according to Dino, is psychological: physical alterations are consequent upon the lover's fantasies, which run from joyful images to fearful ones:

Deinde, cum dicit, *Move cangiando colore,* loquitur auctor de motibus ipsius amoris, idest de diuersis alterationibus quas hec passio inducit in corpus. . . . Nam in amore corpus alteratur nunc ad istum colorem, nunc ad illum qui est oppositus; similiter etiam alteratur nunc

[13] G. Favati, "La glossa latina di Dino del Garbo a 'Donna me prega' del Cavalcanti," p. 98, in *Annali della Scuola Normale Superiore di Pisa,* Serie II, vol. XXI (1952), fasc. I–II, pp. 70–103. This article includes a transcription from MS. Vaticanus Chigianus L. V. 176 of the text of Dino del Garbo's commentary. Favati states that there are inaccuracies in the transcription by Otto Bird of the same manuscript in "The Canzone d'Amore of Cavalcanti according to the Commentary of Dino del Garbo," in *Medieval Studies* (1940), vol. II, pp. 160–74.

ad risum nunc ad planctum. . . . Similiter etiam in amore corpus nunc alteratur ad gaudium et spem, nunc ad timorem et desperationem. . . . Causa autem istarum diuersarum alterationum quas amor inducit in corpus est propter diuersitatem ymaginationum que representantur sibi de re quam amat: nunc autem representatur sibi aliquid de ipsa propter quod gaudet letatur et sperat; nunc vero representatur sibi aliquid propter quod timet tristatur et desperat. Et secundum hoc accidit quod in ipso diuersimode mouetur color naturalis et spiritus . . . (*ibid.*, pp. 98–99).

Next, when he says, *"It moves, changing color,"* the author speaks of the motions of love itself, that is of the diverse alterations which this passion produces in the body . . . For in love the body changes now to this color, now to the opposite; similarly also it alternates between laughter and tears . . . Similarly also in love the body changes now to joy and hope, now to fear and desperation . . . Moreover, the cause of these different alterations which love produces in the body results from the diversity of its imaginations about the thing which it loves: for now it imagines something about the love object on account of which it is joyful, happy, and hopeful; now, however, it imagines something which causes it to be apprehensive, sad, and desperate. And consequently it happens that the natural color and spirit are moved in diverse ways . . .

Del Garbo's commentary on the phrase *et di cor volontate* (stanza II, l. 6) declares that love "has its essence in the sensitive appetite" (Favati, p. 91). He explains Cavalcanti's reference to the possible intellect (stanza II, l. 8) by saying simply that in human beings love involves intellectual apprehension in addition to sensual passion (Favati, p. 93).

Reading in the following line (stanza II, ll. 7–10) *posança* rather than *pesanza*, he concludes that *passio amoris non habet esse in intellectu possibili* (the passion of love does not have its being in the possible intellect). The essence of love is in the sensitive appetite (Favati, p. 93).

The lover's death is reasonably interpreted not as a direct violence done to its subject by love, but as a cessation of a person's normal activities (*ibid.*, p. 96).

Apropos of the fourth stanza, Dino comments: ". . . Nam istud desiderium in amore adeo est magnum, quod quasi uidetur esse infinitum . . ." (p. 97: For this desire in love is so great that it seems to be almost infinite . . . .).

Like other commentators, Dino had to work with a corrupt text. All in all, his commentary is the most enlightening of those written during the Renaissance.

Contemporarily with Dino's commentary or a few years after it there appeared another commentary, attributed to Egidio Colonna.[14] The author's comments are less disciplined than those of Dino, and he prefers to cite Ovid rather than Aristotle or Arabic philosophers. His commentary shows a literary rather than a scientific tendency; he creates his own fanciful images to interpret those of Cavalcanti. He agrees with Dino that their poet's love is an irresistible sensual passion;[15] the power of the appetite in the soul is sovereign (*Il Canzoniere*, p. 103).

Again, apropos of the first lines of the third stanza, the commentator declares that the poet writes of a love that is a "passion of the appetite," devoid of morality because it is not generated by reason.

> . . . Dice l'autore che l'amore non è uertu naturale ne uertu morale, e cio è che dice *Non è uertute.* Unde rimane che l'amore è passione del appetito e cio è che l'autor dice non è uertute e proua spitialmente che non è uertu morale pero che non se genera da la ragione . . . (*ibid.*, p. 102)

> . . . Where the author says, "It is not a virtue," he means that love is neither a natural nor a moral virtue. Whence it follows that love is a passion of the appetite, since the author says that it is not a virtue and proves especially that it is not a moral virtue, because it is not generated by reason. . . .

The commentator relates Cavalcanti's statement that love "discerns poorly" (stanza III, l. 6) to the popular belief that love is blind (*Il Canzoniere*, p. 104).

Man can increase love at will, but lacks the power to diminish it. Love is an overpowering passion which robs the soul of its free will and replaces it with its own infinite desire.

---

[14] The authorship of this work is discussed in the appendix to this book.
[15] *Il Canzoniere Vaticano Barberino Latino 3953 (già Barb. XLV. 47)*, ed. Gino Lega, p. 99. The Ms. Vaticanus Barberinianus Latinus 3953, transcribed in this volume, contains the commentary, attributed to Egidio Colonna, on Guido Cavalcanti's *Donna mi prega*.

. . . L'omo per se medesimo lo po cressere quanto uole ma nol po menomare quanto uole e cio è che dice Ouidio (*ibid.,* p. 108).

. . . As Ovid says, man by himself can make it grow as much as he wishes but cannot minimize it as much as he wishes.

. . . Fa dimostramento la gran signoria che [l'amore] ae sopra l'animo la quale signoria è tanta da poi che l'amore è salito in sul feruore che l'animo è in tutto seruo si che no li rimane da niuna parte liberalitate (*ibid.,* p. 116).

. . . He demonstrates the dominion which [love] has over the soul— a dominion so great, after love has become fervent, that the soul is servile in everything, remaining free in nothing.

The fourth stanza opens as follows:

> L'essere è quando lo voler è tanto
> ch' oltra misura di natura torna.

Its being is when desire is such that it exceeds the measure of nature.

The commentator interprets *oltra misura* as meaning "infinite," and agrees with Dino's expressed view upon the stanza that love, or desire, is almost infinite.

Quanto a la prima parte è da sapere che l'altecça del amore se dimostra per lo suo uolere che quanto al uolere tanto è l'amore e per questa uia dimostra che l'amore è quasi cosa infinita perciò che 'l uolere il quale è suo essere e suo atto è infinito . . . (*ibid.,* p. 109).

As for the first part it must be known that the depth of love is shown by its desire, for the degree of love is equal to the degree of desire. In this way he demonstrates that love is an almost infinite thing, since the desire which is its act and essence is infinite. . . .

Cavalcanti addresses his *canzone* to a lady so as to begin it appropriately with that which is responsible for love's own beginning.

. . . Cossì l'amore comincia da le donne e ne le donne tende e pero pose l'autore raxoneuole principio dicendo *donna,* cominciando da quella cosa da la quale amore ae so nasscimento (*ibid.,* pp. 86–87).

. . . Thus love begins with women and tends toward women. Therefore the author began reasonably saying *donna,* commencing with that from which love takes birth.

He calls love an "accident" because he speaks of it of his own volition, unforced.

Quasi dica per mia uoglia mi mouo a dire de l'amore e non per necessitate di comandamento poi dice d'un accidente (*ibid.*, p. 87).

When he speaks of an accident it is as though he said, "By my will I am moved to speak of love and not by necessity of command."

Such an interpretation of Cavalcanti's poem could scarcely be the work of a philosophically trained mind. Other reasons for rejecting the authorship of Egidio Colonna are adduced in the appendix.

The explanation of the opening lines of the second stanza, which contain Cavalcanti's reference to the "darkness" of love, involves an elaborate simile in which the beloved is compared to the sun, the image of the beloved to the sun's ray, love to light, and the privation of love to obscurity (*ibid.*, pp. 93–94).

The obscurity which he at first calls the privation of love is said to be followed by a second obscurity which is the melancholy agitation (*conturbatione*) that arises in the soul after love has been generated, and always accompanies love (*ibid.*, pp. 94–95). The "contrary steps" of hope and desperation, repose and anxiety, confidence and fear, pleasure and displeasure, joy and bitterness, are so many manifestations of love's darkness, which is so powerful that it causes the dominance by the negative emotions of their positive opposites.

E però ben dice l'autore che la oscuritate fa dimora però che l'animo nel lo stato del amore più a melanconia che letitia, più dubio che securtà, più fatica che riposo, più angoscia che diletto, più amaritudine che dolceça, più dispendio che frutto e ciò è che dice Ouidio (*ibid.*, p. 95).

Therefore the author well says that darkness takes residence, because the soul in the state of love has more melancholy than joy, more doubt than sureness, more labor than repose, more anguish than delight, more bitterness than sweetness, more expenditure than fruition—and that is what Ovid says.

The commentator offers three reasons why love is found chiefly in *gente di valore*: love cannot be directed to oneself; it cannot be servile or for a reward (*ibid.*, p. 114); and it must be firm and stable (*ibid.*).

Apropos of line 4 in the fifth stanza, "Non già selvaggie le bieltà son dardo," Pseudo-Egidio speaks of *la beltà, cioè l'amore* (ibid., p. 121)—a quasi-identification which reappears in many love treatises of the sixteenth century. Shortly afterward, however, he declares that while beauty can be seen, love cannot be known by sight.

Of four commentaries on Cavalcanti's *canzone* written in the sixteenth century—by Jacopo Mini, Francesco de' Vieri, Paolo del Rosso, and Girolamo Frachetta—the most noteworthy is that of Paolo del Rosso. His commentary, published in 1568, declares that Cavalcanti's love is a vicious desire of corporeal beauty, often fatal to reason and full of afflictions, itself invisible, and generating only gratitude (*mercede*) in the heart of the beloved—in short, false love, unworthy of the name.

Et questa è la somma de l'oppenione, che ha Guido di tale amore: il quale ridotto in diffinizione sarà affetto ò ver desiderio vitioso di bellezza . . . verso di persona piaciuta, mortifero spesse volte à la ragione e pieno di diverse perturbazioni, acquistantesi (senza esserlo) per la falsa persuasione, nome di amore, & del tutto cosa invisibile, & da cui nasce non reciproco amore, ma mercede nel petto de la cosa amata. Et così è da lui affermato con ragioni filosofiche & naturali (Rosso, *Comento sopra la Canzone di Guido Cavalcanti*, p. 9).[16]

And here is the gist of Guido's opinion of such love: reduced to a definition it is affection or rather vicious desire of beauty . . . toward a person that one likes, often fatal to reason and full of diverse perturbations, acquiring by false persuasion the name of love (without so being); a completely invisible thing, which gives rise not to reciprocal love but to compassion in the breast of the beloved. And thus he affirms it with philosophical and natural reasons.

Paolo del Rosso acknowledges that Cavalcanti speaks from experience (*ibid.*, p. 112), but declares that the latter's love is but sensual passion masquerading under the name of love. Authentic love is that detailed in Plato's *Symposium*, which Paolo views in a Christian and moral light.

. . . Il vero amore [è] quello che risolve Diotima nel convito di Platone, & l'amore del Creatore verso le sue creature: & de le creature verso lui: & del l'un huomo con l'altro quello che intende al bene &

---

[16] *Mercede* is defined as "compassionate recompense of amorous servitude."

salute del animo de la cosa amata; & non à contentare il suo appetito
. . . (p. 24).

. . . True love [is] that which Diotima explains in Plato's *Symposium*, both the love of the Creator toward his creatures and of the creatures toward him; and of one man for another, that which aims at the good and health of the soul of the beloved object and not to appease its appetite.

Del Rosso shows a wide acquaintance with the previous commentaries and related literature, and cites Dante, Pseudo-Egidio, Petrarch, Marsilio Ficino, Giovanni Pico della Mirandola, Leone Ebreo, Mario Equicola, Jacopo Mini, Plato, and Aristotle. His statement that he will abstain from expounding his own opinion and stick to the interpretation of Guido's text is a thrust at the earlier commentaries.

. . . Noi facciamo professione di dare ad intendere qual sia l'oppinione di Guido in questa Canzone contenuta, sopra questo tale amore; e non di trattare d'amore, & dirne l'oppenion nostra, ò d'altra persona alcuna quantunque molto savia & letterata. Et ci parrà d'haver fatto assai se conseguiteremo il fine di questa nostra intenzione, atteso che quelli che in sin qui hanno preso a comentarla . . . l'hanno ò à pena tocca, ò più tosto oscurata che dichiarata (p. 16).

We profess to explain Guido's opinion about love, and not to treat of love stating our opinion or that of any other person however wise and lettered. And we shall think to have done a great deal if we attain this goal of ours, since those who so far have undertaken to comment on it have either skimmed the surface or obscured it rather than explaining it.

Before beginning his "particular declaration" of the *Canzone*, Paolo furnishes his readers with a prose paraphrase of the poem. Like Dino and Pseudo-Egidio he then gives a stanza-by-stanza commentary with special attention to key concepts and obscure phrases. Frequently alternative readings and interpretations are considered (Del Rosso, p. 19).[17]

The *donna* of the ode's initial line is, according to Paolo, a real woman (*ibid.*, p. 19). The "accident" of love can be called *altero*

[17] E.g., Mars' obscurity, p. 32 f.; p. 49 f., he prefers "Egli è creato da sensato Nome," interpreting *Nome* as *Nume,* to "Egli è creato & ha sensato nome." Stanza II, line 5.

because it appertains to appetite and affection (p. 24). "Death" in the third stanza is not intended literally, but refers to man's deviation from the perfect good (p. 87). The vicious affection which Cavalcanti calls love is so powerful that it often kills man's reason and moral virtue. Man can indeed be called dead when his reason, which is his very essence, has been killed (p. 88).

That lovers change their color and pass from laughter to tears is every day attested by their acts (p. 106).

LORENZO DE' MEDICI'S COMMENTARY ON SOME OF HIS SONNETS

Lorenzo de' Medici in his commentary on his own sonnets provides a dual aid to their understanding by recounting, in a way somewhat reminiscent of Dante's narrative procedure in the *Vita Nuova,* the succession of his thoughts and actions relating to his love, and by stating the philosophico-cultural background of the sonnets and of the love story which they relate. Some of the explanations[18] are of the kind one might expect to find in an annotated edition of his lyrics. The theory of love and beauty which furnishes the doctrinal basis for his sonnets is strongly influenced by Ficino and Platonism; but the ascetic tendency of Christian Neoplatonism is replaced by an unworried acceptance of sensual love.

Lorenzo at the beginning devotes several pages to a justification of his commentary and his sonnets, which soon involves a defense of love itself. The objection that his amorous verses and his comments are a frivolous undertaking would be just, he says, only if men were of such nature as to always act perfectly. The sonnet is inferior to no other vernacular verse form; its virtue consists in its difficulty (*Opere,* p. 22). Lorenzo confirms its excellence by a citation from Plato.

È sentenzia di Platone che il narrare brevemente e dilucidamente molte cose non solo pare mirabile tra gli uomini, ma quasi cosa divina. La brevità del sonetto non comporta che una sola parola sia vana . . . (*ibid.*).

[18] E.g., of true and false dreams. Lorenzo de' Medici, *Comento sopra alcuni de' suoi sonetti,* in *Opere,* I, 83.

It is Plato's opinion that to narrate many things briefly and clearly not only seems wonderful in men, but almost divine. The brevity of the sonnet does not allow one word to be in vain.

He praises the *canzone* by a reference to classical tradition; he thinks it similar to the elegy (*ibid.*).

Lorenzo justifies the commentary by an appeal to tradition: Dante himself commented on his *canzoni* and sonnets; Egidio Colonna and Dino del Garbo commented on Cavalcanti's subtle *canzone*. It is not true then that only theological and philosophical writings are worthy of exposition.

Nè io sono stato il primo che ho comentato versi importanti simili amorosi subietti, perchè Dante lui medesimo comentò alcuna delle sue canzoni ed altri versi; ed io ho letto quelli di Egidio romano e Dino del Garbo, eccellentissimi filosofi, sopra quella sottilissima canzone di Guido Cavalcanti, uomo al tempo suo riputato primo dialettico che fussi al mondo, . . . Donna mi prega . . . (*ibid.*, p. 17).

Nor am I the first to have commented on verses about such amorous subjects, because Dante himself commented on some of his *canzoni* and other verses; and I have read those of Egidio Romano and Dino del Garbo, most excellent philosophers, about that very subtle *canzone* by Guido Cavalcanti, a man renowned in his time as the leading dialectician of the world, . . . *Donna mi prega* . . .

There are in addition, Lorenzo mentions, the many commentaries on Dante's *Comedy*.

To those who say that the vernacular is an unworthy means of expression he replies that to be common does not denote inferiority, for every entity is more excellent to the extent that it is more universal and communicable. He believes that Italy shares a common vulgar language.

E però non pare che l'essere comune a tutta Italia la nostra materna lingua li tolga dignità . . . (p. 18).

And thus it does not seem that its being common to all Italy should take away the dignity of our mother tongue . . .

The love which is Lorenzo's subject matter is human love; which, if not the supreme good which Plato celebrated, may be considered good for its beneficent effects, provided that it is constant. Furthermore, nothing that is natural is to be condemned; and nothing is more natural than the desire to be united with a beautiful thing. Sexual desire is ordained by nature for the propagation of the species, and so long as it is fulfilled within the natural order it cannot be blamed.

E mettendo per al presente da parte quello amore, il quale, secondo Platone, è mezzo a tutte le cose a trovare la loro perfezione e riposarsi ultimamente nella suprema Bellezza, cioè Dio, parlando di quello amore che s'estende solamente ad amare l'umana creatura, dico che, se bene questa non è quella perfezione d'amore che si chiama "sommo bene", almanco veggiamo chiaramente contenere in se tanti beni ed evitare tanti mali, che secondo la comune consuetudine della vita umana tiene luogo di bene, massime se è ornata di quelle circostanzie e condizioni che si convengono ad un vero amore, che mi pare siano due: la prima che si ami una cosa sola, la seconda che questa tale cosa si ami sempre (p. 14).

And putting aside for the present that love which according to Plato is the means for all things to find their perfection and rest ultimately in the supreme Beauty, that is, God; speaking of that love which extends only to loving a human creature, I say that even if this is not that perfection of love that is called "the highest good," at least we clearly see that it contains in itself so many goods and avoids so many evils that according to the common usage of human life it occupies the place of good, especially if it is adorned by those circumstances and conditions which are proper to true love, which seem to me to be two: first, that one love only one object; second, that this object be loved always.

A me pare si possa poco biasimare quello che è naturale: nessuna cosa è più naturale che l'appetito d'unirsi colla cosa bella, e questo appetito è stato ordinato dalla natura negli uomini per la propagazione umana, cosa molto necessaria alla conservazione dell'umana spezie (p. 16).

It seems to me that one may scarcely blame what is natural. Nothing is more natural than the appetite of uniting with a beautiful object, and this appetite has been ordained in men by nature for human propagation, a very necessary thing for the conservation of the human species.

Lorenzo's theories of love are a synthesis of Platonism and the lyrical tradition of the early Renaissance, stated with moderation and good sense. Far from being reprehensible, human love is evidence of *gentilezza* and a great soul; it incites men to virtue. It is defined simply as the desire of beauty; hence it rejects ugliness.

Love "is born of the eyes and of beauty," but requires for its preservation other qualities in the beloved, which the lover must know (pp. 14–15).

. . . Pure credo l'amore tra gli uomini non solamente non essere reprensibile, ma quasi necessario ed assai vero argumento di gentilezza e grandezza d'animo, e sopratutto cagione d'invitare gli uomini a cose degne ed eccellenti, ed esercitare e riducere in atto quelle virtù che in potenzia sono nell'anima nostra. Perchè chi cerca diligentemente quale sia la vera difinizione dell'amore, trova non essere altro che appetito di bellezza. E se questo è, tutte le cose deforme e brutte necessariamente dispiacciono a chi ama (p. 14).

. . . Yet I believe that love among humans not only is not reprehensible, but is an almost necessary and very true sign of nobility and greatness of soul, and above all the occasion of encouraging men in worthy and excellent things. It exercises and brings into act those virtues which are potential in our soul. For he who seeks diligently the true definition of love finds it to be none other than appetite of beauty. And if this is so, all deformed and ugly things are necessarily displeasing to him who loves.

Lorenzo's justification of love and love poetry then shifts to a strongly personal plane:

Quali sieno sute le mie maligne persecuzioni per essere assai publiche e assai note, qual sia suta la dolcezza e refrigerio che il mio dolcissimo e constantissimo amore ha dato a queste, è impossibile che altri che io lo possi intendere (pp. 17–18).

My malicious persecutions, although quite public and very well known, and the sweetness and comfort that my sweetest and most constant love has been for them, it is impossible for anyone but myself to understand.

Having finished his prefatory remarks, Lorenzo begins the exposition of his sonnets. The first four are in the nature of a poetic exercise, having been composed to honor the memory of a lady whose death he deplores as public loss (p. 34). The better to satisfy himself and those who suffered more acutely, he forced himself to believe that he had lost a very dear person (p. 35).

Both sonnets and commentary are the work of an author acutely aware of his people's literary traditions.

The succeeding sonnets are for a lady "of the greatest beauty" who wrought in him "an incredible desire" that deprived him of his liberty of thought and action (pp. 35–37). Being unable, in accordance with custom, to describe the beauty and the eyes of his lady, he tries to demonstrate the gentility of her wit and character (p. 52). He carefully describes the special function of the eyes in love and beauty and seeks to define *gentilezza,* "love being not other than a gentle passion" (p. 32). Lovely eyes, the sign of singular beauty, enamor and render *gentili* the object of their glance.

> . . . Diremo in questo modo: farsi gentile le cose che sono vedute da quelli occhi, quando Amore gli muove; per li occhi si presuppone una singulare bellezza, per amore pietà; e dove concorrono queste due cose, nasce, nel cuore di chi vede, gran dolcezza ed amore, il quale, secondo che abbiamo detto, non è mai sanza gentilezza (p. 55).

> . . . We shall speak in this wise: the things that are seen by those eyes, when love moves them, become gracious. Through the eyes one presupposes a singular beauty; through love, pity. And where these two things are both present, there is born in the heart of him who sees a great sweetness and love, which, as we have said, is never without gentility.

Sight is the most worthy sense (p. 97). It is the eyes which tell the heart to flee to the beloved. The comment on the sonnet, *Lasso a me! quand'io son la dove sia,* reads as follows:

> . . . Guardando negli occhi suoi, vedevo Amore rinvolto ne' raggi di que' begli occhi, e mostrandogli la via come potessi fuggire da me negli occhi della donna mia . . . (p. 39).

> Looking into her eyes, I saw Love enveloped in the rays of those beautiful eyes and showing the way by which I could flee from myself into the eyes of my lady . . .

In mutual love there is a reciprocal exchange of hearts, which is the surest token of favor.

> . . . Avendo fatto la donna mia una commutazione del suo cuore al mio, cioè tolto il mio per se e a me donato il suo, come mostra il presente sonetto, nessuno maggior dono mi poteva dare, ne fare più evidente segno che io fussi pieno della grazia sua (*ibid.,* comment on the sonnet, *Lasso! che sent'io più muover nel petto?* p. 110).

My lady having made an exchange of her heart for mine, that is, taken mine for herself and given hers to me, as the present sonnet shows, she could make me no greater gift and give no clearer token that I was full of her grace.

Lorenzo defines *gentilezza* as the perfect and graceful performance of one's function.

Diremo adunque "gentile" essere quella cosa, la quale è bene atta e disposta a fare perfettamente l'ufficio che a lei si conviene, accompagnata da grazia, la quale è dono di Dio (p. 57).

We shall then call *gentile* that thing which is well fit and disposed to do perfectly the office which is proper to it, accompanied by grace, which is the gift of God.

He comments on the sonnet, *Quanta invidia ti porto, o cor beato*, that the phrase *cuor beato* presupposes *gentilezza*: ". . . Quella cosa è veramente beata che è gentile . . ." (p. 66: That thing is truly blessed which is *gentile* . . .).

Many words which Lorenzo repeats from the vocabulary of Dante's *Vita Nuova*—*beato, mirabile, pio, salute*—have lost their theological connotations.

. . . Lasciato il cercare cogli occhi la donna mia, rifuggii al cercarne col pensiero, al quale domandai la salute mia, cioè che lui almeno mi mostrassi la mia donna . . . (*ibid.*, comment on the sonnet, *Quando la bella imagine Amor pose*, p. 101).

Having ceased to seek my lady with my eyes, I took solace in seeking her with my thought, of which I asked my salvation—that it would at least show me my lady . . .

His lady's hand, following her eyes into the poet's heart, lifted out his heart and replaced it with her own: this act he describes as *cosa mirabile ed inaudita* (a marvelous and unheard-of thing); as *amoroso miracolo* (pp. 111–112).

Gentilezza is engendered by supernal beauty, which Lorenzo Platonically identifies with the good and the true. The soul lives to the extent that it fulfills its desire for the beautiful, the good, and the true, which are imparted to it without diminution of the highest beauty.

. . . Essendo una medesima cosa somma bellezza e somma bontà e somma verità, secondo Platone, nella vera bellezza di necessità è la bontà e verità in modo annesse, che l'una con l'altra si converte. E intendendosi per li cuori gentili gli animi elevati, secondo che abbiamo detto, e perfetti, bisogna sia vero che ogni gentil cuore viva d'infinita bellezza, perchè il bello, buono e vero sono obietto e fine di ogni ragionevole desiderio, dando vita a quegli che gli appetiscono; perchè chi si parte dal bello, dal buono e dal vero, si può dire non vivere, perchè fuora di queste perfezioni non si dice esser cosa alcuna. Adunque, come il sole co' raggi suoi fa risplendere le stelle sanza diminuzione della sua luce, così questa somma bellezza infonde come raggi ne' gentili cuori della sua grazia, cioè un lume spirituale, per lo quale vivono e speritualmente relucono . . . (pp. 132–133).

The highest beauty and the highest goodness and the highest truth being the same thing, according to Plato, in true beauty there are necessarily goodness and truth, connected in such a way that the one is converted into the other. And understanding by noble hearts elevated and perfect souls, as we have said, it must be true that every noble heart lives in infinite beauty. For he who departs from beauty, goodness, and truth may be said not to live, because outside of these perfections nothing may be said to be. Thus as the sun with its rays causes the stars to shine without diminution of its own light, so does this highest beauty infuse noble hearts with its grace—a spiritual light—by which they live and spiritually shine.

Lorenzo cites a three-fold "Platonic" division of beauty according to whether it is predicated of soul, of body, or of voice (p. 46). Bodily beauty depends upon proportion and a certain subjective appeal of grace and comeliness.

La bellezza del corpo e grazia d'esso pare che proceda dall'essere bene proporzionato, di grazioso aspetto, ed in effetto da una certa venustà e leggiadria, la quale qualche volta piace non tanto per la perfezione e buona proporzione del corpo, quanto per una certa conformità che ha cogli occhi ai quali piace, che dal cielo o dalla natura procede; e tutto questo è obietto ed indizio degli occhi (p. 46).

It seems that beauty and grace of body proceed from being well proportioned, of gracious appearance, and actually from a certain loveliness and grace, which sometimes is pleasing not so much for the perfection and good proportion of the body as through a certain conformity that it has with the eyes to which it is pleasing, which proceeds from heaven or from nature; and all this is the object and manifestation of the eyes.

The object of the poet's heart is the eyes and the beauty of his lady (p. 58). The essence of love is the transformation of the lover into the beloved.

E, considerando veramente, Amore non è altro che una trasformazione dello amante nella cosa amata; e, quando reciproco, di necessità ne nasce la medesima trasformazione in quel che prima ama, che diventa poi amato, per modo che maravigliosamente vivono gli amanti l'uno nell'altro, chè altro non vuole inferire questa commutazione di cori (p. 112).

And considering truly, Love is simply a transformation of the lover into the object of love; and when reciprocal, it necessarily gives rise to the same transformation into him who first loves, who then becomes loved, so that lovers live marvelously in each other, for this exchange of hearts means nothing else.

To achieve this perfection the lover must first "die" in respect to less perfect things (p. 24). There are three steps in love—to know beauty, to love it, to enjoy it (p. 58). Knowledge necessarily precedes love (p. 41), just as it precedes the will (p. 72). Every strong love procedes from strong imagination, and makes its subjects melancholy (p. 115). Lorenzo for his· part declares that he is numbered among those who have loved "with very great fervor" (*ibid.*). Lovers are subject to many kinds of pain, but all in all the sources of pain are two: jealousy and privation; in the latter case pain is vented by tears, sighs, or thoughts. Love necessarily includes hope (p. 67); but all lovers are subject to torment, especially at night, when for astro-medical reasons all infirmities are more likely to afflict the person who is ill (p. 78). Lovers are more wretched than non-lovers because of their greater desire (p. 82). Although happiness is the end of love and its motivating factor, few are the lovers who attain it; their unhappiness in the process is almost insupportable.

. . . Io guidico che la dolcezza degli amanti sia rara, e qualche volta assai grande, ma le infelicità loro essere quasi continue, ed il dolore, sanza comparazione, maggiore . . . (p. 91).

. . . I believe that lovers' sweetness is rare and sometimes very great, but their unhappiness is almost continuous and their pain immeasurably greater.

The lover's happiness consists in uniting inseparably with the beauty which he desires—an act very difficult of attainment.

. . . L'amore desidera ed è mosso da un fine che si chiama "felicità" e "beatitudine", la quale consiste nel congiugnersi con quella bellezza che l'amore appetisce e con essa inseparabilmente stare. Ed insino a tanto che a questo fine di beatitudine non si perviene, amore non solamente non è bene, anzi è pena e tormento insopportabile, più e manco secondo la grandezza dell'amore (pp. 47–48).

Love desires and is moved by an end which is called "happiness" and "beatitude," which consists in joining with that beauty which love desires and staying with it inseparably. And until one arrives at this end of beatitude love not only is not good, but is rather a pain and an unbearable torment, greater or less according to the degree of love.

Lorenzo's language is frequently as Platonic as that of the *trattati d'amore*, but his real attitude toward love is frankly sensual. For example; when he writes about the sonnet, *Candida, bella e delicata mano*, that "in the ladder of love one ascends from step to step," the steps he has in mind are anything but Platonic. The first "step" is from looking into his lady's eyes to touching her hand (p. 61). Lorenzo almost reverses the traditional Platonic ladder of humanist love treatises in which the senses occupied the lowest rung on the ladder:

. . . Presupponedo che Amore muova tutti li atti che abbiamo detto della donna mia, cioè il vedere, il cantare, il parlare, il ridere, il sospirare ed ultimamente il toccare, manco affezione mostra il vedere che il cantare, manco il cantare che il parlare; e così dico di tutti gli altri insino al tatto (p. 120).

. . . Presupposing that Love motivates all the actions of my Lady that we have named, that is, seeing, singing, talking, laughing, sighing, and ultimately touching; seeing shows less affection than singing, singing less than talking, and so I say of all the others up to touching.

GIROLAMO BENIVIENI

Dante was not the only author of love poems who was moved by "fear of infamy" to alter their import by a prose commentary. Girolamo Benivieni (1453–1542), the son of a Florentine notary and a member of the Platonic Academy in Florence headed by

Marsilio Ficino under Medicean auspices, in his later years repented for religious reasons the love lyrics of his youth. Being unable to suppress them, he appended a commentary which interpreted them in a theological sense. It is apparent that the strong religious element in his character became progressively more severe and ascetic as he grew older.

In his preface to Luca della Robbia he refers to his eclogues as *ineptie veramente puerile* (*Opere*, p. 73 r). Indeed, they do not merit detailed analysis. They contain no important philosophical doctrines and are mediocre as poetry. They are composed in *terza rima,* perhaps in tribute to Dante, Benivieni's admiration of whom is expressed in a *Cantico in laude di Dante Alighieri Poeta Fiorentino, & della sua oltre à ogni humano concetto divinamente composta commedia.* Benivieni sees his eclogues as chaste in thought, but occasionally marked by "immature license" (p. 78 v) in expression. The purpose of the arguments—one for each of the eight eclogues—is to remove the "sinister opinion" into which they may have fallen by penetrating the "veil" of occasionally "tender and licentious words" which covers the true sense, "pure in itself" (pp. 73 v–74 r). Read in conjunction with the arguments, the eclogues will be freed of any "occasion for scandal" and their author of any possible blame (p. 74 r).

A few examples of his interpretations will suffice. In the first eclogue the character Moelibeo represents the author and Phileno, his desire of praise. In their "mystic sense" they signify respectively the soul's superior part, desirous of God, and its inferior part which loves mundane and corruptible things.

The fourth eclogue, dealing with historical events in Florence— the state of quiet in 1478 and the subsequent "storm" and premature death of Giuliano de' Medici—is interpreted in a theological sense by the argument:

Allegoricamente per el Tauro sottomettente el collo al gioco, & trahente Apollo dalle onde salse sopra lorizonte verso il mezzo di, sintende el libero arbitrio dellhuomo sottentrante al giogo di Christo, & elevante in virtu di quello lanima per cognitione & amore da el turbido quasi mare delli appetiti sensitivi sopra lo orizonte, che è termino fra el di & la notte, cioè fra le tenebre del peccato, & la luce della gratia, &

fra la ignorantia & la scientia, & conducente a verso mezzo di, cioè verso essa luce della divina gratia . . . (p. 93 v).

Allegorically the Bull submitting its neck to the yoke and pulling Apollo from the briny waves over the horizon toward the south signifies the free will of man taking the yoke of Christ and thereby elevating the soul by cognition and love from the turbid sea, so to speak, of the sensitive appetites, over the horizon, which is the border between day and night, that is, between the shadows of sin and the light of grace, between ignorance and science, and leading toward the south, that is, toward the light of divine grace . . .

The fifth eclogue again laments the death of Giuliano de' Medici and illustrates the vanity of things, particularly of human affections. The second praises Giovanni Pico della Mirandola; the third praises the glory, which Benivieni admired as a youth, of poetry and of the exercise of arms. The theme of the sixth eclogue, entitled *Laura*, is the author's "most ardent" love of poetry. In the seventh, entitled *Pico*, Giovanni Pico della Mirandola and Lorenzo de' Medici sing their allegorical loves. The eighth, in a pessimistic tone, gives "some . . . precepts of this pastoral exercise."

THE COMMENTARY OF GIOVANNI PICO DELLA MIRANDOLA ON BENIVIENI'S *Canzone d'amore*

In 1486 Benivieni undertook "to reduce to a few verses that which Marsilio [Ficino] in many pages most elegantly describes" (*Opera Omnia* of Pico della Mirandola, I, 733).[19] The conciseness and obscurity of his *Canzone d'amore* are reminiscent of Cavalcanti's ode, although it lacks the latter's technical skill. Indeed, Benivieni's *Canzone* also brought forth a learned commentary, from the pen of Giovanni Pico della Mirandola. Its doctrine of love, however, is altogether different from that of Cavalcanti's poem. Love's spiritual beneficence, its divine origin, and its ascensive impetus in Benivieni's *Canzone* relate it to the sonnets of Guinizelli, of *stilnuovo* poets, and of Dante, which express some vaguely Platonistic sentiments in conjunction with Christian and chivalric concepts of love. Benivieni's ode, as the author himself tells us, is derived directly from Ficino's *Commentary* on the *Symposium*.

[19] See section entitled "Marsilio Ficino" in Chapter II.

Giovanni Pico della Mirandola, a kindred spirit and a fellow-member of the Platonic Academy, wrote an exhaustive prose *Commentary* in three books, of which the first two treat generally of Neoplatonic philosophy, and the third is a particular commentary on Benivieni's *Canzone*. The publication of the *Canzone* and the *Commentary*, however, was long postponed, for the authors wished to see, Benivieni relates, "whether it could by some revision from Platonic become Christian" (*ibid.*). "There were born in our minds some shadows of doubt as to whether it were proper for a professor of Christ's law, wishing to treat of love, especially heavenly and divine, to treat of it as Platonic and not as Christian."

Also, says Pico in the third book of his *Commentary*, whereas natural and moral philosophy treat of vulgar love, it is the theologian's prerogative to speak of divine love.

Upon the premature death of Pico, Benivieni "decided to leave this *canzone* and the commentary together with many other of [his] verses *in arbitrio della polvere*" (subject to dust)—a decision reversed only by the "efforts and desires of others," who prepared the publication of the poem together with other "books and commentaries" of Pico before Benivieni could prevent it. He therefore cautions that "in all those places where this *Canzone* . . . following the doctrine of Plato departs in any way from Christian truth, may the authority of Christ and his saints, as well as the irrefragable reasons brought forth in opposition by our theologians, especially by the angelic doctor St. Thomas of Aquinas, weigh more heavily [with the reader] than the opinion of an unbeliever (*uno huom gentile*)"—that is, Plato. Benivieni insists that he is merely reciting *sanza alcuna approbatione* (without approval) the opinion of others: the title itself, *Canzone d'amore composta per Hieronymo Benivieni Cittadino Fiorentino, secondo la mente et oppinione de' Platonici,* openly declares his wish "to treat of Love not according to Catholic truth, but according to the mind and opinion of the Platonists."

He feels that Plato scholars, "reading attentively will find in his commentary many clarifications (*lumi*) by means of which their mind's eye can more easily and perhaps with new perspective penetrate to the intimate concepts (*medolle*) of some of the more remote senses of so great a Philosopher."

It is evident from the tone of approval and gratitude toward Pico in this introduction that the latter's commentary agrees substantially with Benivieni's intended meaning. It is even possible that the idea of a commentary may have arisen in conversations about the poem between the two friends. The utility—indeed, the necessity—of such a commentary is occasioned by the poem's obscurity, an inevitable result of the ambitious attempt to concentrate into 154 verses a large body of Neoplatonic doctrine. The evident debt of Benivieni and of Pico to Ficino is acknowledged by themselves. The poem and its "particular" commentary (Book III), may therefore be studied as if they were a unified work produced by the collaboration of two authors.

The first book of Pico's *Commentary* treats of standard Neoplatonic themes: three modes of being of all things including Ideas —causal, formal, and participatory; one God, the source of everything; the unity of the intellect, created *ab aeterno* by God; three natures—God, angelic nature, and rational nature; the *anima mundi* and its relation to the soul of man, whose central position as *vincolo et nodo del mondo* gives him the name of Microcosm.

The second book largely follows Ficino's Platonic exposition of love and beauty. Desire follows knowledge of good things; beauty is a kind of harmony compounded with the undefinable quality of grace. Beauty may be either corporeal or intelligible. The birth of love signifies the desire of material Chaos for the perfection of angelic Forms. Love is of three kinds: angelic, human, bestial.

The esthetic effect of Benivieni's poem is conditioned by its abstract content. We are here not in the realm of lyrical or phantastic poetry, but in the intellectual world of concepts and their interrelations. We shall therefore examine the poem and its commentary with the purpose of discovering its philosophic content.

Stanza I. The love of which the poet speaks, Pico comments, is not the vulgar love which Cavalcanti names in the poem, *Donna mi prega,* but heavenly love, of which the former is but a weak image.[20] Man's soul is rational, but heavenly love is the function of the intellect, which man can experience only by elevating him-

[20] Page references are omitted, as the stanza numbers are sufficient to locate Pico's comments in his *Opera Omnia,* I, 733 ff.

self to angelic status. The sovereign position held by celestial love with regard to man caused the poet to say that Love "forces" his wit (l. 5). The superior virtue of love, however, does not debase itself in descending (l. 14) into man's heart, the *stanza* or habitation of his soul, but rather pulls man upward by its virtue to Faith. The poet's humility results from the fact that his appetites are governed and restrained (l. 1). He says (ll. 7–8), *Il cor vien meno et la lingua repugna a tanta impresa* (The heart falters and the tongue refuses such an enterprise), because he fears himself incapable of reaching the heights of celestial love; but with the help of Love itself, he hopes to discover its mysteries.

Pico's commentary, based on no explicit indication in the poem itself, states, in keeping with Platonic dialogues, that the ascensive motive power of love begins in the friendship of a man for a beautiful and inspiring youth. It is for this reason he declares, that Benivieni in contrast to Cavalcanti, who adopted a feminine name, *Donna,* calls Love by a masculine name, *Amore*—masculinity in the Pythagorean tradition symbolizing perfection, femininity imperfection. Rational love should dominate vulgar love, which is localized in the sensitive appetite, an inferior part of the soul, as every order of being in nature governs its inferiors and is governed by its superiors. The great hierarchy whose extremes are God and brutes is reproduced in the order of the "little world" of the human soul—sense, imagination, reason, and intellect. A chaste rational love such as that of Socrates for Alcibiades and other Athenian youths, has no desire of "anything dirty" (*sozza*), but "is excited by the exterior corporal beauty to look inside that of the soul" whence it came, and the lover is led to higher degrees of spiritual perfection. Thus Socrates, excited by the beauty of Phaedrus on the bank of the river Ilissus, sang the highest mysteries of theology. This motive is taken up in the sixth, seventh, and eighth stanzas, which describe six degrees in the hierarchy of beauty and love.

Stanza II. The second stanza (ll. 1–2) declares Love's divine origin *dal divin fonte dell'increato ben* (from the divine fount of uncreated good), and its all-pervasive effects. Its function on the human plane is to "force" man to the sky—a process described in the later stanzas. In the second half of this stanza the poet invokes

Love and Apollo—the former because he who would speak of love must first be transformed into Love, by Love himself; the latter because the gift of eloquence was attributed to Apollo, as well as to the muses. Love's three effects—[*Amore*] *muov' el ciel, l'alme informa, e'l mondo regge* (1. 4:[Love] moves heaven, informs the souls, and governs the world)—are to be understood not in terms of "effective" causation—for it is God who produces the ideas in the angelic mind; the mind which makes the soul shine with ideal splendor; and the sky's own soul which moves it—but in the sense that none of these effects would follow from its principal cause were it not for love, which converts the soul to mind and the mind to God.

Stanza III. The subject of the third stanza is angelic love. Here Benivieni describes the ever-working cyclical nature of love. When the "divine sun," or, as Pico interprets the stanza, the abundance of ideas, descends into the angelic mind, the latter is inflamed with desire of God. The more completely the angelic mind embraces God, the more ardently does it desire him. The *vero ciel* is God, for as God is the first among all things, so is the sky first among corporeal things. Only intelligible or spiritual things are called "true" by the Pythagoreans and ancient theologians.[21] Truth is the philosopher's goal, appearance the sophist's. The "divine sun" which "descends" is the light of the ideas emanating from God, the source of spiritual light. Ideas for Pico are the substantial forms of the angels; they resemble Dante's circle of angels and blessed spirits who contemplate and serve God. The *frondi* (1. 4) again refer to the ideas, which are called "alive" because through them the angels derive the power of performing their intrinsic operation, which is to understand. *Lei chel suo primo ben ricerca et vuole* (1. 5: That which seeks and wants its first good) refers to the ideal light which kindles in the angelic mind such a heat and insatiable thirst that the lover, or angelic mind, is transformed into the beloved, ideal beauty:

[21] Pico, following Ficino's acceptance of Gemistus Pletho's belief, considered authentic the writings preserved under the names of Zoroaster, Hermes Trismegistus, Orpheus, and Pythagoras, which modern scholars attribute to late antiquity.

Quinc'el primo disio che lei transforma
Al vivo sol dell'increata luce
Mirabilmente alhor s'incende e infiamma (ll. 9–11).

Hence the first desire which transforms it to the living sun of the uncreated light then marvelously kindles and flares.

The phrase *increata luce* (uncreated light) refers to God. The ideas occasion "innate desire" (1. 6) because, although received from God by the angelic mind, they are possessed by the latter not as accidents, but as substance.

The parentage of Venus, *chi Cypri honora* (she who honors Cyprus), is attributed in accordance with the *Symposium* to Plenty (*Poro*) and Poverty (*Penia*), which Pico interprets in Book II of his *Commentary* as the abundance of ideas and unformed, actless matter, respectively.

Stanza IV. Perfect cognition of anything, says Pico, entails the understanding both of its essence (*la natura sua propria*) and its properties. The third stanza declares the nature of love; the fourth, its properties and effects. By Venus, *la bella Cyprigna* (1. 2), is intended ideal beauty. The poet says that love is of the beautiful. So holy a name as love, comments Pico, can be attributed to the desire of nothing that is ugly or deformed. Lines 5–8 describe the power of love to awaken in us the dormant desire of the soul for "that celestial and intelligible beauty" which the oppression of the body has made it forget. Love's instrument in this quickening is the sensuous beauty of bodies, which leads ultimately to the divine source of all beauty. The next five lines (ll. 9–14) describe the emergence of man's higher life from the death of his lower functions. Pico explains that *morendo el cor* (the heart dying) means that the human part of the soul must die in order that man may become an angel—an extension of the poetic concept of death held by poets of the *dolce stil nuovo*. When man is completely absorbed by his higher calling, says Pico, the operation of his lesser potencies, excepting only those of the vegetative soul, are suspended, so that the soul may be said to be separated from the body—the soul's "first death." To achieve complete union with the heavenly Venus a second death is necessary, in which the soul, kissing and embracing Venus in an indissoluble bond, becomes one with the soul of Venus.

Closing his comments on the fourth stanza, Pico declares that while love is the cause (*cagione*) of the production of all things, it is not to be attributed, in the sense given it "by Plato and our poet," to God, "because in him it would be an imperfection"—a position similar to that taken by Leone Ebreo. Love in Benivieni's poem has the meaning of the desire and attraction of all things toward ideal beauty.

Stanza V. The fifth stanza describes the birth of the vulgar Venus, or sensuous beauty, a reflection of the celestial Venus depicted in the two preceding stanzas. That visible things can be seen only in light is true of both the intelligible and the corporeal world. The forms which illuminate matter are rays of the intelligible sun. Likewise, sensuous light is an emanation from intelligible light. As the angelic mind, seeing imperfectly in itself the heavenly Venus, or ideal beauty, amorously desires to convert itself to the "paternal sun," or God, so does the vulgar Venus seek its heavenly counterpart.

Stanza VI. The sixth, seventh, and eighth stanzas reconstruct the Platonic ladder of love. The sixth stanza describes how the particular beauty of an individual body kindles the fire of love in another's soul. In explanation of this process, Pico first expounds the nature of corporeal beauty, in the manner of other Florentine humanists, including Ficino and Lorenzo de' Medici. Two things are apparent: the "material disposition of the body," consisting in the proper "quantity," or proportion and position of parts, and quality, which is in figure and color; and a certain "grace" (*gratia*), which alone inflames the lover's heart. Common opinion holds that the second component of beauty has its origin in the first; not so Pico, who declares that we frequently see a body perfect in the first respect, but utterly lacking in the second, and vice versa. He therefore attributes the second "effect"—that which alone excites love—not to the body, but to the soul.

The Plotinian scheme of universal emanation and return is admirably reflected, as the commentator observes, by the structure of the *canzone* itself, which first describes celestial beauty and love in stanzas III and IV, then relates in the fifth stanza how from them arise their earthly counterparts, and in the concluding stanzas shows "how from sensuous beauty one rises by ordered steps to intelligible beauty." Pico writes that this process, known to but few, is what Plato in the *Philebus* calls "deducing unity into multitude, and reducing multitude to its unity." "Following then the author, this order shows how through six steps (*gradi*) beginning with material beauty man happily arrives at beauty's first source."

1. The first and most imperfect degree of beauty is that of a specific body, such as of Alcibiades or Phaedrus, which presents itself to the eyes.

2. The image received by the eyes is reformed internally by the soul, though still in material and phantastic form.

3. The soul "with the light of the active intellect," separating that received form from all particularity, considers the nature of corporeal beauty in itself, and turns to the universal beauty of all bodies. This degree is the highest attainable by a soul centered upon the senses. The second and third degrees are expressed by lines 14–15 of the sixth stanza, the "sweet error" of whose closing lines signifies that the beloved appears to the lover "much more beautiful" than he is per se, because the lover sees in him the image of beauty which his soul has formed.

4. The soul, considering that it has come to know beauty universally and knowing that everything which is founded in matter is particular, concludes that the universal quality of beauty proceeds not from the exterior sensuous object, but from its own intrinsic light and virtue. Divesting beauty of its material cloud he is able to see the image of ideal beauty imparted by the intellect (stanza VIII, ll. 6–11).

5. Ascending to the intellect itself, the soul sees Venus, or ideal beauty, in her true form—not as an image. Venus cannot be seen in "total plenitude," however, by a particular intellect.

6. Hence the soul tries to "unite its own particular intellect to the universal first mind, first among all creatures and universal habitation of ideal beauty." Here the soul must end its journey and rest as on the Sabbath.

In line 6 of the sixth stanza Benivieni speaks of the individual soul's derivation from its parent star. The commentary explains that the imperfections of the matter which receives the souls from the several planets determine the difference of souls originated by the same planet. The kinship of souls descended from the same planet, however, explains the special attraction which they have on earth for each other.

The soul is said in line 4 to be impressed in the heart because the latter, being naturally a source of life and heat, is the most appropriate abode of the soul.

Stanza VII. The seventh stanza begins with the thought that ends the sixth stanza, and the eighth is likewise connected with the seventh to indicate that love should not stop in its ascent. The soul from the idealized image of its beloved elevates itself *di grado in grado* (by degrees) to the divine source of beauty. The "three mirrors" (l. 9.) which reflect the divine light are named in line 11: mind, spirit, and body, which respectively signify angelic nature, rational nature, and the world of sense. The closing lines of the stanza relate the soul's formation of one concept of manifold bodily beauty (the third degree of love).

Stanza VIII. The eighth stanza describes the soul's ascent to a "more perfect beauty" (ll. 7–8), the immaterial image of ideal beauty—the fourth degree, whence it contemplates *entro alla sua mente* (within its mind) the true form of unimparted beauty— the fifth degree—in so far as it can be seen by an individual intellect. In a final flight the soul strives for union with the "universal and first mind." [22]

Stanza IX. The *congedo, Canzon, io sento Amor chel fren raccoglie* . . . (I feel Love gathering the rein . . .), signifies, according to Pico, that "to him who arrives at the sixth degree, it is not permitted to proceed further, because that is the end of the amorous journey." There is, however, another love, which goes on to "love God in Himself, not as the author of ideal beauty." Such love, however, lies beyond the scope of Benivieni's poem, which treats of love as "desire of beauty, which according to the Platonists is not found in God, because of his simplicity." The poet calls his poem *temerario ardir* (rash boldness) because ancient theologians op-

[22] Pico's paraphrase of *più chiaro et apperto Lum,* ll. 14–15.

posed the publication of divine matters. Hence he feigns himself to have been constrained by love. The sense of the poem's closing lines is that the *Canzone* is directed only to the intellectual elite who are "informed and dressed" by divine love.

In the last paragraph of Pico's *Commentary* we find a further explanation of the poem's obscurity: like the ancient Egyptians who sculptured the Sphinx before their temples, the poet has written of divine love *sotto Enigmatici velamenti* (under enigmatic veilings). The poem and its exposition are thus seen to constitute a mystery explained. This fact, one may conjecture, helps to explain their popularity during the Renaissance.

Renaissance Neoplatonism tried to combine with the classical ideal of beauty the Christian ideal of religious and moral perfection. The difficulty of this fusion is shown by the fact that the preaching of a Savonarola could influence such men as Benivieni and Pico to forsake Platonistic philosophy for revivalist religion. Under Savonarolan influence Benivieni eventually composed a *Canzone dello amore celeste e divino secondo la verità cristiana e della fede cattolica* (Canzone of celestial and divine love according to Christian and Catholic truth).

POMPEO DELLA BARBA'S EXPOSITION OF A PLATONIC SONNET

In April, 1548, Pompeo della Barba, in his own words "Professor of Philosophy and of Medicine," [23] delivered a lecture to the Florentine Academy entitled, *Spositione d'un sonetto platonico, fatto sopra il Primo effecto d'Amore, che è il separare l'anima dal corpo de l'Amante, dove si tratta de la immortalità de l'anima secondo Aristotile, e secondo Platone* (Exposition of a Platonic sonnet, composed upon the first effect of Love, which is to separate the lover's soul from his body, wherein one treats of the immortality of the soul according to Aristotle and according to Plato). The sonnet itself is attributed to *un Amico nostro*. It reads as follows:

> L'Ombre a gl'amati corpi ognhora intorno
> Vagando stanno a' lor sepolcri appresso,
> Sciolte da cruda mano, ond'è che spesso

[23] Page 22 of his work cited in this paragraph.

Fra 'l volgo hor questo hor quel ne pate scorno,
Miser, la spoglia mia pur fa ritorno
A l'empio sito ognhora, ove lo stesso
Spirto gli svelse, & hor se n'va con esso
Chi ne begl'occhi suoi ne porta il giorno.
Ombre felici, almen non è disdetto
A voi l'Urna fatale, el sacro loco
Che v'asconde il mirare l'amico aspetto.
Questo infelice corpo a poco a poco
(Privo del amoroso e caro oggetto)
A forza manca in sempiterno foco.

Shades are ever wandering around their beloved bodies near their tombs, divided by a cruel hand, whence it happens that often now this one now that among the people is mocked by them.

Wretchedly my corpse too always returns to the impious site where the one who wrung its very spirit and now goes with it carries its life in her [or his] beautiful eyes.

Happy shades, at least the fatal urn is not denied you, the sacred place which keeps you from looking at the friendly presence.

This unhappy body little by little (deprived of the dear and loving object) perforce is absent in everlasting fire.

Pompeo devotes only a few pages toward the end of the commentary to the specific exposition of the sonnet, for he dislikes to comment "word by word" as do some expositors who weary the reader with obvious matters (p. 93). The specific commentary, in Chapter VII, declares the sonnet's meaning to be that, like the soul which hovers over its dead body, the lover seeks his beloved in whom the lover's soul dwells.

The previous six chapters restate many motives—mainly Platonistic—current in Florentine humanist writings on love, and pay special attention to poetic and philosophical concepts of death. Pompeo declares (p. 14): "Amore non è altro che morte" (Love is nought but death).

Plato was right to call love a bitter thing (*ibid.*). Love connotes sickness (p. 22).

The proper function of the soul is thought (p. 14); and as the lover thinks not of himself but of his love object, he is dead in himself (pp. 14–15). If his love is reciprocated, however, he lives in another. Love is *dolce-amaro:* sweet because voluntary, bitter because it is death (p. 15).

Chapter I, *Del vario significato d'Amore,* posits three modes of love: natural, sensitive, and rational-voluntary (p. 25). Natural love is the work of the world soul (p. 27); rational love is for three *beni:* honest, useful, pleasurable. Useful love is the least worthy. The sonnet treats of pleasurable love. There are two Veneres, celestial and libidinous.

The second chapter (pp. 33 ff.), *De le cause, e de le generatione d'amore secondo i Peripatetici* ("Of the causes and generations of love according to the Peripatetics,"), finds the efficient cause of love in the stars, its material cause in the heart, and its final cause in the beloved object. Chapter III, *In quanti modi si muore secondo i Platonici, e per che Via l'anima s'unisce al corpo* (In how many ways one dies according to the Platonists, and by what way the soul is united with the body), accurately summarizes Plato's theory of ideas (pp. 49–50) and posits two kinds of death—of the soul and of the animal being (p. 39). The Greeks called the body a bond (*vincolo*) and a tomb (p. 40); the Platonists say that the soul dies when it is infused into the body (*ibid.*). There is also a praiseworthy philosophical kind of death which consists in the separation of the soul from the body and its perturbations and passions (pp. 53–54). Philosophy is the "desire for wisdom, or a conversion from base and fleeting things to celestial and divine things" (p. 54).

The fourth chapter deals with spirits and demons and with the souls that hover about tombs. Plato's opinions about immortality are found to conform with Christian truth; Plato and his followers "have held that the soul remains after the body and is immortal" (p. 74). "Vedete dunque quanto il divino Platone sia conforme a la verità Cristiana . . ." (p. 73: See then how conformable is the divine Plato to Christian truth . . .).

The following chapter, entitled *"Se l'anima (come vogliono alcuni) secondo Aristotile rimane dopo al corpo"* (Whether the soul, as some have it, according to Aristotle remains after the body), declares that all the philosophers who have spoken naturally and according to reason have held that the human soul is mortal.

Among these thinkers he numbers Aristotle, noting that he, Pompeo, is in agreement with Pietro Pomponazzi (p. 79), and Lucretius.

. . . Conchiudiamo dunque (secondo Aristotile) l'anima nostra essere mortale, il che ci conferma ancora l'Epicureo Lucretio . . . E così tutti gli altri che naturalmente e con ragione hanno parlato, sono stati del medesimo parere . . . (p. 82).

. . . We conclude then (according to Aristotle) that our soul is mortal, which is further confirmed for us by the Epicurean Lucretius. . . . And so all the others who have spoken naturally and with reason have been of the same opinion. . . .

The sixth chapter, reminiscent of the last chapter of Pomponazzi's treatise *On Immortality,* is entitled "Quello che s'habbia per certo à tenere dell'anima secondo la verità Cristiana" (That which one may hold for certain about the soul according to Christian truth). It concludes the problem with the following declaration:

Nè è contra le religione Cristiana il veder che non si possa con ragioni naturali provare l'anima esser immortale, anzi accrescie il merito di chi così la crede, come in verità è eterna, incorroptibile, e da Dio creata immortale . . . (p. 83).

Nor is it against the Christian religion to see that one cannot with natural reasons prove the soul immortal; on the contrary it increases the merit of him who so believes, as in truth it is eternal, incorruptible, and created immortal by God.

CHAPTER II

Love Treatises

LOVE and lovers are a frequent theme in the Platonic dialogues. As Christian writers recognized a sacred and a profane love, so the classical world treated love both philosophically and sensually. Plato in the *Symposium,* where love is an aspiration, and in the *Phaedrus,* where love is a divine madness, related the two loves in a highly imaginative way. Some eighteen centuries later Florentine humanists and philosophers drew inspiration and doctrine from these dialogues.

Love is the one subject about which Socrates claims knowledge (*Symposium,* 177 d). Love generally in Plato's dialogues is not a relation between man and woman, but between two men, or more frequently a man and a youth, lover and beloved. In the *Symposium* the stage is set for Socrates' famous speech—the Diotiman ladder of love, which enjoyed the greatest vogue among Renaissance authors of love treatises—by the preceding encomiums of five speakers. The first, Phaedrus, praises love as the oldest god, inspirer of virtue and the sense of honor in men. Pausanias distinguishes two Aphrodites—a transient, earthly love of body and an enduring, heavenly love of soul. Eryximachus, the doctor, identifies love with the cosmic force of attraction. Next Aristophanes describes love as a quest for the other half of the divided self. Following him, the young poet Agathon, who is celebrating his triumph as a tragedian, glorifies love as the best and the most beautiful of gods, superlative in all qualities—a brilliant speech the eulogistic hyperbole of which irritates Socrates.

The preceding speakers have praised love indiscriminately. Socrates in his simplicity has imagined that the topics of praise should be true, and will speak after his manner only the truth about love. Love itself is not beautiful, as Agathon called it, but of the beautiful, which it lacks. Socrates will repeat the tale that Diotima, his instructress in the art of love, once told him:

Love is not a god, but a demon, intermediary between gods and men. The child of Poverty and Resource, he is in want like his mother and a hunter of wisdom like his father. Love is not of the other half, unless by that we mean the good. What men really love is the unending possession of the good; when they love the beautiful they love the good. The object of the lovers' pursuit is birth or reproduction in beauty, whether of body or of soul. Love is for the sake of immortality, whose semblance ordinary men achieve by begetting children of the flesh. Pregnant, creative souls bring forth just institutions, immortal poems, and other works of wisdom and virtue.

Next Diotima revealed the greater mystery of love. The desire of the beautiful begins in youth with the love of a particular beautiful body, which is generalized into the love of all bodily beauty, whence the lover rises through successive stages of loving beautiful souls, institutions, laws, and sciences to the boundless love of wisdom. On that grown strong, he suddenly perceives the changeless idea of beauty itself. Contemplating and conversing with the divine essence of beauty, he will be able to create not images of beauty but realities, becoming ever more virtuous, to be the friend of God, and immortal, if mortal man may.

The speech finished, Socrates' spell is ruined by the sudden intrusion of his lover, the drunken Alcibiades, who proceeds to praise not love, but Socrates himself. The picture of divine love is shattered by the unexpected appearance of love in the flesh.

Coincident with the Renaissance itself was a "rebirth" of Platonism. In the fifteenth century there appeared in Italy a conspicuous number of literary works showing a Platonic influence. In the preceding century Petrarch had treasured a Plato manuscript, which he was unable to read. His vague aspiration, whetted by his acquaintance with Cicero, St. Augustine, and the *Timaeus*, to revive the Platonic philosophy, was realized a century later by Mar-

silio Ficino. In the first half of the fifteenth century Leonardo
Bruni translated into Latin six of Plato's dialogues—the *Apology,
Crito, Gorgias, Phaedo, Phaedrus,* and part of the *Symposium*—
and the *Letters.* An intensification of Platonic studies followed the
arrival in Italy in 1438 of Gemisthus Pletho, his pupil Bessarion,
later a Cardinal of the Roman Catholic Church, and other Greek
scholars. The greatest impetus to the study and diffusion of Platonic
and Neoplatonic ideas was given by Ficino's translation, with commentary, of the complete works of Plato and Plotinus. His *Com-
mentarium in Convivium Platonis de Amore,* written in 1469,
printed in 1484, and translated by himself into the vernacular,
formulated for the first time the doctrine of Platonic love.[1] For over
a century thereafter Platonic love was a frequent theme of Italian
literary endeavor.

The Platonic *trattato d'amore* is a literary genre which began
with Marsilio Ficino's commentary on the *Symposium* of Plato,
and achieved great vogue in the sixteenth century. It frequently
took dialogue form and was usually written in Italian rather than
in Latin. There continued to be authors who wrote of love as a
human biological and emotional phenomenon devoid of philosophical implications. Some treatises were written in a popular vein
without philosophic pretenses, such as the *Ragionamenti di messer
Francesco Sansovino, nel quale brevemente s'insegna a' giovani
uomini la bella arte d'amore* (Discussions of Messer Francesco Sansovino in which young men are briefly taught the fine art of love);
and the *Specchio d'amore—Dialogo di messer Bartolomeo Gottifredi nel quale alle giovani s'insegna innamorarsi* (Speculum of love
—Dialogue of Messer Bartolomeo Gottifredi in which young
ladies are taught how to fall in love). These dialogues undoubtedly
reflect to a certain extent attitudes toward love then current among
the social classes to whom such works were addressed. Mario Equicola[2] mentions also the biological approach to love of Battista da
Campo Fregoso:

Battista vuole che amor proceda da desiderio di emittere fuora il

---

[1] Ficino coined the term "Platonic love" (*amore platonico*) in a letter to
Alamanno Donati. See Ficino, *Opera omnia,* p. 716.

[2] Mario Equicola, *Libro di natura d'amore,* p. 27 v.

seme genitale . . . (Battista holds that love proceeds from the desire to emit semen . . .).

However, a large number of writers chose to treat love "Platonically" as an intellectual, nonsexual, or even anti-sexual phenomenon. Marsilio Ficino, and others after him, limit love to sight, hearing, and thought. The appetite, which follows the other senses, is not love, but lust or frenzy.[3] Mario Equicola is not alone in speaking (*Libro di natura d'amore*, p. 71 v) of *la spurcitia del coito* (the filth of coitus). The *trattatisti* overlook the existence of emotional, psychological, and esthetic factors in sensual love, which they identify with animality. Castiglione, for instance, writes that sensual lovers experience only the same pleasures that irrational animals feel.[4]

These writers profess in regard to sexual love a severe contempt which is tempered by an almost grudging admission of the necessity of sexual intercourse in order to propagate the human race—an achievement which they describe, after Plato, as a result of the individual's desire for immortality. Sexual activity in itself is identified with ugliness and bestiality. Yet, discussion of the philosophical problems of "divine" and "Platonic" love often lapses into a consideration of "doubts" (*dubbi*) concerning "practical" questions of "human" or "vulgar" love.

These writers inherited from the dialogues of Plato the concept that male youths rather than women excite love in men.

Così è pregno il corpo degli uomini (come vuole Platone) Così è pregno l'Animo: Et amendui per gli incitamenti di Amore, sono stimolati a partorire. Ma alcuni o per natura o per uso sono più atti a il parto dell'animo che del Corpo. . . . I Primi seguitano il Celeste Amore: I Secondi seguitano il vulgare: I Primi amano i Maschi più tosto che le Femmine, & Adolescenti più tosto che Puerili: perchè in essi, molto più vigoreggia lo acume dello Intelletto: il quale è suggetto attissimo, per la sua eccellente Belleza a ricevere la disciplina, la quale per natura generare coloro appetiscono (Ficino, *Sopra lo amore*, p. 182).

As men's bodies are pregnant, as Plato says, so are their souls; and both by the incitements of love are stimulated to give birth. But some either by nature or by habit are better suited to the birth of the soul

---

[3] Ficino, *Sopra lo amore o ver' convito di Platone*, Oration I, chapter iii, p. 17.
[4] Castiglione, *Il libro del cortegiano*, IV, liii, 476–77.

than of the body . . . The former pursue celestial love; the latter, vulgar love. The former love males rather than females, and adolescents rather than children: for in them the acumen of the intellect is much more vigorous. Such a one is a very apt subject because of his beauty to receive the discipline that they by nature desire to generate.

Ad eccitare il disio amoroso dello intelletto giudicò Platone, & altri valenti huomini esser più acconcia la bellezza del Giovane, che della giovane Donna, anzi quegli che amano Donne sono da lui stimati fecondi, & gravidi più tosto di corpo, che d'animo (Nobili, *Trattato dell' Amore Humano,* p. 16 v).

Plato and other worthy men judged the beauty of a youth to be more fit than that of a young lady to excite the amorous desire of the intellect. Moreover he considered those who love women to be fecund and gravid rather in body than in soul.

Scholars having been taxed at least from the time of Dante with the charge of homosexuality,[5] the *trattatisti* of love were careful to make plain their abhorrence of such a vice. Ficino (*Sopra lo Amore,* Oration VI, chap. xiii, p. 183) calls it *nefaria scelerateza, la quale Platone nelle sue leggi, come spezie di omicidio, agramente bestemmia* (nefarious wickedness, which Plato in his laws bitterly curses as a kind of homicide). Mario Equicola writes as follows of the *horrendo vitio* (*Libro di natura d'amore,* p. 114 r):

Non voglio che in questa opera s'intenda . . . parola alcuna d'amori puerili & concubiti contra natura. . . . Esterminemo puerili coiti, ove il paziente ha in odio l'agente (*ibid.,* p. 112 r-v).

I do not want a single word to be heard in this work about the love of boys or copulations against nature. . . . Let us abolish coition with boys, where the passive one hates the active one.

Lorenzo de' Medici likewise declares:

E però sono sommamente da dannarsi quelli, i quali l'appetito muove ad amare sommamente le cose che sono fuori di quest'ordine naturale e vero fine già proposto da noi . . . *Comento* . . . , p. 16).

---

[5] *Inferno,* XV, ll. 106–8, Brunetto Latini:

   In somma sappi che tutti fur cherci
     e litterati grandi e di gran fama,
     d'un peccato medesmo al mondo lerci.

In short, know that all were great and renowned clerks and men of letters, stained on earth by one same sin.

And therefore those whom the appetite moves to love things which are outside this natural order and true end already proposed by us are highly to be condemned.

Tullia d'Aragona writes that men who love male youths lasciviously do so outside the ordering of nature and are worthy of punishment by divine and canonical laws.[6]

The treatise writers could avoid the idea of homosexuality by two devices. First, they could attribute only an intellectual, or intellectual and moral, fervor to those men who loved youths.

Certo riguardando la Natura delle cose mi par verisimile, che la bellezza del Maschio non sia sì atta a svegliare concupiscenza carnale, come quella della Donna, la quale a questo fine fu ordinata di accendere in noi desio di generare corporalmente: & in ciò mi giova di prestar fede a Platone, & a i suoi imitatori, i quali amando Maschi, come non si sono lasciati trasportare in quel dishonesto, & in tutto alla Natura repugnante appetito, così mostrano d'esser venuti in ardente disiderio di giovar loro, & di rendergli valorosi, & scientiati . . .[7]

Certainly observing the nature of things it seems to me probable that the beauty of the male is not as apt to awaken carnal desire as that of the woman, which was ordained to arouse in us the desire of generating corporally. This fact encourages me to lend credence to Plato and his imitators, who in loving males, as they did not let themselves be carried away by that dishonest appetite, altogether repugnant to nature, thus show that they ardently desired to help them and to make them valorous and learned.

Secondly, they could attribute not to men but to women the personal beauty which excites men to love and impels the lover to seek ever higher forms of beauty. The first of them to choose clearly the latter course was Pietro Bembo.

Because of his great prestige and literary following, Bembo's *Asolani* became one of the main sources of this stream of litera-

---

[6] Tullia d'Aragona, *Della infinità di amore*, in *Trattati d'amore del Cinquecento*, ed. by Zonta, p. 227.

[7] Nobili, *Trattato dell'amore humano*, p. 16 v. Cf. Guiseppe Betussi, *Il Raverta*, in *Trattati d'amore del Cinquecento*, ed. by Zonta who writes as follows (p. 10) of love between two persons of the same sex: "Può essere vero e perfettissimo, mentre abbia risguardo alle bellezze dell'animo, ed è lecito; si come diventa illicito quando tende ad altro fine" (It can be true and most perfect while it is concerned with the beauties of the soul and it is licit; just as it becomes illicit when it tends toward another end).

ture, along with the love dialogues of Marsilio Ficino and Leone Ebreo, which almost alone of that vast body of treatises have philosophical importance.[8] The philosophical elements, as we shall see, soon became stereotyped; the author's main effort was to express with literary grace, in polished prose, sentiments and theories that were far from original. An indication of the preponderance of the literary motive over the philosophical is that the most frequently quoted author is not Plato, but Petrarch! Frequently lectures on love were delivered in academies, where interest in Petrarch, especially in the sixteenth century, often ran high.

In the treatises under consideration, love is a concept of multiple derivation: Christian charity, Plato's love, the friendship of Aristotle and of Cicero, and the love of *stilnuovo* poets and of Petrarch are all importantly represented.

A salient feature of many *trattati d'amore* is the fashionable *dubbi* or doubts about love, which are likely to be discussed after or during the philosophical exposition of love. A few of them, perhaps, entered Italian literature from the treatise *De amore,* on courtly love, of Andreas Capellanus. Some seventy such *dubbi* are found in a fifteenth-century treatise on love by Giovanni Iacovo Calandra of Mantua. Those cited by Equicola[9] from Calandra are found widely in the subsequent literature.

Propone circa settanta dubbi d'amore, de quali noi habiamo eletti questi. Quali sia maggior difficulta fenger amore, over amando dissimular non amar: qual donna è da piacer piu, o la bella simplice, o la deforme accorta. Se amor puo esser senza gelosia: qual è maggior forza d'amor, se fa il savio pazzo, o se fa il pazzo savio, Se amante po morire per troppo amore. Naturalmente chi è piu costante l'homo o la donna. Se seria meglio o peggio nel mondo non essendovi amore. Se di fama uno se puo inamorar di donna: qual sia maggior incitamento a virtu l'honore, o desio di piacere all'amata: qual donna ama piu la timida o l'ardita, qual sia piu difficulta acquistar la gratia della donna, o in quella mantenerse. Chi piu facilmente se persuade esser amato

---

[8] The works on love and beauty of Francesco Cattani da Diacceto are philosophical; they follow fairly closely the lead of Diacceto's predecessor, Ficino. Giovanni Pico della Mirandola is not, strictly speaking, the author of a *trattato d'amore,* although the second book of his commentary on Benivieni's *Canzone d'amore* expounds Platonic theories of love and beauty.

[9] Equicola, *Libro di natura d'amore,* p. 38 r-v. Calandra's tract is not extant.

l'huomo, o la donna: qual sia maggior segno ad una donna d'esser amata, oltra la perseverantia: qual sia piu potente passione, amore, o odio. Se per magica si puo flettere animo duro. Se è possibile che uno avaro ami.

He proposes about seventy doubts concerning love, of which we have chosen these: Which is more difficult, to feign love or, loving, to conceal it. Which lady is more pleasing, the simple beauty or the clever ugly one. Whether love can be without jealousy. Whether love is more likely to make a wise man crazy or a crazy man wise. Whether a lover can die from too much love. Who is naturally more constant, man or woman. Whether the world would be better or worse if there were no love. Whether one can fall in love with a lady from her renown. Which is a greater incitement to virtue, honor or the desire to please the beloved. Which woman loves more, the timid one or the bold one. Which is more difficult, to acquire the favor of a lady or to keep it. Who is more easily persuaded that he is loved, man or woman. What is the clearest sign to a woman that she is loved, besides perseverance. Which is the more powerful passion, love or hate. Whether a hard heart can be turned by magic. Whether it is possible for a miser to love.

Medical explanations of the concomitants of love are frequently encountered in these love treatises, partly because the two chief Renaissance sources of the literature, Marsilio Ficino and Leone Ebreo, were physicians. Medical references are by no means limited to them, however, and indeed a modicum of medical knowledge could not be lacking in any lettered person of that time. Similarly, astrological explanations of amorous attraction are common in the treatises.

The aristocratic appeal, if not the snob appeal, of Platonic love is especially evident in the treatises which have a court setting or were written for a courtly audience. Castiglione, for example, declares through his character Pietro Bembo, appropriately introduced in *The Book of the Courtier* to expound the theory of Platonic love:

E perchè mi conosco indegno di parlar dei santissimi misteri di Amore, prego lui che mova il pensiero e la lingua mia, tanto ch' io possa mostrar a questo eccellente Cortigiano amar for della consuetudine del profano vulgo . . . (*Il libro del Cortegiano*, IV, lxi, 485).

And because I know myself to be unworthy of the most sacred mysteries of Love, I pray him to move my thought and tongue so that I may show this excellent Courtier how to love apart from the custom of the profane crowd. . . .

Similarly, Giuseppe Betussi understands vulgar love, in contrast to celestial love and the celestial Venus, as the kind of love practised by vulgar people.

Quali sono queste Veneri?
. . . Una celeste e l'altra volgare. . . . Per la celeste s'intende quel desiderio e quello amore intellettuale e perfetto, che può rendere l'anima astratta da tutte le altre cose alla contemplazione spirituale. Per l'altra s'intende quel libidinoso e biasimevole appetito, che ad altro non tende, eccetto che a godere quella ombra di bellezza vana; e ben si dice Venere e Amor volgare, perciochè è quello che segue il vulgo, il quale, sì come meno intendente e più rozzo investigatore delle perfette bellezze, più difficilmente le apprende e meno le conosce (Betussi, *Il Raverta*, p. 30).

What are these Veneres?
. . . One is celestial, the other vulgar. . . . By the celestial one is meant that intellectual and perfect desire and love which can draw the soul toward spiritual contemplation and away from all other things. By the other is meant that lustful and blameworthy appetite which tends only to the enjoyment of that vain shadow of beauty. And well may one say vulgar Venus or Love, since it is that sought by the multitude, which, being a less skilled and refined investigator of perfect beauties, apprehends them and knows them with greater difficulty.

MARSILIO FICINO

To Marsilio Ficino, who first used the term "Platonic love," [10] the words signified an intellectual love between friends based on the individual's love of God. Such relationships were the foundation of his Academy.

Ficino's commentary on Plato's *Symposium* takes the form of seven orations attributed to various participants in a commemoration, which actually took place in the villa in Careggi under the auspices of Lorenzo de' Medici, on Plato's traditional birthday and date of death, November 7. Each speaker expounds one of the speeches made in praise of love by a character in Plato's *Symposium*. Christianizing tendencies are immediately in evidence. In the dedication of his Italian translation of the commentary (p. 3) to Ber-

[10] Kristeller, *The Philosophy of Marsilio Ficino*, p. 286.

nardo del Nero and Antonio Manetti, Ficino says that Diotima was inspired by the Holy Spirit. Greek gods and demons become Christian angels.

. . . Gli Dii, o vero Angeli, come vogliono i nostri Teologi, maravigliandosi della Belleza divina quella amano (*Sopra lo amore* . . . , Oration I, chap. I., p. 8).

. . . The gods, or rather angels, as our theologians prefer, marveling at divine beauty love it.

Et quelli buoni [demoni], che di noi ànno custodia, sono per propio nome da Dionisio Areopagita chiamati Angeli governatori del Mondo inferiore: la qual cosa non discorda da la mente di Platone (*ibid.*, VI, iii, 131).

And the good [demons] who have custody of us are called by their own name by Dionysius the Areopagite, governing angels of the inferior world—which does not disagree with Plato's mind.

Poro is described as *scintilla del sommo Dio* (a spark of the highest god); *Penia* as the poverty present in the Angel at its creation (*ibid.*, VI, vii, 142). Love is partly rich and partly poor because people desire neither that which is entirely in their possession nor that which they altogether lack (*ibid.*, p. 143).[11]

As Plato teaches, there are two Veneres, heavenly and Vulgar (Oration II, vii, 39). The former is the intelligence of the Angel; the latter, the power of generation in the *anima mundi*.

The ideas become the "Angelic Mind," (*ibid.*, I, ii, 10) which turns toward God as the eye toward the sun (*ibid.*, I, ii, 13). The basis of Ficino's cosmology is the emanative system of Plotinus, which, following Plotinus himself, Ficino attributes to Plato:

Iddio prima crea la Mente Angelica: Dipoi l'Anima del Mondo, come vuole Platone: Ultimamente il corpo dello Universo (*ibid.*, p. 10).[12]

God first creates the angelic mind; then the world soul, as Plato states; lastly, the body of the universe.

Ficino inherited from George Gemisthus Pletho the tradition that Plato was the continuer of a kind of inspired pagan theology

[11] Cf. Plato, *Philebus* 35.
[12] The term and concept of angelic mind are peculiar to Ficino, not derived from Plotinus. See Kristeller, *The Philosophy of Marsilio Ficino*, pp. 167–68.

handed down by Hermes Trismegistus, Zoroaster, Orpheus, and Pythagoras. Like many Renaissance scholars after him, Ficino accepted as genuine the apocryphal works of these "authorities" which Pletho had canonized. Ficino also attributed to Pletho's public lectures on Platonism in Florence Cosimo de' Medici's idea of founding a Platonic academy. Whatever Cosimo's motives, Ficino liked to think of his own work as a continuation of Pletho's. However, the only major idea which Ficino took from Pletho was the tradition mentioned above, which became very widespread. Here is an example of this theme from Ficino's commentary on the *Symposium:*

Orfeo nella Argonautica, imitando la Teologia di Mercurio Trimegisto. . . . Nel seno di esso Caos collocò l'Amore. . . . Platone nel Timeo similmente descrive il Caos (p. 9).

Orpheus in the *Argonautica,* imitating the theology of Hermes Trismegistus . . . placed Love in the heart of this Chaos. . . . Plato describes Chaos similarly in the Timaeus.

Love is "desire of beauty" (*ibid.,* I, iii, 16) or "desire of enjoying beauty" (*ibid.,* II, ix, 49).

Love's ethical utility results from the sense of modesty (*vergogna*) and the desire to be excellent, both of which it engenders (*ibid.,* I, iii, 15). Sight and hearing, as subsequent treatise writers repeated ad infinitum, are the spiritual senses (*ibid.,* V, ii, 89), alone capable of perceiving beauty. Love desires only "temperate, modest and honorable things (*ibid.,* I, iii, 17). The *rabbia Venerea* or "appetite for coitus" is a "foolish perturbation" contrary to love. The lover is dead in his own body, alive in that of his beloved (*ibid.,* II, viii, 42). The beloved is constrained to love the lover (p. 47). Love is ubiquitous. Eryximachus says: "Che lo amore è in tutte le cose, et inverso tutte, creatore di tutte, et maestro di tutte" (*ibid.,* III, i, 51: That love is in all things and toward all, creator of all, and master of all) and "Adunche questo tanto Dio perchè egli è in ogni luogo, et è dentro a tutte le cose, dobbiamo temere come potente signore" (*ibid.,* III, iv, 61: Then we must fear this great God as a powerful lord, since he is in every place and is inside all things).

The sixth oration, on Socrates' speech, posits five classes of love:

(*ibid.*, VI, viii, 147 f.: How there are two loves in all souls, and in ours, five). The extremes of love are the good "demon" or "eternal love of seeing divine beauty," by whose stimuli men are motivated to study philosophy and to observe justice and piety; and the bad demon or "occult stimulus to generate children." Although the second demon is called bad, both demons actually are good, "inasmuch as the procreation of children is necessary and honest, like the search for truth (*ibid.*, p. 148)." By the second demon "we are continually incited to sculpture in the image of children some similitude of supernal beauty (*ibid.*)." It is called bad "because of our disordinate use" which "diverts the soul to vile mysteries, withdrawing it from its principal good, which consists in the speculation of truth."

Between the two demons there are three "middle" loves or motions or affections:

1) Divine love or the contemplative life, which from the sense of sight advances to the consideration of divine and spiritual matters.

2) Human love or the active life, which continues to delight in seeing and conversing with the person loved.

3) Bestial love or the voluptuous life, which from sight enters the "concupiscence of touch (*ibid.*, p. 149)."

This classification of three kinds of love, either with or without reference to the two demons which Ficino posits as extremes, was very widely repeated in the subsequent literature of Platonic love.

The steps in Diotima's ladder of love are Body, Soul, Angel, God. However, although we may love God, we cannot know him in this life (*ibid.*, IV, vi, 80; VI, xiii, 181).

In the first chapter of the seventh oration, Ficino mistakenly identifies Guido Cavalcanti's theory of love with Socratic love. Cristoforo Marsupino addresses these words to Ficino, who has just expounded Socrates' speech:

[Guido Cavalcanti] seguitò lo Amore socratico in parole, et in costumi. Costui con li suoi versi brevemente conchiuse ciò che da voi di Amore è detto (*ibid.*, VII, i, 205).

[Guido Cavalcanti] pursued Socratic love in words and in habits. With his verses he briefly stated that which you have said about love.

Ficino then proceeds to elaborate upon the words *Sole et Raggio* (p. 207: sun and ray), which he erroneously attributes to Cavalcanti's *Canzone*.[13]

In the seventh oration Ficino devotes ten chapters (Chapters III–XII) to the consideration of vulgar love. As a physician, he is able to describe its medical causes and symptoms. Vulgar love is a *male d'occhio* carried by spirit from the blood of one person to the eye of another. The effects of love are not unlike those described by the learned physician Dino del Garbo and by Petrarch and earlier poets of the Tuscan school.

The lover, Ficino tells us in Chapter VI of Book II, cannot be satisfied by any particular love, for not knowing God, he does not know what he really desires and seeks. Hence it is that lovers always feel fear and reverence on seeing the beloved person. They are hot or cold as they alternate between audacity and timidity.

The moral love which thrives upon conversation with the beloved, in which only the spiritual senses of sight and hearing are brought into play, may appear to resemble the "pure love" described by Andreas Capellanus in his courtly code and by other writers. Marsilio Ficino allows the element of sensual desire in moral love, checked by reason and fear of offending the beloved. Andreas Capellanus attributes the origin of all virtues to love and particularly to pure love. However, when it is observed that the "Platonic" element of overcoming sensual desire is characteristic of Ficino's moral love, while the value of courtly "pure love" is the very in-

---

[13] Ficino apparently had read the commentary of Pseudo-Egidio. That author mentions *sole* and *raggio* as follows: "*Prende suo stato si formato come diaffan dal lume duna oscuritate.* Quasi dica come il diaffanno essendo prima sotta una oscuritate isguardato dal sole et illuminato dal suo raggio prende suo stato perfetto e luminoso cossi lanimo essendo prima quasi sotto una oscuritate isguardato da la cosa de fuori per la uertu de la ditta ymagine prende suo stato perfetto cio e stato damore nela qual simigliança asomiglia lautore la cosa de fuori al sole la ymagine de la cosa al raggio del sole. lamore al lume. la priuation del amore ala oscuritate" (*Il canzoniere Vaticano Barberino Latino* 3953, ed. by Gino Lega, pp. 93–94: It takes its state formed like a diaphanous body from the light of a darkness. As though he said, as the diaphanous body, being first in darkness, when beheld by the sun and illuminated by its ray takes its perfect and luminous state, so the soul, being first so to speak in darkness, when beheld by the outside thing takes its perfect state—that of love—by virtue of the said image. In this comparison the author likens the outside thing to the sun, the image of the thing to the sun's ray, love to light, the privation of love to darkness).

tensification of sensuality by the unfulfillment of desire, the apparent similarity between these two kinds of love utterly vanishes. Castiglione's allowance of the kiss in Platonic love may be considered a courtly concession, although he disguises the sensuality of the kiss by metaphysical legerdemain. Furthermore, analysis of the virtues sought by courtly love will reveal their mundane nature in contrast to that of Platonic and Christian virtues.

In Platonic philosophy love is defined in terms of beauty. Love is desire of beauty or desire of birth or reproduction in beauty. Since Platonic love theory involves a whole system of ethics, beauty is a key concept in the moral realm. By its association with truth and goodness, beauty is related to the gnosiological field as well. The beauty which one loves cannot be unknown. Some Renaissance writers use the terms "love" and "beauty" almost interchangeably.[14] For these reasons it is important for us to identify the conception and status of beauty in the writings of Ficino and of the other humanists and philosophers whom we shall examine.

Plato and the Greeks generally considered beauty to be the result of harmony and proportion among the parts of a thing. Plotinus objected that simple things in which there is no proportion of parts, such as the sphere and light, can also be beautiful. Beauty for him becomes an intangible spiritual essence.

Tradunt enim ferme omnes, commensurationem quandam partium et invicem et ad totum una cum coloris gratia pulchritudinem pertinentem ad oculos procreare, atque in eo pulchritudinem omnium esse sitam, ut moderata commensurataque sint. Sed apud eos, qui id opinantur, nihil simplex, solum vero compositum necessario erit pulchrum, ipsisque totum formosum erit. Partes vero singulae nullam habebunt propriam pulchritudinem, solum vero quatenus ad totum conferunt, pulchra dicentur; quanquam oportet, si modo pulchrum est totum, partes quoque esse formosas; non enim ex turpibus constat pulchrum. Oportet autem partes omnes pulchritudinem accepisse. Colores insuper pulchri, sicut et ipsum solis lunem, cum simplicia sint, neque ex commensuratione habeant pulchritudinem, apud illos exclusa a pulchritudine relinquentur. Aurum quoque quonam pacto illis erit pulchrum? coruscatioque nocturna, siderumque spectaculum? Similiter in vocibus, quod simplex fuerit, id erit a pulchritudine alienum. . . .[15]

---

[14] See Francesco de' Vieri's interchange of the two terms, reported on page 149 of this book.

[15] Plotinus, *Enneads*, I, VI, I, as translated by Ficino.

Nearly all teach that a certain commensurateness of parts, both toward each other and to the whole, together with grace of color, creates beauty in relation to the eyes, and that all beauty resides in moderation and proportion. But according to those who think thus nothing simple, but indeed only a compound necessarily can be beautiful, and for them the whole will be beautiful, yet the single parts will have no beauty of their own, and indeed only in so far as they contribute to the whole may they be called beautiful. Nevertheless, if the whole is beautiful, the parts must be beautiful; for the beautiful is not made up of ugly things. On the contrary, it is necessary for all the parts to partake of beauty. Moreover, beautiful colors, like the very light of the sun, since they are simple and do not derive their beauty from commensurateness, remain excluded from beauty by those persons. How then, too, can gold be beautiful to them? The nocturnal shining and the spectacle of the stars? Likewise with sounds, the simple one will be without beauty. . . .

Ficino, leaning now toward Plato and now toward Plotinus in his exposition of the *Symposium,* shows a certain inconsistency in defining beauty, which is reflected in some later writers. In the third chapter of the first oration beauty is called "a certain grace which . . . is born from the correspondence of several things" (". . . La Belleza è una certa grazia, la quale . . . nasce da la corrisponden- zia di piu cose . . ." (*Sopra lo amore* . . . , p. 6): if beauty of soul, from the correspondence of several virtues; if bodily beauty, from the correspondence of colors and lines; in the case of sonant beauty, from the correspondence of voices. In the fifth oration, Chapter III, the opinion that beauty is proportion is rejected (*ibid.,* 93), on the grounds that simple things can be beautiful. Beauty is then defined, in accordance with its above-quoted description as "splen- dor of divine beauty" (*ibid.,* II, iii, 26), as a spiritual essence, the "splendor of the face of God" (*ibid.,* V, iv, 96).

In Chapter III of the second oration, *Come la belleza è splendore della bontà divina: et come Dio è centro di quattro cerchi,* goodness, according to "the ancient theologians" is put in the center of four circles of beauty—mind, soul, nature, and matter.

"Questo raggio dipinge in questi quattro cerchi, tutte le spezie di tutte le cose: et noi chiamiamo quelle spezie, nella Mente Angelica, Idee: nell'Anima, ragioni; nella Natura, semi: et nella Materia forme" (*ibid.,* II, iii, 30–31).

This ray [of beauty emanating from the goodness of the center] paints in these four circles all the species of all things; and we call these species ideas in the angelic mind; in the soul, reasons; in nature, seeds; and in matter, forms.

Beauty thus is subordinate to the good. In Chapter V of the same oration, this relationship is confirmed: to the good is assigned a status like that of the supra-existential one in the Plotinian hierarchy; beauty is an outgoing, all-penetrating act, derivative of goodness.

. . . Il bene è essa supereminente essenzia di Dio: La Belleza è un certo atto, o vero raggio di quindi per tutto penetrante . . . (II, v, 35).

. . . The good is this supereminent essence of God; beauty is a certain act or rather ray penetrating everywhere therefrom.

Like love, beauty is everywhere (*ibid.*). Divine beauty gives birth to love (II, ii, 23). Personal beauty, which is exterior perfection, results from the interior perfection of moral goodness.[16]

Ficino's commentary is the prime source for subsequent *trattati*. His statements are so widely repeated that their source is frequently overlooked. It was customary in the Renaissance to cite by name mainly classical authors, rarely recent or contemporary writers. Furthermore, Ficino was considered to be a faithful interpreter of Plato throughout his writings. Later authors fail as did Ficino to recognize the mutual antagonism of some of the speeches in the *Symposium,* and Plato's occasional playfulness, as in the fable of Aristophanes. The medieval and Renaissance expectation of "hidden doctrine" in ancient, exalted writings remains.[17]

The two traditions—that of prose treatises on love and that of love lyrics and commentaries on them—frequently coincide in their theoretic content. Many of the motives which we have traced in the first chapter appear also in the *trattati d'amore* in such profusion that the attempt to trace source lines becomes impracticable if not

[16] Some later writers disputed this point. Giuseppe Betussi, for example, in *La Leonora,* in *Trattati d'amore del Cinquecento,* ed. by Zonta, p. 323, declares that the "Pythagorean" rule that a beautiful body encloses a beautiful soul often errs.

[17] See Leone Ebreo, *Dialoghi d'amore,* pp. 98 f.; Bruno, *Eroici furori,* in *Opere italiane,* "Argument."

impossible. For example, did Ficino say that the lover's soul lives in his beloved because Plato had said so or because early Tuscan poets said so? [18]

A comparison between Dante and Ficino will be instructive. Both authors believe in a hierarchy of being, basically Neoplatonic, which includes God, intelligences, souls, and bodies. It is not surprising, therefore, that their theories of love should offer striking similarities. In both, love is an ascending process the ultimate goal of which is unity with God. For both, love is ubiquitous, the controlling force in both the human realm and the divine. Love is a mystery, its esoteric doctrines known but to a select circle. To the *stilnuovo* motive of the *cor gentil* there corresponds the Platonic rejection of vulgar and "bestial" conduct in love. The spirits of love enter through the eyes and convey to the lover the image of the beloved. Love's effects are severe and unmistakable; but its net result in any proper love is the moral betterment of the lover, who strives to be worthy of his loved one. As Ficino associated love with knowledge and philosophy in his exposition and development of Diotima's ladder, so also does Dante in the *Convivio*. In both authors the love of another human being becomes a *scala coeli* whereby man leaves behind the conditions of his sensuous existence and enters the higher world, knowing God to the extent allowed to the human soul.

However, there are many differences between the love theories of Ficino and those of Dante, in both the worldly realm and the celestial. Ficino does not share all the *stilnuovo* motives adopted by Dante—for example, the theme that love is intensified by the death of the loved one. Neither does Ficino employ the troubadour theme of exalting the lady with praise and service. In fact, male friendship rather than the love of woman remains the basis of moral love. Dante extended the troubadour conception by emphasizing the supernatural quality of the *donna angelicata* and her theological symbolism. For all of Ficino's desire to reconcile Platonism with Christianity, his concept of love is basically Platonic, that of Dante

[18] Ficino appears to credit Plato as his source: "Platone . . . disse, Quello Amatore è uno animo nel proprio corpo morto: et nel corpo d'altri vivo" (*Sopra lo amore* . . . , II, viii, 42: Plato . . . said, That lover is a soul dead in his own body and alive in another's body).

Christian and chivalric. Through Dante's wealth of lyric invention there is woven the Christian emphasis upon such words as *salus, novus, humilitas,* descriptive of Beatrice's effect upon those who know her, especially Dante. Dante's love is the spiritual emotion of *caritas.* Ficino defines love Platonically as desire of beauty or desire to enjoy (*fruire*) beauty. When love begins to transcend material limitations, as in the love of beautiful institutions, laws, and sciences the praise of any particular love object must cease. In Dante, on the other hand, the praise of Beatrice, at the corresponding point in the ascent of the ladder, may continue as before; for the poet's praise of that particular love object symbolizes his divine love. Especially in the *Divine Comedy* Beatrice is herself, like the Virgin Mary, a direct intermediary between man and God.

Nor is there in Dante, who did not know the *Symposium* or the *Phaedrus,* an equivalent of the theme of divine madness or of Ficino's concern with Platonic myths about the origin of love. But the greatest basic difference between their theories of love, which alone has important philosophical and religious ramifications, is the monism of Dante's doctrine and the dualism of Ficino's theory. In the *Divine Comedy* love is the sole source of good and evil, universalized to include even the world of physics. There is one native tendency in man's soul, love for God, corrupted by original sin. However, Ficino's man, like Pico's and, later, Bruno's, is torn by a dual impulse. His soul wishes to obey now the "good demon," now the "bad demon" of Plato's *Symposium.* Ficino, Pico, Bruno, and many others in the Renaissance declare that man's soul hovers on the horizon of the spiritual and material worlds, ready to obey either of its contrary impulses.

LEONE EBREO

Leone Ebreo's *Dialoghi d'amore* is not only a treatise on love, but also a detailed synthesis of philosophical doctrine centering in a restatement of the Neoplatonic position.

The universe is designed by a divine architect; its perfection is in the unity and the harmonious functioning of its parts (*Dialoghi d'amore*, p. 163), which are beautiful and worthy to the extent to which they participate in the eternal life of intellect and forms. The end of human life is happiness, which is impossible without love, the universal unifying force (*ibid.*, pp. 164–5). The essence of man is his intellective soul, which by divine wisdom and virtue renders him immortal (pp. 279–280). Except for a few passages which extol the Jewish faith and Mosaic teaching it is hard to believe that we are not reading the work of an Italian Neoplatonist such as Pico or Ficino.

Leone Ebreo or Jehudah Abarbanel, born in Lisbon, was personal physician to Ferdinand and Isabella of Castile until the expulsion of the Jews from Spain in 1492. In addition to his medical studies, he was well versed in Latin and Arabic scholastic learning, Talmudic and Cabalistic doctrine, and in astrology, which was related to medicine.

After 1492 Leone resided in Naples and Genoa. He did not become a Christian. His dialogues were probably written during 1501 and 1502 and probably in Italian, as there is no evidence of an autograph in Spanish or another language.[19]

The love of Filone for Sofia, depicted in the introduction and the digressions, forms an ornamental frame for these dialogues. In their philosophical discussions Filone strives to satisfy the doubts and questions of Sofia. Leone Ebreo defines love not in terms of beauty, as Ficino did, but in terms of the good.

   . . . L'amore è de le cose che sono buone o ver stimate buone . . . (*Dialoghi d'amore*, p. 6).

   . . . Love is of things which are good or are considered good. . . .

[L'amore] è affetto volontario di fruire con unione la cosa stimata buona (*ibid.*, p. 13).

[Love] is a voluntary affection to enjoy in union the thing considered good.

Love is an affection of the will. Its object, however, is something judged by the intellect to be good. Cognition must precede love.

---

[19] Santino Caramella, editor, in Leone Ebreo, *Dialoghi d'amore.*

. . . Bisogna che il conoscimento preceda all'amore: chè nissuna cosa si potria amare, se prima sotto spezie di buona non si conoscesse . . . (p. 8).

. . . Knowledge must precede love, for nothing could be loved if it were not first known under the species of good. . . .

Immoral love, as for the Platonic Socrates, is the result of false judgment (p. 9).

. . . Molte volte quella che è stimata buona e amabile, è gattiva e debbe esser aborrita (*ibid.*).

. . . Many times that which is considered good and lovable is bad and must be abhorred.

In Ficino, as in Dante, love and morality are identified primarily with the will. By deriving "bad desires and dishonest loves" (*ibid.*) from erroneous judgment Leone is in this instance closer to Plato's often stated position than is the Florentine *alter Plato*.

In the first dialogue, *D'amore e desiderio*, Leone says that people love things which they possess and desire things that they do not have (p. 5). This criterion for distinguishing between love and desire was widely repeated by later authors, who sometimes cited Leone as their authority.[20] Returning to this distinction in the third dialogue, *De l'origine d'amore*, Leone modifies his position and extends the definition of love. Because possession is a temporal thing, it involves an element of lack, and the distinction between love and desire is lost. Subsequent writers took Leone to task for equating love with desire.

. . . Abbiamo prima diffinito altrimenti l'amore ch'il desiderio: perchè dicono il desiderio essere affetto volontario d'essere o avere la cosa stimata buona, che manca, e l'amore essere affetto volontario di fruire con unione la cosa stimata buona che manchi. . . . E aviamo mostrato che l'amore, non ostante che qualche volta sia di cosa posseduta, nondimeno presuppone sempre qualche mancamento di quella, come fa il desiderio. . . . Sì che in effetto, ben speculato, il desiderio e l'amore è una medesima cosa . . . e però in fin di quel nostro parla-

[20] E.g., F. Paolo del Rosso, *Comento sopra la canzone di Guido Cavalcanti*, p. 114. Betussi in *Il Raverta*, p. 6, also takes issue with Leone's position, although he does not mention him by name in this connection.

mento abbiamo diffinito l'amore essere desiderio d'unione con la cosa amata . . . (*Dialoghi d'amore*, p. 207).

. . . We have previously defined love differently from desire; because they say that desire is a voluntary affection to be or to have the thing judged good, which is lacking, and love is a voluntary affection to enjoy in union the thing judged good which is lacking. . . . And we have shown that love, despite the fact that it is sometimes for a thing possessed, nevertheless presupposes always some lack of it, as does desire. . . . So that in effect, thoroughly considered, desire and love are one and the same . . . and therefore at the end of that discussion of ours we defined love as desire of union with the thing loved . . .

Sofia. S'ama pur la cosa posseduta, e quella non manca già.
Filone. Non manca la presente possessione, ma manca la continuazione di quella . . . (*ibid.*, p. 210).

Sofia. Yet one loves the thing possessed, and that is not lacking for the present.
Filone. Not the present possession, but its continuation, is lacking. . . .

Not love, but pleasure (*gaudio*), is now said to result from possession; love, like desire, is of that which is lacking (*ibid.*).

Ficino's commentary is primarily an exposition and interpretation of Plato's *Symposium*; only by derivation is it also a treatise on love. The dialogues of Leone Ebreo, on the other hand, are from beginning to end an exhaustive treatise on love. Leone's book is consequently more comprehensive than Ficino's work in its consideration of love, treating of cosmic questions about love which do not occur in Plato's *Symposium* or in Ficino's commentary upon it. Leone himself declares that Plato in the *Symposium* spoke only of human love and not of God's love, whereas he is discussing universal love.

Sofia. . . . Ma come mi consolerai di Platone che, essendo quel che è, nieghi che in Dio sia amore?
Filone. Di quella spezie d'amore, del quale nel suo *Convivio* disputa Platone (che è sol de l'amore participato agli uomini), dice il vero, che non ne può essere in Dio: ma de l'amore universale, del quale noi parliamo, sarebbe falso negare che in Dio non ne fusse (*ibid.*, p. 217).

Sofia. . . . But how will you console me about Plato, who, being who he is, denies that there is love in God?
Filone. Plato says the truth about that kind of love which he dis-

cusses in his *Symposium* (which is only about the love bestowed to men), that there can be none of it in God. But concerning universal love, of which we are speaking, it would be false to deny that it is in God.

Platone in quel suo *Simposio* disputa solamente de la sorte de l'amore che negli uomini si truova, terminato ne l'amante ma non ne l'amato: però che questo principalmente si chiama amore, chè quel che si termina ne l'amato si chiama amicizia e benivolenzia. Questo rettamente lui diffinisce che è desiderio di bellezza. Tale amore dice che non si truova in Dio, però che quel che desia bellezza non l'ha nè è bello, e a Dio, che è sommo bello, non gli manca bellezza nè la può desiare, onde non può avere amore, cioè di tal sorte (pp. 217-8).

Plato in his *Symposium* discusses only the kind of love that is found in men, limited in the lover but not in the loved one: for this kind mainly is called love, since that which ends in the loved one is called friendship and benevolence. Plato rightly defines this love as a desire of beauty. He says that such love is not found in God, because that which desires beauty and doesn't have it is not beautiful, and God, who is the highest beauty, does not lack beauty nor can he desire it, whence he cannot have love, that is, of such a kind.

Leone's more comprehensive approach to love determines a different classification of love from that employed by Ficino and by subsequent essayists, who followed Ficino's terminology. By human love Leone usually means man's love of God, or sometimes of another human; and by divine love, the Creator's love of the created. Other *trattatisti* call human love the sensual love of human beings; whereas by divine love they mean man's love of the deity. To make the conventional distinction between vulgar and divine love, Leone speaks of "sensual" and "spiritual" love, the latter resulting from rational cognition, the former from sensuous cognition (p. 331). However, toward the end of the third dialogue he mentions the Platonic classification of three kinds of love adopted by Ficino.

[Platone] divide li generi d'amore in tre, come Aristotile, ma in altro modo, che è: amore bestiale, amore umano e amore divino. . . . E chiama amore umano quello che è circa le virtù morali. . . . E chiama amore divino l'amore de la sapienza e de l'eterne cognizioni . . . (pp. 367–68).

[Plato] divides love into three kinds, like Aristotle, but in another way, namely: bestial love, human love, and divine love. . . . And he calls human love that which is about the moral virtues. . . . And he calls divine love the love of wisdom and eternal knowledge. . . .

Love is the force which binds together the inferior and superior worlds in a union desired by both entities. God is the cause, the material world his effect. The world constitutes plurality unified (pp. 157–58). Lover, loved, and love are three entities only when they are in potency; in act they are one and the same. In God, who is pure act, their unity is pure and simple (p. 255).

As for Ficino, Pico, and Bruno, the two worlds meet and are joined in the soul.

[L'anima è] mezzo fra il mondo intellettuale e il corporeo (dico mezzo e vinculo, con quale l'uno con l'altro si collega) . . . (p. 178).

[The soul is] midway between the intellectual world and the corporeal (I say midway and a bond, by which the one is connected with the other). . . .

This cosmic dichotomy explains the dual impulses of the human soul, for man is a microcosm, and his soul is an image of the world soul.

. . . L'anima è mezzo fra l'intelletto e il corpo: non solamente dico l'anima del mondo, ma ancora la nostra, simulacro di quella; ha adunque la nostra anima due faccie (come t'ho detto de la luna, verso il sole e la terra), l'una faccia verso l'intelletto suo superiore, l'altra verso il corpo inferiore a lei (p. 331; cf. p. 187).

. . . The soul is midway between the intellect and the body—I speak not only of the world soul, but also of ours, its simulacrum. Our soul has then two faces (as I told you about the moon, toward the sun and toward the earth), one face toward the intellect, its superior, the other toward the body, its inferior.

By loving divine beauty man can unite the inferior world with the divinity (p. 265). The sensual impulse in men's souls is not the sheer bestiality described by Ficino and others, but is tinged with the desire to ameliorate the object of desire by imparting to it something of the beauty which the soul derives from the intellect.

Con questo[21] si giunta un altro amore gemino de l'anima al mondo

---

[21] Leone refers to the soul's love of the beauty of the divine intellect, which he likens to the love of the female for the perfecting male.

corporeo a lei inferiore, come del maschio a la femmina, per farlo perfetto imprimendo in lui la bellezza che piglia da l'intelletto mediante il primo amore: come che l'anima, ingravidata de la bellezza de l'intelletto, la desidera parturire nel mondo corporeo . . . (*Dialoghi d'amore,* p. 195).

To this love is joined another twin love of the soul for the corporeal world inferior to it, as of the male for the female, impressing into it the beauty which it takes from the intellect through the first love—as though the soul, impregnated with the beauty of the intellect, desired to bring it forth into the corporeal world. . . .

Nevertheless, the soul enamored of sensual beauty can be neither beautiful nor happy until it is purged of sensuality and comes into unimpeded possession of its intellective light, which is happiness (*ibid.*, p. 333).

Almost the entire second half of the book is needed for Filone to reply to Sofia's fivefold question about love in the third and principal dialogue:

. . . Dì se nacque, quando nacque, dove nacque, di chi nacque e perchè nacque questo strenuo, antico e famosissimo signore (p. 204).

. . . Tell whether this zealous, ancient, and most famous lord was born, when he was born, where he was born, of whom he was born, and why he was born.

The first love is that of God for himself; the second, his love of the created world.

Il primo amante si è Dio conoscente e volente, il primo amato è esso Dio sommo bello (p. 253).

The first lover is God the knower and willer; the first beloved is the same God, the highest beauty.

Il primo amore, di poi di quello intrinseco uno con Dio, fu quello per il quale il mondo fu fatto, o ver prodotto: il qual nacque quando il mondo [nacque] . . . essendo egli causa del nascimento del mondo. . . . (p. 257; cf. p. 370).

The first love after the one intrinsic in God was that by which the world was made or rather produced: which was born when the world [was born] . . . it being the cause of the world's coming into being. . . .

Love was born when beauty was born, for every loved thing is beautiful (pp. 309–10). Love's birth was in the angelic realm, from whence it descended through the degrees of the inferior world, where only man, in whose corruptible body there is an immortal intellect, can resemble the angel by loving divine beauty (p. 265). The person loved is the efficient cause of love, which the beloved generates in the lover. The beloved is likened to a father, the lover to a mother who gives birth to love (p. 229). Similarity of complexions is the chief cause of love in men, as conformity of nature causes love among celestial bodies (p. 97).

Two mutual lovers are no longer two, but one, in their unity, or four,[22] as each transforms himself into the other and is both lover and loved.[23] The end of love is pleasure (*diletto*)—beautiful pleasure. The end of the appetite[24] is pleasure that is not beautiful. Pleasure consists in union with the pleasurable. Carnal love is good and honest when moderated by the intellect and directed toward reproduction.

. . . [Il] fine d'ogni amore è la dilettazione de l'amante ne la cosa amata (*Dialoghi d'amore*, p. 358).

. . . The end of every love is the delight of the lover in the thing loved.

. . . De l'amore è fine il diletto bello, e de l'appetito è fine il diletto non bello (*ibid.*, p. 359).

. . . The end of love is beautiful delight, and the end of the appetite is delight which is not beautiful.

. . . Non è altro la dilettazione che l'unione del delettabile . . . (p. 364).

. . . Delight is nought but union with the delightful.

Sofia. E sono alcune di queste carnali dilettazioni che sono pur veramente buone?

[22] *Dialoghi d'amore*, p. 222. This apparently inconsequential statement was widely repeated after Leone.
[23] The transformation of the lover into the beloved was a favorite theme of Ficino.
[24] Although it appears that Leone here wavers and again distinguishes appetite from love as other essayists did, he is perhaps using "appetite" in the specific sense of a sensual passion.

Filone. Sì, quelle che sono temperate necessarie a la vita umana e a la progenie; le quali, se ben sono dilettazioni carnali, sono e si chiamano oneste, però che sono misurate e temperate da l'intelletto, principio de l'onestà . . . (p. 362).

Sofia. And are there some of these carnal pleasures which are yet truly good?

Filone. Yes, those which are temperate and necessary for human life and progeny; which, although they are carnal pleasures, are honest and are so called, since they are measured and tempered by the intellect, the source of honesty.

Diotima's account of love is examined and interpreted in the third dialogue. Love's parents, *Poro* and *Penia*, represent respectively the active intellect and the potency of matter. In the generation of love *Poro*, inebriated with the nectar of the divine ideas, was motivated by a desire to improve the material world; *Penia*, or matter, desired the perfection of the forms which she lacked (p. 310).

Leone for his own part prefers to say that beauty is the father of all love, and that love's mother is the knowledge of beauty, mixed with lack (p. 312). Love is a kind of perfection in potency, which lacks the actual possession of the beauty which it desires: hence it is said to be a mean between beauty and ugliness. The myth of *Poro* and *Penia* is thereby made to symbolize the intermediate position of the possible intellect and material forms between unformed matter and separate forms or angels which are truly beautiful. Not even the angels, however, possess the immense eternal beauty of the divinity, which they know (p. 311).

E d'ambidue [Poro e Penia] nacque l'amore però che l'amore dice perfezione, non in atto ma in potenzia, e così l'intelletto nel corpo generabile, che è forma potenziale e intelletto possibile e per essere intelletto conosce le cose belle, e per essere in potenzia gli manca la possessione di quelle e desia la bellezza attuale: e questo è quel che dice che è mezzo fra il bello e il brutto, perchè l'intelletto possibile e le forme materiali sono mezzo fra la pura materia totalmente informe e fra le forme separate e intelligenzie attuali angeliche che sono vere belle (pp. 310–11).

And love was born from both [*Poro* and *Penia*], for love means perfection, not in act but in potency, and thus the intellect generable in the body, which is potential form and possible intellect, because it is intellect, knows beautiful things, and, because it is in potency, lacks the possession of them and desires actual beauty. It is for this reason that love is said to be midway between the beautiful and the ugly, because the possible intellect and material forms are midway between pure matter, totally formless, and separate forms and angelic intelligences, which are true and beautiful.

Ne mostrò adunque Diotima in questa sua favola che l'intelletto possible è participato de l'intelletto, agente o in atto, angelico o ver divino, e che la possibilità non gli viene da la sua propria natura intellettuale . . . ma solamente da la compagnia de la bisognante materia privata d'ogni atto e pura potenzia (p. 311).

Diotima then showed us in this fable of hers that the possible intellect partakes of the intellect, active or in act, angelic or divine, and that its possibility does not come to it from its own intellectual nature . . . but only from the company of needful matter bereft of all act, pure potency.

Diotima's ladder of love also finds its counterpart in Leone's philosophy. By cognition and love of beauty man himself becomes pure and beautiful. Material beauty should be loved in so far as it induces love and knowledge of perfect incorporeal beauty (p. 357). The philosopher ascends in virtue and science from the minor beauties to major ones, and thence to the love and knowledge not only of the most beautiful intelligences who move the stars, but of the very highest beauty which is the "giver of every beauty, life, intelligence, and being" (*ibid.*). In becoming beautiful he is but returning to his progenitor, beauty, in his native land, which is wisdom. This "sweetest union" (*soavissima unione*) is the ultimate felicity and beatitude of pure intellects (*ibid.*, pp. 357–58).

The theory of knowledge in the *Dialoghi d'amore* is more thoroughly developed than in more conventional love treatises. Knowledge, as in all Platonistic writers, is closely related to love. "The greatest beauty is the first wisdom" (p. 345). The intellect is the highest part of the soul. Knowledge must precede love (p. 8; p. 44). Love does not outstrip knowledge, as Ficino and Bruno hold, but is limited by it. Such limitation of knowledge is consistent with Leone's preceding identification of love with possession (p. 5). The infinite God "is loved to the extent that he is known" (p. 32). He is "loved with knowledge and love" (p. 43). Love of God is never devoid of ardent desire of the knowledge which one lacks; and as knowledge increases, so does love.

. . . Non è mai spogliato l'amor divino d'ardente desiderio: il quale è d'acquistare quel che manca del conoscimento divino; di tal modo che, crescendo il conoscimento, cresce l'amore de la divinità conosciuta (p. 33).

Divine love is never without ardent desire: to acquire that which is lacking in divine cognition; so that, knowledge increasing, love of the known divinity increases.

The end of wisdom is to know God, who is supreme wisdom and goodness and the origin of every good thing (p. 32).

Direct knowledge of divine beauty is impossible in this life (p. 275), where the most one can know is the finite beauty of the active intellect, which mirrors the ultimate divine beauty and makes man desire it.

Beyond discursive knowledge, the divine intellect can show to a meritorious and well-trained reason the ideal essences and the supreme beauty of the first intellect in "intuitive, unique and most abstract cognition" (p. 326).

This kind of knowledge is the Platonic *raptus,* which Leone calls "copulative" knowledge, from the union of the human mind with God. Here more than ever knowledge and love are in intimate relation to each other. Love is *desiderio di fruir con unione, o veramente desiderio di convertirsi con unione ne la cosa amata* (p. 45: desire of enjoying with union, or rather desire of converting oneself, with union, into the thing loved). Strong love and desire, says Leone, cause the intellect to lose itself in contemplation and to rise, enlightened by divine grace, to a superhuman knowledge and union with God. When he is in ecstasy, the lover is totally unaware of himself, intent only upon the object of his contemplation (p. 176). Some blessed men in contemplating divine beauty with extreme desire even abandoned their bodies altogether (p. 178). The intellect in such a state is more divine than human.

Questo tanto amore e desiderio fa che siamo astratti in tanta contemplazione, che'l nostro intelletto si viene a sollevare: in modo che, illuminato d'una singulare grazia divina, arriva a conoscere più alto che l'umano potere e l'umana speculazione; e viene in una tale unione e coppulazione col sommo Dio, che più presto si conosce nostro intelletto essere ragione e parte divina, che intelletto in forma umana (p. 45).

This so great love and desire causes us to be abstracted in such contemplation that our intellect begins to rise; illuminated by a singular divine grace it arrives at a higher knowledge than that of human power and human speculation; it comes to such union and copulation with highest God that our intellect is more readily known to be a divine part and reason than an intellect in human form.

This extraordinary divine knowledge perfects the created intellect and constitutes man's happiness (p. 46). Again, intellectual activity has the primacy in the achievement of beatitude which Christian writers like Ficino perforce attributed to moral and theological virtues.

Le virtù morali sono vie necessarie per la felicità; ma il proprio suggetto di quelle è la sapienza (p. 36).

The moral virtues are necessary ways to happiness; but their proper object is wisdom.

Copulative knowledge is intermediate only between angelic and human intelligence (p. 275). However, from sacred scriptures we know that Moses achieved immediate angelic "copulation with divine beauty" (*ibid.*). In all, there are five degrees of intellect: the human intellect in potency, ignorant; the human intellect in act (*in abito*), wise; the copulative intellect; the angelic intellect; and the divine intellect (*ibid.*, p. 274–75). The human intellect sees divine beauty in the enigmatical form of the corporeal universe; the angelic intellect sees it directly according to the angel's finite capacity; the divine intellect sees its immense beauty and is the equal of its object, as though the sun should see itself (p. 277). Man's intellect does not have a particular essence, but is all things in potency (p. 41), like the soul conceived by Giovanni Pico della Mirandola. Its ultimate beatitude is achieved when its potencies, which are of all things, are actualized. Man then knows all things (p. 36; p. 41).

Man's rational soul is an image of the world soul, the beauty of whose forms it can see and love (p. 326). The world soul is the origin of all forms and souls (p. 325). God is unformed, because in himself he is highest form (*somma forma*, p. 242).

Matter desires forms as the female desires the male—a Platonic simile repeated by many *trattatisti*—and receives them successively.[25]

Leone, like Ficino, is persuaded by Platonic tradition to ascribe Neoplatonic doctrines to Plato. Specifically, he attributes to Plato the Plotinian doctrines of the One, and of emanation.

[Platone] tiene che l'intelletto e sapienza divina, che è il verbo ideale, non sia propriamente il sommo Iddio, nè manco in tutto altro e distinto da lui, ma che sia una sua cosa dependente ed emanante da lui e non separata ne distinta da lui realmente, come la luce del sole. Questo suo intelletto, ovvero sapienza, chiama opifice del mondo, idea di quello, e continente ne la sua simplicità e unità tutte l'essenzie e forme de l'universo, le quali chiama idee . . .[26]

[Plato] holds that the intellect and divine wisdom, which is the ideal word, is not really the highest God, nor yet wholly other and distinct from him, but that it is a dependent thing of his emanating from him and not really separate or distinct from him, like the light of the sun. He calls this intellect or wisdom the fabricator of the world, its idea, containing in its simplicity and unity all the essences and forms of the universe, which he calls ideas . . .

Leone here confuses the demiurge with the ideas, as Giordano Bruno confounded it with the *anima mundi*.

Leone writes extensively of the astrological and medical correspondence between the cosmos and man the microcosm. Like Marsilio Ficino, Iacopo Mini, Pompeo della Barba, and Flaminio Nobili, Leone Ebreo was both a physician and a Neoplatonic philosopher. The seven planets have special significance for the seven cavities (*busi*) of the head (*Dialoghi d'amore*, p. 84 f.). The three worlds—generable, celestial, and intellectual—are found in the different operations of man divided even into definite parts or organs of the body (*ibid.*, p. 90 f.).

[25] Bruno attacks the doctrine that matter desires forms as the female desires the male. However, he describes as the end of the physical universe the successive information of matter by innumerable forms.

[26] Leone Ebreo, *Dialoghi d'amore*, p. 348. Elsewhere on p. 348 the attribution to Plato of the belief in an unnamable occult God—"ipse"—is even more specific.

Ancient poets artistically enclosed in the literal sense of their poems moral and allegorical senses for many reasons—to avoid revealing to everyone their excellent secrets; for brevity; to mix historical and fictional diversion with intellectual truth; and to preserve knowledge unchanged (pp. 98–100). Hence we may look to pagan mythology for ancient doctrine. Leone devotes more pages than subsequent writers of love treatises to the interpretations, largely astrological, of the myths of pagan gods (pp. 112–54). Of Aristophanes' fable in the *Symposium* he says: "La favola è bella e ornata; e non è da credere che non significhi qualche bella filosofia" (p. 291: The fable is beautiful and ornate; and it is not to be doubted that it signifies some fine philosophy).

The heavens, being composed of form and matter, are naturally dissolvable; but divine omnipotence, as Plato teaches in the *Timaeus,* rules that they shall not dissolve (pp. 111, 243, 245). Ancient theologians who were Plato's masters state that the material world is corrupted and renewed every seven thousand years (p. 247). This doctrine of the cosmic year is confirmed by astrologers who say that when the eighth sphere revolves one time, everything returns to its primitive condition (*ibid.*).

Leone proceeds to reconcile Platonic cosmology with that of Moses: "*Sofia.* Mi piace vederti fare Platone mosaico e del numero de' cabalisti" (p. 251: *Sofia.* I like to see you make Plato Mosaic and one of the cabalists). Even more startling is the fact that Plato is depicted as borrowing Aristophanes' fable in the *Symposium* of the halving of primeval man from the Hebrew story in Genesis of the creation of man.[27] Plato's philosophy in general is seen to follow Mosaic theology,[28] and to this alleged fact is attributed Plato's superiority to Aristotle.

Come ch'io sia mosaico ne la teologale sapienzia, m'abbraccio con questa seconda via, però che è veramente teologia mosaica: e Platone,

[27] *Dialoghi d'amore,* pp. 291–300. Pompeo della Barba cites Leone's Biblical derivation of the Platonic myth, in *Spositione d'un sonetto platonico,* p. 21. Giovanni Pico della Mirandola, in his *Oration on the dignity of man,* par. 2, also says that Moses and the *Timaeus* agree on the creation of man.

[28] *Dialoghi d'amore,* pp. 351 f. In ancient times Philo Judaeus and Numenius held that Plato knew the Mosaic doctrines.

come quel che maggior notizia aveva di questa antica sapienzia che Aristotile, la seguitò. Aristotile, la cui vista ne le cose astratte fu alquanto più corta, non avendo la mostrazione de li nostri teologi antichi come Platone, negò quello ascoso che non ha possuto vedere, e gionse a la somma sapienzia, prima bellezza, de la quale il suo intelletto saziato, senza vedere più oltre, affermò che quella fusse il primo principio incorporeo di tutte le cose. Ma Platone, avendo da li vecchi in Egitto imparato, potè più oltre sentire . . . (*Dialoghi d'amore*, p. 351).

As I am Mosaic in theological wisdom, I embrace this second way, for it is truly Mosaic theology; and Plato, having more information about this ancient wisdom than Aristotle, pursued it. Aristotle, whose sight in abstract matters was somewhat shorter, not having the demonstration of our ancient theologians like Plato, denied what was hidden from his eyes and arrived at the highest wisdom, the first beauty, having satiated his intellect with which, he affirmed that that was the first incorporeal principle of all things. But Plato, having learned from the old men in Egypt, was able to see farther.

Beauty is defined in relation to love and knowledge.

La bellezza è grazia, che dilettando l'animo col suo conoscimento, il muove ad amare . . . (*ibid.*, p. 226).

Beauty is a grace which, delighting the soul with its knowledge, moves it to love. . . .

Like Ficino, Leone says that beauty is found only in the objects of the two spiritual senses, sight and hearing (pp. 226–27). The imagination or fantasy also can comprehend the beautiful, though not to the extent to which it can be comprehended by the intellective reason. The latter comprehends in particular corruptible bodies the universal beauties, changeless and immaterial. Beautiful study, beautiful law, and beautiful science arouse the soul to pleasure and love far more than do beautiful material objects. But man's supreme knowledge is in the abstract mind, which contemplating the science of immaterial things, becomes enamored of divine grace and beauty, thereby achieving the ultimate felicity.

Molto più conosce del bello la ragione intellettiva, la qual comprende grazie e bellezze universali, incorporee e incorruttibili, ne' corpi particulari e corruttibili, le quali molto più muovono l'anima alla dilettazione e amore: come son gli studi, le leggi, virtù e scienzie umane, quali tutte si chiamano belle; bel studio, bella legge, bella scienzia. Ma la suprema cognizione de l'uomo consiste ne la mente astratta, qual, contemplando ne la scienzia di Dio e de le cose astratte da materia, si diletta e innamora de la somma grazia e bellezza che è nel creatore e fattore di tutte le cose, per la quale arriva a sua ultima felicità (pp. 227–28).

The intellective reason knows much more of beauty; it comprehends in particular and corruptible bodies universal, incorporeal, and incorruptible graces and beauties, which move the soul much more to delight and love—studies, laws, human virtues and sciences, which are all called beautiful: beautiful study, beautiful law, beautiful science. But the supreme knowledge of man consists in the abstract mind, which, contemplating the science of God and things abstracted from matter, takes pleasure and falls in love with the highest grace and beauty which is in the creator and maker of all things, by which man arrives at his ultimate happiness.

The belief that the beautiful and the good are identical is explicitly rejected. Beauty involves a unique personal relation between the object desired and the person desiring it. What appears beautiful to one person may not be so to another. The nature of goodness is less subjective; that which is good is good in itself, and will therefore appear so to most people. As a consequence, the good can be desired for another whom one loves, while beauty can be desired only for oneself (p. 219). However, love considered in broad terms is not only of good things which are beautiful, but also of good things which are not beautiful; hence love can be either of good things which are lacking to the lover or of good things which are lacking to the beloved. God's perfecting love of his creatures is of the latter sort. Love is as manifold as the species of good—beautiful, useful, honest, pleasurable, etc. (p. 221).

Although beauty is considered as a species of good, Leone usually describes philosophic processes, such as cognition and the accession to the divinity, in terms of beauty, rather than in alternative terms such as goodness, truth, or knowledge. Whether or not by express design, this usage enables him to present his entire philosophy in the guise of a treatise on love, for it is beauty that excites love. Even God loves himself as beautiful. In God there is beauty before love; being beautiful and lovable precedes being a lover (p. 253, p. 311).

Perfect beauty is in the divine intellect; its resplendence produces all the ideas (p. 256). The soul, itself "a splendor" that proceeds from that intellect, falls in love with the superlative intellectual beauty, like the imperfect female who loves her perfecting male,[29] and yearns for happiness in perpetual union with its superior origin (p. 195). The specific object of human love is the beautiful, as Plato said, although generically it is the good, as Aristotle said (p. 228). The latter, defining love universally in terms of the good, includes divine love; Plato, in defining it especially by beauty which the lover lacks, excludes divine love (p. 221).[30]

Leone interprets the two Veneres of Plato as the great Venus or eternal beauty of the intelligible world (p. 311), and the inferior Venus who represents the participatory beauty of bodies (p. 312). Thus there are two kinds of beauty, intellectual and corporeal, corresponding to the two sorts of love (p. 196). Leone for his own part posits a threefold division of beauty: God, the beautiful which beautifies; beauty, the first ideal intellect; and beautified beauty, or the created universe (p. 349). The highest divine beauty is immense and infinite, altogether incommensurate with created beauty (p. 266).

The beauty of every created thing is the perfection wrought in it by the highest creator. Corporeal beauty is the resplendent image of the spiritual world (p. 318).

Forms do not completely succeed in removing the "deformity" of matter by the form and beauty which they impart (p. 321). Matter is never as beautiful as the forms which inform it (p. 322) and which always abide separate from matter (p. 323). Form without body is *bellissima;* body without form, *bruttissimo* (p. 325).

Ideas, essentially beautiful, are the divine *prenotizie* of the created universe, pre-existent in the creative intellect (p. 336). Prior to the beauty of "partial" ideas is the beauty of the idea of the whole universe. The multifariousness of the idea of the universe is existent only in parts of the created universe; the idea in itself is simple and

---

[29] A simile repeated by later *trattatisti*—e.g., Romei.

[30] As previously pointed out, Leone means by divine love God's love for creation.

indivisible (p. 342). In human and angelic intellects the unity of the multiform beauty infused there by God is greater in proportion to the intellect's clarity and nearness to the "first and true beauty of the intellectual idea which is in the divine mind" (p. 343). The beauty of the idea of the world is the beauty of the intellect itself (*ibid*). In other words, knower, what is known, and knowledge —like lover, loved, and love—are identical in the godhead (p. 255).

Leone, like Ficino, substantially repeats the Plotinian objections to the definition of beauty as proportion. Such a concept of beauty, he declares, does not include the lucid beauty of the sun, the moon, and the stars; only the whole of a thing, and not its parts, could be beautiful (p. 319). Leone considers light the most beautiful thing in the corporeal world (p. 320). It makes beautiful every color and colored object (p. 322). Colors are beautiful because they are forms (*ibid.*).

Beauty is primarily a spiritual essence. Matter, in itself without form or beauty, becomes beautiful by participation in the spiritual world.

Higher in the scale of beauty than beautiful material objects is the cogitative beauty which resides in the human mind. This beauty is truly formal and spiritual, and exercises a twofold function: it disposes the mind to participate in doctrinal beauty—by which Leone presumably means the beauty inherent in ordered thought—and it expresses itself in artistic creation.

Le bellezze de la cognizione e de la ragione e de la mente umana manifestamente precedeno ogni bellezza corporea: però che queste sono vere formali e spirituali, e ordinano e uniscano li molti e diversi concetti de l'anima, sensibili e razionali, e ancora porgeno e participano bellezza dottrinale ne le menti disposte di ricevere bellezza, e ancora bellezza artifiziale in tutti li corpi che per artifizio son fatti belli (p. 323).

The beauties of cognition and reason and the human mind manifestly precede all material beauty, since they are true, formal, and spiritual, and order and unite the soul's many diverse concepts, sensible and rational, and further offer and bestow doctrinal beauty to minds disposed to receive beauty, as well as artificial beauty to all bodies which are made beautiful by artifice.

Leone's *Dialoghi d'amore* soon became a widely quoted, authoritative, and enthusiastically accepted source for writers of love treatises. Giuseppe Betussi refers to him as "quello ebreo che sì divinamente n'ha scritto" (*Il Raverta*, p. 4). Tullia d'Aragona, following the lead of Benedetto Varchi, does not hesitate to prefer Leone above all other writers on love:

Tra tutti quelli . . . che abbiano scritto di Amore . . . a me piace più Filone che niuno.[31]

Among all those . . . who have written of love . . . I like none better than Filone.

Varchi's words are as follows:

Ultimamente venne in luce il Dialogo di Filone Ebreo, diviso in tre libri; nei quali si tratta, benchè alcuna volta oscuramente o confusamente, così a lungo delle cose d'amore e così veramente, che io per me lo prepongo a tutti gli altri.[32]

Lately there came to light the dialogue of Filone Ebreo, divided into three books, in which matters of love are treated at such length and so truly—though at times obscurely and confusedly—that I for my part prefer it to all the others.

Leone's influence on subsequent writers appears to have equaled that of Ficino.

PIETRO BEMBO

The literature of Platonic love enters a new phase with the publication in 1505 of Pietro Bembo's *Asolani*. Written almost contemporaneously with Leone's *Dialoghi d'amore*—Bembo began this work by 1497—the *Asolani* is in marked contrast to the other two chief sources for the genre of love treatises. The primarily philosophical interest of Ficino's commentary on the *Symposium* and of Leone Ebreo's love dialogues is replaced by a predominantly literary tone and intent in the three dialogues of the *Asolani*. This tendency prevailed among subsequent writers. The literary orientation im-

---

[31] Tullia d'Aragona, *Della infinità di amore*, p. 224. By "Filone" Tullia means Leone Ebreo.

[32] Benedetto Varchi, *Sopra alcune quistioni d' amore, in Opere*, II, 536.

parted to the genre by Bembo is an important factor in the wide popularity it enjoyed in the sixteenth century.

Pietro Bembo (1470–1547) was a young man when he wrote the *Asolani,* but he had already assimilated the broad humanistic culture which was to make him famous. He studied Greek at Messina in the school of Constantine Lascaris; a confirmed Ciceronian, he wrote elegant Latin prose and verse. He had a good knowledge of Provençal and Italian literature. His critical acuteness and talent for cultural synthesis helped win for him the enormous prestige which enabled him to determine the stylistic and esthetic ideals of the literature of his age.[33] He was the chief exponent of Petrarchism, which was to run hand in hand with Platonism for the better part of a century.

The *Asolani* is the first bona fide case of a prose work written in Tuscan by a non-Tuscan author.[34]

Petrarchan, Boccacian, and Dantean motives abound and often intermingle. Gismondo thinks on his *donna gentile* and her *treccia d'oro* (golden tress).[35] The settings and the characters are reminiscent of *The Decameron;* the verses, as we shall see are studiously replete with Petrarchan motives; Gismondo's defense of love in the second dialogue is courtly, sensual, gallant, and virtuous. He speaks of their conversation after Dante as a *convito* or *vivanda,* and declares: "E di sua propria man mi detta Amore" (*Gli Asolani,* p. 132: And of his own hand Love dictates to me).

Bembo is interested in linguistic expression for its own sake; yet his style in the *Asolani* is heavy and archaic, and less polished than in the *Prose della volgar lingua,* published in 1525, which codified the poetic taste of the *cinquecento* according to the models of Petrarch and Boccaccio, and upheld Florentine as the most excellent Italian dialect.

Gallant and mundane, the *Asolani* gives to the discussions of love

[33] Giuseppe Betussi in *La Leonora* (*Trattati d'amore del Cinquecento,* ed. by Zonta, p. 340), calls him "mio reverendissimo ed eterno Bembo" (my most reverend and eternal Bembo). Varchi calls him "il secondo Petrarca" (the second Petrarch).

[34] The *Arcadia* of Jacopo Sannazzaro, written except for the last pages between 1480 and 1485 and published in 1504, alternates poetically oriented rhythmic prose passages with classicizing eclogues.

[35] Pietro Bembo, *Gli Asolani,* in *Gli Asolani e le rime,* p. 132.

a courtly setting in Asolo in the castle of Caterina Cornaro, former queen of Cyprus. The formal framework is imparted by a *tenzone* about love among the three male protagonists, Perottino, Gismondo, and Lavinello, whose discussion is heard and abetted by three charming damsels. In the third dialogue the audience is augmented by the presence of the queen and her other guests.

The *canzoni* with which the discussions are interspersed appear at first glance to tie the work to the tradition of prose commentaries on verse. However, the prose passages are in no sense a commentary upon the *canzoni;* rather, the latter are an adornment of the prose body, and there is no pretense of commentary as there is in Dante's *Convivio.* The verses themselves, however, are purely Petrarchan.

Ostensibly, the *Asolani* was composed to teach its readers "not to err," since "not to love" is impossible (pp. 3–4). The first book consists of Perottino's development of the thesis that *amare senza amaro non si può, nè per altro rispetto si sente giamai . . . alcuno amaro, che per amore* (p. 16: one cannot love [*amare*] without bitterness [*amaro*], nor does one ever experience bitterness from any other cause than love).[36] The untoward results of love are practically without number. Only the sweet thought of death gives pleasure to Perottino, and holds him from suicide (*Asolani,* p. 25). The lover's torment and the antithesis of his life, which kills him, to the death that vivifies him are expressed in the following verses:

> Quand'io penso al martire,
> Amor, che tu mi dai, gravoso e forte,
> Corro per gir a morte,
> Così sperando i miei danni finire.
> Ma poi ch'i' giungo al passo,
> Ch'è porto in questo mar d'ogni tormento,

[36] Cf. Petrarch's lines (*Trionfo d'Amore,* I, 76–8):

> Questi è colui che 'l mondo chiama Amore:
> amaro, come vedi, e vedrai meglio
> quando fia tuo, com'è nostro signore.

(This is he whom the world calls love, bitter as you see and shall better see when he is your master as well as ours.)

Paolo del Rosso (*Comento,* p. 36) quotes these verses in his commentary on Cavalcanti's *Canzone.*

Tanto piacer ne sento,
Che l'alma si rinforza, ond'io nol passo.
    Così 'l viver m'ancide,
Così la morte mi ritorna in vita:
O miseria infinita,
Che l'uno apporta e l'altra non recide.
                        (ibid.)

When I think of the affliction, oppressive and severe, that you give me, O Love, I run toward death, hoping thus to end my troubles.

But when I reach the crossing which is a harbor in this sea of every torment, I feel such pleasure thereat that my soul grows stronger, whence I do not cross it.

Thus living slays me, thus death returns me to life: O infinite misery, which the one brings and the latter does not cut off.

As in practically all the treatises, arbitrary explanations are offered of the god Love's traditional attributes. He is depicted nude to show that lovers have nothing of their own, but belong to others; a boy because he makes his followers boyish; winged, because lovers think to soar to heaven through the air of their hope. He holds a burning torch—bright for pleasure, but burning most painfully. His bow and arrow signify that love's wounds are like those a good archer might inflict, all the more fatal for their being aimed at the heart *(ibid., pp. 30–31)*.

For every sweet solace of love there are a thousand pains. The first sweetness of Perottino's love has vanished, leaving only sorrowful memories. He finishes his story in tears, which move his listeners also to weep.

The next day, in the second dialogue, Gismondo replies point by point to Perottino's diatribe and extols love as the author of every pleasure. *Amore* (love) is no more *amaro* (bitter) than *donne* (women) are *danno* (harm). Rather, says Sabinetta, young ladies . . . are useful *(le giovani . . . giovano, p. 63)*. The lover burns with a sweet fire (p. 66); he "feigns" (p. 70) that his heart and that of his beloved change places. "Meco 'l cor vostro e 'l mio con voi dimora" ("Your heart lives with me and mine with you," p. 71). The point of Aristophanes' myth of the hermaphrodite in Plato's *Symposium* is that in loving another, one loves the other half of himself (p. 74). Perottino is but the shadow of a lover; for if he truly loved, his love would be temperate (p. 82). Gismondo's song to his chaste lady, *Sì rubella d'Amor nè sì fugace* (pp. 83–84), illustrates the dominance of Petrarchan motives. It ends with these words:

> *Asprezza dolce* è mio *dolce tormento,*
> Dolce miracol, che veder non suolse,
> *Dolce ogni piaga,* che per voi mi resta
> Beata compagnia.
> Quanto Amor vaga, par beltate onesta
> Nè fu giamai nè fia [Italics mine. J.C.N.].

A sweet harshness is my sweet torment, a sweet miracle which is not often seen, sweet every wound, which because of you remains my blessed company.

Such chaste beauty, as gracious as Love, never was and never shall be.

The italicized phrases are hollow repetitions of Petrarch, which will reappear in nearly all love lyrics for the next two centuries. The Dantean words, however—*miracol, beata,* and *onesta*—have completely different meanings from those Dante intended: *miracolo* and *beata* bear not the faintest trace of their theological origin, while *onesta* means not "worthy of honor," but "chaste."

Love is infinitely good, and can never be fully known (p. 89). Excited by feminine beauty, it incites the courtly virtues. Gismondo, in the *canzone, Se'l pensier, che m'ingombra,* sees the beauty of his lady and his thoughts of love preserved and reflected in an idyllic landscape. Love is always pleasurable, to young and old, to the good and to the wise (p. 115). All kinds of amorous adventures, earned and stolen, true or false, are desirable.

In the third book, Lavinello declares that both Perottino and Gismondo have "passed beyond just measure in their judgment" (p. 125). Love can be either good or bad. All love is desire, and all desire is love (p. 126). One's love will be good if he loves in his "gentle and amorous lady" her qualities of *ingegno* (wit), *onestà* (honesty), *cortesia* (courtesy), *leggiadria* (loveliness), and the other parts of the soul more than those of the body, which should be loved only as ornaments of the soul (p. 128). Good love is desire of beauty, as the best ancient definers tell us (p. 129). Beauty itself is defined as a grace born of proportion, predicable equally of soul and body.

[La bellezza] non è altro che una grazia che di proporzione e di convenenza nasce e d'armonia nelle cose, la quale quanto è più perfetta ne' suoi suggetti, tanto più amabili essere ce gli fa e più vaghi, et è accidente negli uomini non meno dell'anima che del corpo (p. 129).

[Beauty] is a grace which is born of proportion and suitability and harmony in things, which, the more perfect it is in its subjects, the more lovable and charming it makes them for us. It is a quality in men's souls no less than in their bodies.

The sense of hearing is directed toward beauty of the soul, sight toward bodily beauty (*ibid.*). However, Bembo says with Ficino that if only the eyes, the ears, and thought are involved in the appreciation of beauty, love will be good. With the "material senses" not beauty but "dirty things" are desired (p. 130). There follow three *canzoni*, treating in part of the three innocent manners of pleasure (*diletti*) which are felt in "loving well." The last of the *canzoni* declares that the body is a prison.

Lavinello then relates what a saintly hermit told him. Love is not the same as desire, which possession replaces with pleasure. However, one cannot desire without loving (p. 142). Will is the source of love and hate (*ibid.*). To love well one must follow reason, not sense (*ibid.*, p. 143). Unerring nature gave to man the will power to descend through sense to animal kind and to rise by reason to the superior species: man can become either a dirty beast or a god (p. 146). Body is a fleeting and discordant mixture of the four elements, whereas the soul, altogether pure and immortal, is eager to return to its maker, except that, enclosed in its carnal prison, it may lose itself in earthly loves. As though they had drunk the beverage of Circe, men who seek false beauties become animals (p. 147). Beyond the material world there is a divine, illuminated, changeless world (pp. 154–55), visible to the soul's eyes, the home of true life, of which this world is but a shadow and image (p. 155). The soul's true satisfaction is in divine love (p. 156), which makes a death a happy event (p. 158) and leads man to eternal bliss, whereas bad love condemns him to eternal pain (p. 159). The Christianizing of Platonic love is complete.

FRANCESCO CATTANI DA DIACCETO

Francesco Cattani da Diacceto (1466–1522), the chief disciple of Marsilio Ficino, may be considered a link between Ficino and sixteenth-century Italian Platonists. Some sixteen to twenty years after Ficino's death, Diacceto was active in the Medici Academy, which considered itself a revival of the Platonic Academy.[37]

Diacceto composed two treatises on love, *De amore libri tres* and a shorter *Panegyricus in Amorem,* both translated into Italian by himself. The *Tre libri d'amore,* like the author's even more comprehensive treatise, *De pulchro,*[38] differs from all subsequent *trattati d'amore* in being primarily a metaphysical work.

Diacceto does not wish to minutely interpret Plato;[39] appropos of Plato's myth of the parentage of love—Plenty and Poverty—he refers his readers to the *Commentary* of "our leader Marsilio, where the nature of love according to the understanding of Plato is divinely explained" (*Tre libri d'amore,* pp. 128–29).

The *Tre libri d'amore,* like the *De Pulchro,* is given a strongly Plotinian flavor by Diacceto's insistence on the ultimate superessentiality and unknowability of God in his innermost unity; and by the comprehensive ontological scale ranging from supra-being to nonbeing.

Et però Plotino, et gli altri Platonici niegono Iddio esser essentia, o intelletto: ma . . . [è] ricco della sua semplicissima Unità. Solamente noto a se medesimo, solo ammiratore, et cultore dell'abisso della sua divinità. Questa è quella divina caligine, la quale tanto celebra Dionisio Areopagita splendore della Christiana Theologia, alla quale non aggiune virtù alcuna rationale, o intellettuale (*ibid.,* pp. 35–36).

And therefore Plotinus and the other Platonists deny that God is essence or intellect; rather . . . is he rich in his most simple unity,

---

[37] Kristeller, "Francesco da Diacceto and Florentine Platonism in the Sixteenth Century," in Biblioteca Vaticana Studi e testi, vol. 124, *Miscellanea Giovanni Mercati,* p. 276.

[38] No attempt is made here to summarize the *De pulchro,* which is even farther than the *De amore* and the *Panegyricus* from being a *trattato d'amore.* The reader is referred to the article by Kristeller cited in the preceding footnote.

[39] Francesco Cattani da Diacceto, *I Tre Libri d'Amore . . . con un Panegirico all'Amore,* p. 98. Diacceto's *Opera omnia* were published in Basel in 1563.

known only to himself, the sole admirer and cultivator of the abysm of his infinity. This is that divine fog so celebrated by Dionysius the Areopagite, splendor of Christian theology, to which he does not add a single virtue rational or intellectual.

The natural issue of such a doctrine is negative theology.

Adunque molto più appropinqueremo a Dio procedendo per le negationi, che per l'affermationi . . . (p. 37).

Thus we shall approach much nearer to God proceeding by negations than by affirmations. . . .

The *Panegirico* contains a clearer statement than the *Tre libri d'amore* of the ontological hierarchy. First there is God, infinite goodness, infinite simplicity; second, the angelic nature; third, rational nature, or the soul; fourth, shadow-like corporeal nature; and fifth, matter, cause of all evil, much nearer to nonbeing than to being (*Panegirico* [Rome, 1526], pp. 13–15).

Happiness is achieved through the maximum possible possession of God by the intellect and the will together in man's whole being (*I tre libri d'amore*, pp. 56–57). The human soul lives the life of the gods when "in the most pleasant meadow of the intelligible truths it completes justice, beauty and goodness" (*ibid.*, p. 93). Understanding these essences, it will act accordingly and become a "colleague" of the world soul (*ibid.*). The soul has two inclinations: "to produce and govern the body" and "to divine things" (*ibid.*, p. 60). The individual soul should be guided by the world soul (p. 64), the soul a mistress, the body its subject (p. 19). As the body is governed by the soul, so should the latter be ordered by the angelic nature, or intellect (pp. 22–23). Like Ficino and Pico, Diacceto considers the soul's position to be intermediate between the spiritual and corporeal worlds.

Adunque diremo essere due nature nell'anima: una per la quale rappresenta la Natura Angelica; l'altra, per la quale inclina al corpo. Onde è detta dal divin Platone nel Timeo, sustantia meza, come quella, che posta in mezo fra l'Angelico, et il corpo partecipa dell'una, et dell'altra natura (p. 23).

Then we shall say that there are two natures in the soul: one by which it represents the angelic nature; the other by which it inclines toward body. Whence it is called by the divine Plato in the *Timaeus* a middle substance, being that which, placed between the angelic and the material, partakes of both natures.

The natural hierarchy is expressed by the Neoplatonic metaphor of light: the angel is completely lucid, the soul partly so, and the body altogether dark. Truth is changeless; bodies are in continual generation and corruption (pp. 7–8), owing to the matter of which they are composed. The universe itself is animated (p. 18).

Diacceto adds little to the Platonic theories of love and beauty. He defines love with Ficino as "desire of beauty" or desire to enjoy beauty and to generate beauty in beauty.

Ogni appetito, et ogni desiderio si puo chiamare amore in un certo modo benche pigliando propriamente l'amore sia solamente desiderio di bellezza. . . . (p. 44).

Every appetite and every desire can be called love in a certain way, although taking it properly love is only desire of beauty. . . .

[L'amore è] uno intenso desiderio di fruire, et di fingere la bellezza (p. 84).

[Love is] an intense desire of enjoying and forming beauty.

E . . . l'amore desiderio di fruire et generare la bellezza nel bello, secondo il divin Platone difinisce nel Simposio (p. 99).

Love is . . . the desire to enjoy and generate beauty in the beautiful, as the divine Plato defines it in his *Symposium*.

There are two kinds of beauty and two kinds of love, celestial and vulgar, corresponding to the two Veneres (p. 85). Angelic love is directed toward understanding (pp. 43–44). Cognition precedes desire; desire precedes action (p. 91). The object of cognition is truth; the good is the object of desire (p. 100).

. . . Alla cognitione che è circa il vero, seguita l'appetito, che è circa il bene (p. 102).

. . . After cognition, which is of the true, follows appetite, which is of the good.

One is likely to fall in love with a person who is under the influence of the same planet (Ficino, *Sopra lo amore*, VI, vi). The lover lives without soul in his beloved (Diacceto, *I tre libri d'amore*,

p. 123) unless he receives his beloved's soul in reciprocation (*ibid.*, p. 128). Love is a "grave malady" with pains in the heart caused by violence wrought in the spirit by the love object (p. 120). The spirit, "being generated by a very subtle exhalation of blood, takes its origin from the heart" (p. 111). The sick soul, delighted by the divine aspect of its beautiful spectacle, especially resplendent in the eyes, is deceived by the voluptuousness which "a certain demon" mixes with love as "a very sweet bait," so that the deadly poison is not felt to penetrate (p. 121). The fate of the soul depends on the way in which it pursues bodily beauty, which can prove to be either a *scala dei* or the calamitous ruin of the soul.

L'anima nostra, poiche è discesa nel corpo mortale se usa per istrumento la bellezza corporale alla divina bellezza, guidata dall'amor celeste, recupera le perdute delizie della vita intelligibile. Ma se fatta ebbra, quasi da poculi di Circe, precipita nella generatione, ingannata dall'amore volgare, diventa serva di tutte quelle calamità, che ha seco congiunte la Natura corporale (pp. 98–99).

Our soul, after it has descended into the mortal body, if it uses bodily beauty as a means to divine beauty, guided by celestial love, recovers the lost pleasures of the intelligible life. But if made drunk, as though from the goblets of Circe, it rushes headlong into procreation; deceived by vulgar love, it becomes the slave of all those calamities which corporeal nature carries with it.

Sensible beauty can excite one toward intelligible beauty (p. 87), which proceeds from the interior perfection of the angel, or intelligence (p. 53). Beauty is a species of the genus "good." The good is autonomous; beauty in some way participates in the good (p. 54). Beauty is thus defined as a grace, a flower, a splendor of goodness (p. 55. Cf. p. 105). It is distinguished from the good as the extrinsic from the intrinsic (p. 53). It precedes love or appetite as the desirable must desire (p. 55). The first beauty, generated by divine goodness, arouses love in the angel, which, having thereby become "all beautiful," expresses its beauty throughout nature. This is the process to which the phrases "celestial love" and "celestial Venus" refer.

Ma . . . sendo la prima bellezza una gratia, uno splendore, un fiore della perfetione interiore, la quale meritamente chiamiamo bontà; che maraviglia è se nella potentia intellettuale dell'Angelo eccita un' intensa appetito? . . . Questo è l'amore, et la Venere celeste, celebrata nel Simposio, nell'oratione di Pausania (pp. 54–55).

But . . . the first beauty being a grace, a splendor, a flower of the interior perfection which we rightly call goodness, what marvel is it if in the intellectual potency of the Angel it excites an intense appetite? . . . This is the love and the heavenly Venus celebrated in the *Symposium* in the oration of Pausanias.

The *Panegirico allo amore* largely repeats ideas expressed in the *Tre libri d'amore*. Nothing is more welcome to the gods than the praise of love (Diacceto, *Panegirico allo Amore*, p. 3). The soul is enraptured by beauty, an exterior grace, because it promises an entry into the infinite perfection of divine goodness (*ibid.*, p. 4). The greater one's knowledge of beauty, the greater one's participation in the divinity (p. 5). Beauty is found only in the company of goodness; neither goodness nor beauty is inherent in matter (p. 15). The body is the "prison" or "tomb" of the soul (p. 20), but is a vehicle of divine beauty, which is manifested especially in the face and the eyes (pp. 21–22).

MARIO EQUICOLA

The *Libro di natura d'amore* of Mario Equicola occupies an independent position in the field of Renaissance love literature. It is almost encyclopedic, covering the philosophical, religious, moral, poetic, mythological, biological, medical, and astrological aspects of love. Despite the superficiality of the book it enjoyed a high reputation among subsequent authors of love treatises: Equicola's name is frequently mentioned with those of Ficino, Bembo and Leone Ebreo. In 1563 Thomaso Porcacchi published a "corrected and reformed" edition,[40] declaring in a dedicatory letter his amazement that Equicola lacks a polished style, although he lived "in the times when the great Bembo flourished" and was very friendly with him. To say that Equicola was an eclectic would be an understatement. He declares in the Proem to the first book of six:

[40] *Mario Equicola d'Alveto di natura d'amore, di nuovo ricorretto, et con somma diligentia riformato per Thomaso Porcacchi.* Venice, 1563.

. . . Quanto vi apparecchio è stato ne campi di philosophia, et theologia con diligenza per me raccolto . . . (Equicola, *Libro di natura d'amore*, p. 3 r).

. . . Whatever I set before you has been diligently harvested by me in the fields of philosophy and theology. . . .

The first book is a cursory review of late medieval and Renaissance literature on love in both verse and prose, which serves the author *qual ramo all' uccellino* (as a branch serves a young bird) as a preparation for his own treatise. The authors he discusses are Guittone d'Arezzo, Guido Cavalcanti, Dante Alighieri, Francesco Petrarca, Francesco da Barberino, Jean de Meung, Martin Franch, Giovanni Boccaccio, Marsilio Ficino, Giovanni Pico della Mirandola, Giovanni Francesco Pico della Mirandola, Francesco Cattani da Diacceto, Battista del Campo Fregoso, Battista delli Alberti, Platina, Pier Hedo di Fortuna, Pietro Bembo, Maestro Battista Carmelita Poeta, and Giovanni Iacovo Calandra. With unwitting irony he says of Petrarch:

Questo è quello che non solamente l'uno, et l'altro Guido cacciò di nido: ma è quello ch'a tutti la gloria della lingua tolse . . . (*ibid.*, p. 8 v).[41]

He is the one who not only chased both Guidos from the nest, but took from everyone the glory of our tongue. . . .

Giovanni Pico is a "new heavenly swan"; Diacceto, "the beloved disciple of Marsilio Ficino."
· The abundance of Equicola's "harvest" may be observed, for instance, in the chapter on Cupid in the second book, where in the space of a few pages (pp. 64 v–70 v) there is a succession or rather conglomeration of fifty-four quotations from or references to the following classical authors: "Phaedrus" (of Plato), Hesiod, Archesilaus, "Pausanias" (of Plato, three times), Plato (twice), Aristotle, Socrates, Cicero (five times), Propertius (four times),

---

[41] Dante in *Purgatory*, XI, ll. 97–99, writes:
"così ha tolto l'uno all'altro Guido
la gloria della lingua; e forse è nato
chi l'uno e l'altro caccerà del nido."
Thus one Guido has taken from the other the glory of the language; and perhaps one is born who will chase them both from the nest.

Claudianus, Philostratus, Meleager (twice), Archelaus, Varro, Pliny (twice), Alexander of Aphrodisias (four times), Vergil (three times), Ovid (twice), Seneca (three times), Homer, Themistius, Moschus, Catullus (twice), Aristophanes (twice), Quintilian, Eustachius,[42] Lucian, Apuleius, Calvus, Menander, Demosthenes, and Josephus.

In the second book he begins to discuss theories about love, which are not so much his own as traditional opinions which he thinks worthy of repetition. In the Proem to the first book he states: . . . Intendo usare in confirmatione de mie opinioni l'authorità solamente de antiqui Greci, & Latini . . ." (p. 4 r: . . . I intend to use in confirmation of my opinions the authority only of the ancient Greeks and Latins . . .).

He identifies beauty with the good (p. 40 r), refers to love as *una cupidità* (p. 39 r), and describes it as "desire of the good, which we wish to have always" (p. 39 v). He repeats many motives from the *Symposium* and the *Phaedrus,* calling love *quella cupidità per la quale semo tirati a generare et parturire nel bello* (that desire by which we are drawn to procreate and give birth in beauty). He adds: "Dicese anchor demone, mezzo tra 'l bello et non bello" (*ibid.*: It is further called a demon, midway between the beautiful and the not beautiful).

The soul, immortal, is incarcerated in the mortal body (*ibid.,* p. 42 r). Platonic themes are perhaps predominant throughout the book. On the last page Equicola concludes as follows: "Tra philosophice sette, eligemmo la academia. La verità christiana sempre abbracciamo . . . (p. 222 r: Among philosophical sects we choose the Academy. We always embrace Christian truth . . .).

He considers all kinds of love as aspects of self-love.

". . . Noi non amamo se non noi stessi . . ." (p. 41 r: We love only ourselves . . .).

". . . Chi ama se stesso è amatore di Dio" (p. 53 r: . . . He who loves himself loves God).

The highest self-love is that of the Christian martyrs (p. 52 v). Christian charity—by the authority of Augustine—is love of the

[42] "Eustachio autor greco"—perhaps Eustratius, the commentator on Aristotle's *Ethics.*

good; man's love of God is not desire (*cupidità*) but charity (p. 57 r). God alone returns love surely and immutably to those who love him (p. 221 v). Equicola's considered definition of love, however, has a sensual flavor:

Dicemo adunque amor esser cupidità d'animo che procede da sensi con pensieri di conseguire il desiderato & fruire la opinata bellezza di quello: fruir al presente intendemo haver la cosa desiderata a tuo piacere, in tua potestà & arbitrio (p. 74 r).

We say then that love is a desire of the soul which proceeds from the senses with the thought of attaining the desired and enjoying its supposed beauty. By "enjoying" we mean here having the thing desired at your pleasure, in your power, and at your disposition.

When it is remembered that the beautiful which one desires is identical with the good, such a definition of love can be applied also to divine love. "Love" itself is such an ample word that it includes all the affections (p. 53 r).

Concludemo . . . amor essere desiderio d'haver & usar & fruire quel che ne credemo bello: mutamo quel bello & in suo luogo dicamo buono: forse in grandissima parte seria diffinitione anchor del divino amore perche buono & bello se converteno come di sotto mostraremo (pp. 74 v–75 r).

We conclude . . . that love is desire of having and using and enjoying that which we believe beautiful. Let us change that "beautiful" and say in its place "good"; perhaps in very large part it would further be the definition of divine love, because good and beautiful convert into each other, as we shall demonstrate below.

However, love seeks beauty, desire seeks pleasure (p. 74 v).

God's love, as Hebrew, Christian, and Platonist agree, was the cause of the creation of the world. However, God's emotions in the Bible are to be understood metaphorically (*ibid.,* Book III, *Del amore di Dio,* p. 91 v f.).

Love is natural, sensitive, or intellectual; or by the Platonic division, contemplative, voluptuous, or visual and conversational (*ibid.,* pp. 70 v–71 v). There are three kinds of *beni*: contemplative, civil, and voluptuary, whose respective ends are the true good, honor, and pleasure (p. 47 r). Everyone desires and loves (p. 39 v). The model lover, like Castiglione's model courtier, should be modest, civil, lettered, a dancer, a good conversationalist, and so forth (*ibid.,* Book V, *Virtù, diligentia, modi, et arte* . . .).

Beauty, according to Plotinus, is of two kinds: corporeal and incorporeal. Plato recognizes three kinds, objects respectively of sight, of hearing, of thought. Bodily beauty requires proportion.[43] The highest beauty of the souls is the cognition of truth and true wisdom (*ibid.,* Book II, p. 80 r).

BALDASSARE CASTIGLIONE

Il libro del Cortegiano by Baldassare Castiglione differs from most of the works examined in this chapter in that it is not a treatise on love. Like Bembo's *Asolani* it has a courtly setting: the court of Urbino, ruled by Duke Guidobaldo da Montefeltro, whose wife, Duchess Elisabetta Gonzaga, presides over the conversations of a happy company of courtiers and guests. The topic proposed for the first night's discussion permeates the entire four books: "formar con parole un perfetto Cortegiano" (to form with words a perfect Courtier, *Il libro del Cortegiano,* I, xii, 36). The second book discusses the effective practice of the courtier's good qualities, and examines the varieties of jokes and humor. The perfect lady of court is propounded in the third book. In the fourth the prince himself and the courtier's relation to the prince are dealt with, and toward the end the question arises, whether the courtier should be in love? Indeed he should be (*ibid.,* IV, xlix, 469); yet since the conversers have said that he must induce the prince to be virtuous, he must almost necessarily be old, "since wisdom very rarely comes before years" (*ibid.*). How, then, can he be in love? Appropriately, Pietro Bembo is called upon to answer the question.

In order to reply, Bembo must "declare what love is, and in what the happiness consists which lovers can have," (*ibid.,* IV, li, 471–72). The elderly person is much more able than the youth to love in a completely praiseworthy and happy way without vexations. Love, "as defined by ancient savants," is "desire to enjoy beauty" (p. 472). Desire is naturally of the good; but in order to desire one

---

[43] *Libro di natura d'amore,* Book II, "Che cosa è bellezza," pp. 77 f. Equicola indicates the ideal bodily proportions.

must first know—by sense, by reason, or by the intellect. Will is based on intellective knowledge and since intellection is directed only to intelligible things, the will is nourished only by spiritual goods. Man, naturally rational, is poised between the extremes of sense and intellect, capable of leading a life common with the animals or with the angels (p. 473).

Beauty too can be desired on any of these three planes. The essential characteristic of beauty, whether natural or artistic, is proportion (*ibid.*). Beauty in bodies is "an influence [*flusso*] of divine goodness," which adorns its subject with "a remarkable grace and splendor" (*ibid.*, IV, lii, 473). The way in which the soul acts in its desire to enjoy this beauty "as a good thing" is of crucial importance; guided by sense, it will run into error, thinking that by possessing the body it will enjoy (*fruir*) beauty. Acting without reason or knowledge, the pleasure it experiences can only be false.

Essendo adunque l'anima presa dal desiderio di fruir questa bellezza come cosa bona, se guidar si lassa dal guidicio del senso incorre in gravissimi errori, e giudica che 'l corpo nel qual si vede la bellezza, sia la causa principal di quella, onde per fruirla estima essere necessario l'unirsi intimamente più che po con quel corpo, il che è falso: e però chi pensa, possedendo il corpo, fruir la bellezza, s'inganna, e vien mosso non da vera cognizione per elezione di ragione, ma da falsa opinion per l'appetito del senso: onde il piacer che ne segue esso ancora necessariamente è falso e mendoso (p. 474).

The soul then being taken with the desire of enjoying this beauty as a good thing runs into very grave errors if it lets itself be led by the judgment of the senses and judges that the body in which beauty is seen is the principal cause thereof; whence in order to enjoy that beauty, it thinks it necessary to unite as intimately as possible with the body, which is false. And therefore he who thinks by possessing the body to enjoy beauty, is deceived and is moved not by true cognition and rational choice, but by false opinion and sensual appetite: whence the pleasure that follows from it is also necessarily false and lying.

In short, sensual love is a deceit. It is not surprising that such lovers are pale, afflicted, tearful, sorrowful, complaining or silent, desirous of dying, completely unhappy. Strong-blooded youths of vigorous flesh may be excused for succumbing to sensuality; but they are thereby prevented from enjoying the true graces and goods of love. Older persons can more easily guide their desire by reason and perfectly possess beauty, benefiting their souls with the good effects which the spiritual possession of beauty entails (IV, liii, 477). Youths who love with their reason may even be called "divine" (IV, liv, 478).

The courtier who sees a beautiful woman should call upon his reason and remember "that the body where that beauty shines is not the fount whence beauty is born" (IV, lxii, 486). Beauty, incorporeal, is "a divine ray" which loses much of its excellence by its very conjunction with matter (*ibid.*). The courtier should love in his lady the beauty of her soul not less than that of her body; he will generate beauty in beauty by seminating virtue in her soul and reaping "with remarkable delight" the fruits of beautiful conduct (p. 487). At this point Bembo's discourse is interrupted with enlivening contrast by the declaration of Signor Morello da Ortona:

Il generar, disse, la bellezza nella bellezza con effetto, sarebbe il generar un bel figliolo in una bella donna; ed a me pareria molto più chiaro segno ch'ella amasse l'amante compiacendol di questo, che di quella affabilità che voi dite (IV, lxiii, 487–88).

Actually generating beauty in beauty, he said, would be to generate a beautiful child in a beautiful woman; and it would seem to me a much clearer sign that she loved the lover if she obliged him in this rather than in that affability of which you speak.

Bembo can only answer:
"Non bisogna, signor Morello, uscir de' termini" (p. 488: One must not, Signor Morello, go beyond the limits).

Sensual love is always bad, except possibly in young people; in them it can even be thought licit, since to win the grace of a lady a lover may accomplish virtuous things, thereby deriving a little *dolce* from much *amaro* (IV, liv, 477–78). To the older, nonsensual lover a lady may concede pleasant laughter, private conversations, jokes, the touching of hands, and even a kiss, in which their souls[44] as well as their bodies may meet. The lover's spirits, which are subtle vapors of the blood, issue from his eyes and receive

---

[44] The kiss here appears as a variation on the well-known theme of lover's exchange of souls.

the image of his lady's beauty (*Il libro del Cortegiano,* IV, lxv, 490–91). Beauty is properly the object of vision and of hearing (*ibid.,* IV, lxii, 486).

The courtier should use his lady's love as a step toward a higher and more sublime love (IV, lxvii, 492–93). Accumulating knowledge of all kinds of bodily beauty, he will form a universal concept of the beauty of bodies (p. 493). Then turning inward to the objects of the mind's eye, having purged his soul by philosophical studies, as though awaking from a deep sleep, he will see "a ray of that light which is the true image of angelic beauty." Enraptured and aflame he will rise with his intellect to the contemplation of divine beauty. His soul, flying to unite with the angelic nature, abandons sense and even reason; for having become an angel it understands (*intende*) all intelligible things without veil or cloud, and is supremely happy (IV, lxviii, 494–95). Alienated from oneself, one can be transformed into the object of love (IV, lxx, 498).

The reader should not be surprised that Castiglione's ethereal flight ends in a more complete optimism than those of Ficino and Bruno; Castiglione is not a philosopher. Nor should he register surprise at the severity of Castiglione's love theory, more rigorous and less compromising than that of Ficino and other Platonist philosophers—which might seem discordant in a book that is characterized by gallantries, fine manners, wit, urbanity, and courtly vanity. It is the very unpracticality of the book, and its social, if not moral, isolation, typified by the author's unwillingness to investigate deep moral problems, which require an unreal and ethereal vision of love. What more un-Machiavellian approach to the life of the state can be found than that which counsels the courtier to frankly and truthfully persuade his lord to the pursuit of virtue, goodness, and generosity for his good and that of his subjects? (IV, v, 412)[45] Nevertheless, the passage on love is written with a brilliance of style, particularly in the fervor of Bembo's speech, that is an undeniable merit. It is obvious, however, that from the doctrinal standpoint Castiglione offered nothing that had not already been said by Ficino, his primary source, and by Bembo.

[45] The practical result of this naïveté is seen in the fiasco of Castiglione's embassy to the court of Charles V.

BARTOLOMEO GOTTIFREDI

Even in popular treatises on love, we find reflection of current philosophical and poetic concepts of love. In Bartolomeo Gottifredi's *Specchio d'amore*,[46] in which Coppina teaches the young Maddalena about love, we find the statement that beauty of body kindles love, but needs the good parts of the soul to make it last (*Specchio d'amore*, p. 255); and that the flame of love is kindled in the heart by the eyes (*ibid.*, p. 258). The latter statement is common to many schools, both poetic and philosophic; the former is frequently found in Platonizing love treatises of the late fifteenth and the sixteenth centuries. The dialogue of the *Specchio d'amore* is vivacious and entertaining, the topic of discussion frankly sensual love.

. . . Giorno e notte in altro non pensiamo nè bene ci par sentire, finch'al desiato fine non siamo pervenuti. Quivi ogni nostro senso cerca di sodisfare al voler suo con l'operare la sua virtù ne lo amato obbietto; nella qual cosa, restando ingannata la speranza, il fuoco s'intiepidisce, ed a poco a poco, scemando la sua nutritiva cagione, in breve manca (pp. 258–59).

. . . Day and night we think of nothing else, nor does it seem to us that we feel, until we have come to the desired end. Here our every sense seeks to satisfy its desire by performing its function with regard to the object of love. When hope is deceived in this undertaking, the fire cools and, as its nourishing cause abates, it quickly goes out.

The matters discussed are practical: the selection of a lover, how to appear attractive, the bounds of conduct when being courted, etc. In the second of the two parts of the dialogue Coppina dwells on the contrast between the condition of lovers and that of married persons: "Per necessità si marita, . . . e per diletto s'ama" (p. 291: One marries by necessity, . . . and one loves for pleasure).

[46] Written circa 1542, published in 1547. *Specchio d'amore, dialogo di Messer Bartolomeo Gottifredi nel quale alle giovani s'insegna innamorarsi*, in *Trattati d'amore del Cinquecento*, ed. by Zonta.

FRANCESCO SANSOVINO

Of similar character, though converse point of view, is the *Ragionamento*[47] of Francesco Sansovino, first published in 1545, which counsels young men in the art of seduction. Agreeing with Castiglione that old men are more ardent in divine love, Sansovino's Panfilo will counsel his friend Silio in worldly love. The noble love of *cuori gentili* is dismissed in equally summary fashion (*Ragionamento*, p. 154). His reference to Platonic lovers is more than slighting:

Silio. Che gente è quella che non fa stima dello amor delle donne nobili o non nobili?

Panfilo. Sono i platonici, cioè contemplativi della bellezza più perfetta, che essi dicano che consiste nello uomo, col mezzo della quale ascendano alla divina. Ma lasciamoli andare, essendo sospette le loro azzioni (p. 165).

Silio. What people are they who don't appreciate the love of noble or not noble women?

Panfilo. They are the Platonists, that is the contemplators of the more perfect beauty which they say resides in man, by means of which they rise to divine beauty. But let's forget them, since their actions are suspect.

The Decameron is cited as an authoritative volume on the *casi d'amore* (pp. 158, 163, 182). Woman, incapable in war, trade, and government, nevertheless is proficient when it comes to love, of which she is the very object and abode (*albergo*).

Nè per altro è stimata nè per altro aùta cara che per questo effetto . . . (p. 160).

Nor for aught else is she esteemed or held dear than for this purpose. . . .

The *amata* should be a married woman; maidens for many reasons are to be fled (p. 157). The lover should be of medium stature, well-to-do, noble, cultured, prudent, good-looking, practical,

---

[47] Francesco Sansovino. *Ragionamento di Messer Francesco Sansovino nel quale brevemente s'insegna a' giovani uomini la bella arte d'amore,* in *Trattati d'amore del Cinquecento,* ed. by Zonta.

affable, and sweet; unmarried and desirous of remaining free (p. 164). His amorous undertakings will meet with success if he is determined in his attentions.

Sta' saldo nel tuo fermo proposito, perchè amando, pregando, essendo continuo, non è che col tempo non si penetri nei petti di ghiaccio: la servitù finalmente è qualche volta conosciuta (p. 169).

Remain steadfast in your resolute purpose, because loving, begging, being persistent, one cannot fail in time to penetrate hearts of stone: finally, service is occasionally recognized.

The most efficacious instrument of all is praise (p. 167). However, love that is true and not feigned requires no instruction; and the mark of true love is to think always of one's beloved and to be almost transformed into her essence (p. 166). In fine, Panfilo declares that all his advice can be condensed into the words, "Love and you shall be loved" (p. 179). The reason for loving is the joy experienced by two souls who are transformed into each other. With love mankind is made immortal; in love only are we recreated from life's many miseries (p. 180).

In an appendant letter presenting the treatise to Gaspara Stampa, so that she may "learn to flee the deceptions which perverse men use upon candid and pure maidens," the author declares that the treatise was written as a "recreation from graver letters" (Appendix, p. 184).

GIUSEPPE BETUSSI

Of quite different intent from the two dialogues just discussed is that by Giuseppe Betussi entitled *Il Raverta*,[48] which may be considered a hybrid kind of dialogue, mixing philosophical considerations of love with popular "practical" and literary questions about "human" love. The philosophical discussion occupies the first part of the dialogue; the *dubbi* the slightly longer remaining part. On the whole this treatise is typical of its genre. The author repeats rather fully the doctrines of love and beauty expounded by

---

[48] Giuseppe Betussi. *Il Raverta, dialogo di Messer Giuseppe Betussi nel quale si ragiona d'Amore e degli effetti suoi,* in *Trattati d'amore del Cinquecento,* ed. by Zonta.

Marsilio Ficino and Leone Ebreo, adding no original doctrines and few corollaries of his own. Composed in dialogue form, the treatise introduces real persons as interlocutors and does not neglect literary interludes and stylistic embellishments. Seemingly earnest in his exposition of a suprasensible ideal of love, Betussi apparently sees no contradiction in turning his attention to questions which would seem trivial if the Platonistic ideal of intellectual love and beauty were accepted at face value: Who really loves more: the timid person or the daring person? (*Il Raverta*, p. 66). Is it possible for a miser to love? (*ibid.*, p. 64). Which is more difficult, to acquire the favor of the *amata* or to maintain it? (*ibid.*, p. 98). The influence of Leone Ebreo is apparent in *Il Raverta* both in point of doctrine and in the language in which the doctrines are expressed. Betussi's definition of love, while not the same as Leone's, is a modification of the latter's definition:

Amore è uno affetto volontario di partecipare o di essere fatto partecipe della cosa conosciuta, stimata bella (p. 8).[49]

Love is a voluntary affection to partake or to be made a participator in the thing known and judged beautiful.

. Contained in Betussi's definition of love is the idea common to most of the Neoplatonists that knowledge must precede love or desire. He repeats after Leone Ebreo the doctrine that love is generated in the lover by the beloved; hence, being the recipient, the lover is inferior to the beloved (p. 33).

Betussi refers to Leone as "that Jew who wrote so divinely of love" (p. 4). In more than one point he tries to Christianize Leone's concepts. One cannot hope to rise to the perfection of contemplating divine beauty unless one is illuminated by God's grace (p. 45). Leone's triad of beauty, *bello bellificante, bellezza,* and *bello bellificato,* is identified by Betussi with the three persons of the Christian trinity.

E ci sono tre gradi di bellezza: l'autore, quella e il partecipante; e chiamasi "bello bellificante," "bellezza" e "bello bellificato." Bello bellificante è il Padre, cioè il sommo Iddio, autore e produttore di quella ed esso tutto, dal quale ella deriva. Èvvi la bellezza, la quale sua bellezza

[49] Leone defined love as "affetto volontario di fruire con unione la cosa stimata buona" (voluntary affection to enjoy with union the thing judged good).

è la sua somma sapienza, constituita e figurata per il Figliuolo, e pure in sè, chè sono due in uno. Bello bellificato è tutto il mondo applicato allo spirito; le quali tre cose sono tre ed una sola. E questo bello bellificato è Amore, cioè pur lo Spirito santo (p. 40. Cf. p. 41).

And there are three degrees of beauty: the author, beauty itself, and the partaker. They are called "beautifying beauty," "beauty," and "beautified beauty." Beautifying beauty is the Father, that is the highest God, author and producer of beauty and the all from which it derives. There is his beauty, which is his greatest wisdom, constituted and symbolized by the Son, and yet in itself, for the two are one. Beautified beauty is the whole world as applied to the spirit. These three things are three and one only. And this beautified beauty is Love, that is also the Holy Spirit.

Betussi includes the knowledge of beauty in his definition of love; similarly, he incorporates in the definition of beauty the knowledge or perceptive capacity of mind and of the eyes and ears, the organs of the two Platonic "spiritual senses."

La bellezza è un dono dato da Dio, ed uno splendor del sommo bene; cioè una certa grazia, la quale, per la ragion conoscitiva che ne ha la mente o per la persuasione che ne prendono i due sensi spirituali, l'occhio e l'orecchia, diletta e trae a sè l'anima (p. 11).

Beauty is a gift of God and a splendor of the highest good; that is, a certain grace which through the knowledge that the mind has of it or through its pursuasion of the two spiritual senses, sight and hearing, delights the soul and draws it to itself.

There are thus three qualities of beauty: of souls, of bodies, and of sounds (pp. 11–12). The greatest beauties are in the soul, great in proportion to their separation from body in the imagination, the reason, or the intellect (p. 13). God in one passage is said to be beauty itself or goodness itself (p. 15); in another he is called not beauty, "but rather origin and creator . . . of . . . beauty" (p. 39). Knowledge of the highest beauty and of God can be achieved only in a step-by-step process from body to soul to angel to God (p. 15). Hell is simply the deprivation of the eternal light of beauty (p. 46).

Betussi adopts Ficino's classification of love as bestial, human, and divine (p. 19). The divisions of love form a ladder from worldly to heavenly things (p. 10). Loving only the body, one does not love a person, but a shadow, because the person is the soul, in which true beauty exists. The rational soul of man is an image of the world soul (p. 36). The body is its prison and tomb. Man becomes enflamed with love to make himself more perfect through union with the soul of the beloved. The moving cause is beauty (p. 23). Love enters the heart through the eyes (p. 67); the lover is dead in his own body, alive in that of his loved one (p. 68). Love cannot be the same as desire; for if it were, it would be love before it had the thing desired and, having it, would no longer be love (p. 6). Love is described, but not defined, by saying that it is a good circle, perpetually returning from the good to the good (p. 9). The meaning of this description is that the soul, led by its reflections on the beauty of the beloved's soul to the contemplation of God, supreme author of beauty, readily abandons the prison of the body so that it may enjoy true happiness in union with the highest beauty whence it took its origin (pp. 43–44). Such is the theme of the dialogue. The soul is aflame with love of God and thinks no more on miserable human things (p. 44). Signora Baffa, listening to the words of Signor Raverta, exclaims: "Tutta mi sento infiammata di divino zelo" (p. 45: I feel all inflamed with divine zeal).

The Platonic myth of the origin of Love from Plenty and Poverty signifies that the lover desires to participate in that which he lacks, and knows or thinks to abound in the beloved. But to fully understand the mystery of love, which, being eternal, has no origin, one must understand the Trinity (p. 25).

Among the interludes in the discussion are the *canzone* (pp. 20–22) which commends the beauty of body and of soul of Signor Vicino Orsino, to whom the dialogue is dedicated; several pages devoted to the praise of various *rari ingegni* (p. 55 f.;[50] stories from Boccaccio (p. 81), Anton Francesco Doni (p. 83), and others introduced apropos of points under discussion; and occasional stanzas to Signor Orsino upon the death of Signora Adriana dalla Roza (pp. 117–20). Betussi takes a good half of his *dubbi*, which occupy about one half of the dialogue, verbatim from those quoted by Mario Equicola (*Libro di natura d'amore*, p. 38 r-v) from

[50] However, not everyone mentioned is praised.

Giovanni Iacovo Calandra. Of the sixteen *dubbi* listed by Equicola, Betussi repeats fourteen.[51]

La Leonora,[52] a later dialogue by Betussi on beauty, published in 1557, adds but little in a doctrinal way to the content of *Il Raverta*. The dialogue, set in Melazzo, Sicily, belongs to the class of courtly literature. In it Signora Leonora relates a conversation of the previous winter with Annibal Caro. The predominant tone of the dialogue is indicated by such occasional moralistic platitudes as the following: that happiness in this world consists in occupying "these few hours of life" far from vulgar conversations and mundane sensuality (*La Leonora,* p. 309); that by the body, composed of the four elements, we are subject to worldly accidents, and by the soul, which is like a divine breath, we desire to return to heaven; that through the cognition of truth we see the frailty and filth of material things in the light of the beauty of things celestial (pp. 320–21). Being naturally more prone to vice than to virtue (pp. 337–88), we must let our soul dress us in virtue (p. 331); good works purify the soul (pp. 334–35). A personal touch is given to the conversation by Signora Leonora's declaration that she will place her "every hope in that greatest beauty and good, the fount and origin of every beauty and every goodness" (p. 317). A foil for this sentiment is provided by the character Giovan Giorgio, as by Signor Morello in the Platonic episode of Castiglione's *Courtier* (IV, lxiii, 487–88).

Giorgio asks:

Che abbiamo noi a fare degli angeli e degli altri corpi celesti ed incorporei? Noi vorremo sapere quali siano le bellezze più convenevoli e più proprie delle donne e degli uomini, . . . e non tante chimere (*La Leonora,* p. 322).

---

[51] The *dubbi* omitted are the following: "Qual donna è da piacer più, o la bella simplice, o la deforme accorta" (Which woman is more pleasing, the simple beauty or the clever ugly one) and "Se per magica si puo flettere animo duro" (Whether a hard heart can be turned by magic). In another case Betussi alters Calandra's question from "Qual donna ama più, la timida o l'ardita" (Which woman loves more, the timid one or the bold one) to "Chi più merita esser amata: una donna timida o una ardita?" (Who is more deserving of being loved: a timid woman or a bold one?).

[52] Giuseppe Betussi, *La Leonora. Ragionamento sopra la vera bellezza di messer Giuseppe Betussi,* in *Trattati d'amore del Cinquecento,* ed. by Zonta.

What have we to do with angels and other celestial and immaterial beings? We would like to know what are the most fitting and suitable beauties of women and men, . . . and not so many chimeras.

Betussi dwells upon the divine origin of the soul and its innate desire to return to heaven (*ibid.,* pp. 320–21, 327, 328). The knowledge of beauty not only has moral results for the soul in the good works which purify the soul (pp. 334–35), but is itself a moral process: beauty is known through love and love through beauty (p. 314). Beauty itself was given us by God for our moral perfection (p. 335). No true knower of real beauties can fail to love them (p. 342).

. . . Questa vera bellezza si consegue col mezo in gran parte delle virtù morali e teologiche . . . Ne senza parte delle arti liberali possiamo giungere a questo colmo. Perciochè per la virtù di queste ci riduciamo a scoprire mille belli segreti della natura e di Dio (p. 336).

. . . This true beauty is attained in great part by means of the moral and theological virtues . . . But we cannot reach this height without the help of the liberal arts. For through them we are led to discover a thousand fine secrets about nature and God.

Betussi here repeats from Ficino the doctrine—which he attributes with Ficino to "ancient theologians" who saw "that God is in everything and [is] everything" (p. 346)—that goodness is the center of four concentric circles of beauty, manifested in the mind, in the soul, in nature, and in matter (Ficino, *Sopra lo amore,* II, iii, 26).

As Castiglione's *Courtier* closes with the sunrise, *La Leonora* ends with the sunset.

SPERONE SPERONI

In Sperone Speroni's *Dialogo di Amore,* through words already familiar to us from treatises of Platonizing writers there occasionally emerges a tendency toward naturalism which draws him nearer than the more orthodox Platonists to the theories of courtly love. The Platonism of his theory of love derives particularly from Leone Ebreo.

. . . Amore non è altro, che desiderio di alcuna cosa, la quale sia veramente o paja altrui esser bona (*Dialogo di Amore*, p. 21: Love is desire of something which is really good or which seems to be so).

As in Leone's dialogue, the active role is paradoxically attributed to the beloved, who is said to paint his (or her) picture in the face and heart of the lover, who is passive (*ibid.*, p. 29). Love is called a centaur, composed of sense and reason (pp. 21–23); the senses are a ladder to reason (p. 6); and reason should be "the major-domo in the house of love" (p. 40). However, Speroni imparts to these statements apparently consonant with Renaissance Platonism an altogether un-Platonic intention. Foolish is he who neglects his essential appetites and tries to be bodiless like an angel.

. . . I sensi son scala e via alla ragione: onde chiunque è cosi sciocco in amore, che egli non curi delli lor proprii appetiti, ma come semplice intelligenza senza alcun corpo, cerchi senza altro di satisfarne la mente sola, si può dir simile alla persona, che trangugiando alcun cibo senza toccarlo nè masticarlo, più s'inferma, che si nutrichi (p. 6).

The senses are a ladder and path to the reason: whence whoever is so foolish in love that he takes no care of their respective appetites, but like a pure intelligence with no body tries simply to satisfy the mind alone, may be said to resemble the person who, gulping down some food without touching it or chewing it, grows weaker rather than gains nourishment.

To completely despise the worldly pleasures is *operazion non umana, ma angelica senza carne* (p. 39) (not a human action, but angelic and fleshless). Reason should regulate appetite, not suppress it (p. 39). Woman is praised as the "joy and delight of the universe" (p. 36). The role of reason as "major-domo" is not at all that of the rational charioteer in the *Phaedrus;* on the contrary, reason, as in late medieval courtly theories of love, seeks to order the senses in such a way as to secure a good measure of sensual pleasure:

. . . Voi vederete, voi udirete, tu parlerai; intanto dorma la mano, la quale svegliata cessino gli altri, finchè chiamati dalla ragione volentieri servano al senso . . . (p. 40).

. . . You shall see, you shall hear, thou shalt speak; meanwhile let the hand sleep. When it awakens let the others cease, until called by reason they may gladly serve the senses. . . .

However, he who forgets that he is a "man of understanding" will suffer the fabled fate of those who drank Circe's potions. Indeed, lasciviousness and idleness are the two extreme miseries of mortal life (p. 42). Other familiar commonplaces are voiced about love: among love's "privileges" is that of "living in another, dying in oneself" (p. 4); love in one moment burns and freezes, wounds and heals, kills and resuscitates (p. 4); love lives by hope (p. 5). Petrarch is occasionally quoted in substantiation of some minor point of discussion. The dialogue represents three characters: Tullia [d'Aragona], [Bernardo] Tasso, and [Nicolò] Grazia, who is the main speaker. Throughout the dialogue there are references to an impending voyage to Salerno by Tasso, and almost at the end of the dialogue Grazia advises Tullia to hope that Tasso's love for her will rise from sense to the mind and thereby achieve cosmic grandeur. In this way Speroni closes his dialogue on the note of moral elevation common to all Neoplatonic love treatises.

. . . Temete solo, anzi sperate che l'amor suo per se stesso dal senso alla mente salito, ed indi a guisa di Ganimede di terra in cielo portato, saglia tanto alto, che la gloria del mondo ora tenuta infinita, piccola e bassa gli si dimostri (p. 45).

. . . Fear only—on the contrary, hope—that his love, risen of its own accord from sense to mind and then like Ganymede carried from earth to heaven, may rise so high that the glory of the world now held infinite will appear to him small and mean.

TULLIA D'ARAGONA

In a letter to Cosimo I de' Medici, Tullia d'Aragona calls her dialogue, *Della Infinità di amore*,[53] "un ragionamento fatto, sono già più mesi, dentro delle mie case" (a discussion held several months ago within my dwellings). The consensus of scholars is that Benedetto Varchi had a hand in the work, if he did not actually write it. Giuseppe Zonta opines that Tullia probably reconstructed in her dialogue a speech delivered by Varchi in her house (*Della Infinità di amore*, p. 361). The sixteenth-century editor of the

---

[53] *Dialogo della signora Tullia d'Aragona della Infinità di amore*, in *Trattati d'amore del cinquecento*, ed. by Zonta, p. 248.

dialogue, Muzio Iustinopolitano, wrote to Tullia that he had changed the name of the character Sabina, which Tullia for reasons of modesty had originally adopted, to her own name (*ibid.*, p. 246). The other interlocutors are Benedetto Varchi and Lattanzio Benucci.

The form of the dialogue is reminiscent of Giuseppe Betussi's dialogue, *Il Raverta,* in that philosophical and courtly questions are interspersed with lighter conversation of a personal or literary nature. The origin of this form is to be found in Leone Ebreo's *Dialoghi d'amore.* The persistent lovers' quarrel there between Filone and Sofia is the prototype of the amorous caprices of Varchi and Tullia in Tullia's dialogue. The dialogue is livelier than most and occasionally witty:

> *Tullia.* Il dubbio è questo: "Se si può amar con termino. . . ."
> *Varchi.* . . . Io non intendo i termini del quesito (p. 190).

> *Tullia.* This is the doubt: "Whether one can love within terms [limits]. . . ."
> *Varchi.* . . . I do not understand the terms of the problem.

In answer to Tullia's question Varchi states that it appears that one cannot love finitely (*con termine*) (p. 203). From his statement and from experience, which she professes to value above all philosophical opinions (p. 204), Tullia posits the infinity of love, "not in act, but in potency." "Amore è infinito non in atto ma in potenza, e . . . non si può amar con termine: cioè i desideri degli amanti sono infiniti e mai non si acquetano a cosa niuna; . . . come testimonia il Boccaccio . . . nel principio delle sue *Cento novelle*" (p. 216: Love is infinite not in act, but in potency, and . . . one cannot love finitely. That is, the desires of lovers are infinite and are never satisfied by anything, . . . as Boccaccio testifies . . . in the beginning of his *Decameron*). Infinity as here used denotes imperfection. "L'infinito, come infinito, importa . . . imperfezzione . . ." (p. 208: The infinite, as infinite, implies . . . imperfection . . .). In other words, love is an insatiable passion. In its grips the lover wavers between tears and laughter, hope and fear, heat and cold, inclination and disinclination; lovers "live dying" and act as they are said to act by poets, especially by Petrarch, incomparable in the realm of love (p. 216).

The definition of love is a paraphrase of Leone Ebreo's definition: "Amore . . . non è altro che un desiderio di goder con
unione quello che è bello veramente o che par bello allo amante"
(p. 202: Love . . . is a desire to enjoy with union that which is
truly beautiful or which seems beautiful to the lover).

Beauty is the mother of all loves; their father, the knowledge of
beauty (*ibid.*). Only vulgar love has a cessation; honest love,
which springs from reason rather than desire in the gentle and
virtuous souls of noble men has for its end the lover's transformation into the object of love, with the desire that the latter be
transformed into him; so that the two may become one only or
four. Petrarch and Bembo have spoken very beautifully (*leggiadra-
mente*) of this transformation (*ibid.*, pp. 222–23). Vulgar love can
sometimes be the cause of honest love (p. 236). As bodies cannot
penetrate each other, he who desires a union beyond the spiritual
will find no attainment or end of his love (p. 223). Apropos of
these statements Varchi commends Tullia for having read Filone—
that is, Leone Ebreo—whom he prefers among all writers on love,
even above the "miraculous" works of Plato and Marsilio Ficino.

Varchi. Tra tutti quelli . . . che abbiano scritto di Amore . . . a me
piace più Filone che niuno.
Tullia. Avete voi letto Platone, ed il *Convivio* di messer Marsilio
Ficino?
Varchi. Signora sì, e mi paiano amendue miracolosi: ma Filone mi
contenta più, credo perchè non intendo gli altri (p. 224).

Varchi. Among all those . . . who have written about love . . . I
like Filone better than anyone else.
Tullia. Have you read Plato and Messer Marsilio Ficino's *Symposium?*
Varchi. Yes, madam, and both appear miraculous to me; but Filone
satisfies me better, I think because I don't understand the others.

The interlocutor Varchi qualifies his admiration of *Filone* by
saying that when he speaks of the Judaic faith he is to be excused
rather than approved (*ibid.*).

It is observed that Leone contradicts Plato in stating that persons
loved are nobler and more worthy than their lovers (*ibid.*, p. 240).
The *Dialogo d'amore* of Speroni is called *bellissimo e dottissimo*
(very beautiful and very learned, p. 242). The merit of Socratic

love is the superiority of the generation of a beautiful soul to that of a beautiful body (p. 229). Beauty and goodness are the same thing (p. 230). Sight and hearing are the spiritual senses; the other senses are material (pp. 235–36).

If Tullia's picture of love seems more spiritual than might be expected of a courtesan, it might nevertheless be expected that a cultured and famous courtesan such as she should write of love in no other way. Her mode of life required it as a kind of leavening. There is no reason to doubt the genuineness of her participation in and contribution to the literary and philosophical currents of her day. On the contrary, her Petrarchizing sonnets have the warmth of experienced emotions. The Platonism of her dialogue on love is orthodox in terms of Renaissance interpretations of Plato, but spirituality is not exaggerated. There are hints of naturalism in the moderation which she urges: natural things cannot be censured (*biasimate*); but man's appetite should not be unbridled (*sfrenato*) and excessive (*strabocchevole*) (p. 226).

BENEDETTO VARCHI

The opinions attributed to Varchi in the dialogue just examined are consonant with those actually held by him, while those expressed by Tullia herself do not contradict Varchi's doctrines of love. Among Varchi's works are seven lectures and treatises on love and related subjects. The majority of these works lie outside the limits of the love treatise genre, but they may also be briefly examined here because of their related subject matter. These writings are patently the work of a man well versed in the culture of his day and the literature of his country. His style is eloquent and graceful when he does not fall into hyperbole. Yet it would be difficult to find in any of these seven writings an element of originality. The principal source of his doctrines of love is obviously Ficino; the "questions" and "doubts" which he considers are those already abundantly dealt with by other writers. He brings them again into discussion not because they are of vital philosophical concern, but because they are—to the eyes and ears of his age—

belli: appropriate material for Sunday afternoon lectures to the Florentine Academy.

Three lectures take the ostensible form of commentaries on verses:

Dell'amore. Dichiarazione sopra il sonetto di M. Fr. Petrarca che incomincia: L'amor non è ecc;

Della pittura d'amore. Dichiarazione sopra que' versi del Trionfo d'amore, i quali incominciano: Quattro destrier via più che neve ecc;

Dell'amore. Lezione una. Dichiarazione sopra que' versi di Dante nel diciassettesimo canto del Purgatorio, i quali incominciano: Nè creatore, ne creatura mai ecc.

The first of these speeches was delivered at the Florentine Academy the third Sunday of Lent, 1553 (Varchi, *Opere*, II, 496); the second was read in the *studio fiorentino* (*ibid.*, p. 489); the third was given in two parts before the Florentine Academy on successive Sundays in August and September, 1564 (p. 321).

The *Dichiarazione* upon Petrarch's sonnet, like Pompeo della Barba's *Exposition of a Platonic sonnet*, allows the "particular" commentary on the sonnet only a small proportion of the total work, the main purpose of which is the exposition of the Platonic theory of love. Petrarch in his sonnet "raised well . . . many and very beautiful doubts about love, but resolved none of them" (p. 498). Hence, says Varchi,

> . . . Avemo preso . . . a . . . interpretare e scioglier tutte le dubitazioni sopra dette, secondo la dottrina del Filosofo divino, . . . riserbandoci a favellare d'amore secondo Aristotile ad un altro tempo.

> . . . We have undertaken . . . to . . . interpret and resolve all the above-mentioned doubts according to the doctrine of the divine Philosopher, . . . reserving for another time the privilege of speaking about love according to Aristotle.

With these words Varchi avoids identifying himself as a Platonist; indeed, Tullia d'Aragona in her dialogue on love calls him an Aristotelian (*Della Infinità d'amore*, p. 210). He then proceeds to recite amply, but with slight modification in detail, the full five categories of love described by Ficino, whom he does not name in the treatises: the two extremes of love, divine and bestial, between

which are the love that prefers the soul to the body, which it loves
only with the two spiritual senses; that which loves both soul and
body, the latter with the material senses as well; and that which
loves the body more than the soul and "delights in filth [*fango*]
after the manner of pigs" (Varchi, *Opere*, II, 499). Divine love is
"that incredible delight, that immense pleasure, that infinite joy,
which is taken, felt, and enjoyed with ineffable sweetness in the
contemplation of celestial things and particularly of true Being and
the highest Good" (*ibid.*). Upon this "nectar" and "ambrosia" are
nourished those who separate the soul from the body and rise
through wisdom and virtue, the beauties of the soul, to the contemplation of God. Varchi's names for the five kinds of love differ
somewhat from those of Ficino; they are "celestial or divine,
courteous [*cortese*] or honest, civil or human, vulgar or plebeian,
bestial or feral [*ferino*]" (*ibid.*).

Mediante queste cinque sorti d'amore . . . non solo si possono sol-
vere le dubitazioni del presente sonnetto, ma infinite altre . . . (*ibid.*).

Through these five kinds of love . . . not only can one resolve the
doubts of the present sonnet, but an infinity of others . . .

It should be clear that while this tract has the outward form of a
prose commentary on another writer's verses, its content associates
it with the Platonic love treatises which had been written during
the greater part of a century before it.

Varchi then declares that Petrarch loved his *bellissima e castis-
sima Madonna Laura* in three ways at different times: divinely,
honestly, and humanly (p. 500).

Petrarch's sonnet, *S'amor non è* . . . , asks about love:

> Se bona, ond'è l'effetto aspro mortale?
> Se ria, ond'è si dolce tormento?
> > (ll. 3–4)

> If good, whence comes the harsh, fatal effect?
> If bad, whence such sweet torment?

Varchi comments that love may be either good or bad.

> S'a mia voglia ardo, ond'è 'l pianto e lamento?
> S'a mal mio grado, il lamentar che vale?
> > (ll. 5–6)

If I burn by my own will, whence come the tears and lamenting?
If against my will, what good to lament?

Is the lover constrained, asks Petrarch, or does he act by free
will? Theologically, answers Varchi, there can be no doubt that he
acts freely; but philosophically considered, his freedom is highly
doubtful [*dubbiosissima*] (Varchi, *Opere*, II, 502).

"O viva morte . . ." (O living death . . . , 1.7), writes Petrarch.

The lover is dead in himself, Varchi comments, because he does
not operate in himself (Varchi, *Opere*, II, 503).

After the brief scholastic examination of Petrarch's sonnet Varchi
passes on to the solution of other *dubbi* (pp. 504–6).

Only in divine love can one *amare senza amaro* (love without
bitterness). Man alone, the "little world," has within him all the
ways of love, natural, animal, and rational, of which the latter is
proper to him. Lovers seek "the nature of the intellect" even when
they are unaware of their desire. The intellect, imprisoned in the
body, seeks by the knowledge of shadowy earthly beauty to rise to
divine beauty, which being incorporeal, can be enjoyed only by
the soul (pp. 505–6).

[L'amore] non è altro che un appetito dato dalla natura a ciascuna
cosa d'assomigliarsi a Dio quanto può il più, per conseguire la perfezione
e beatitudine sua (p. 505).

[Love] is a desire given to everything by nature of resembling God
as closely as possible in order to attain his perfection and beauty.

Such are the "new declarations" which Varchi with unconscious
irony attributes to his long experience in love (p. 504).

Varchi's commentary on nine lines from the first chapter of the
Trionfo d'Amore, entitled *Della pittura d'amore*, is an explanation
of the reasons why Petrarch and others paint love—vulgar love, at
least—as a beautiful boy, pleasing, rude (*crudo*), nude, red, blind
or with veiled eyes, with wings and blond curly hair, carrying
bow, arrows, and quiver, in a fiery chariot drawn by four steeds.
This work is more properly a commentary upon Petrarch's verses
than is the *Statement* on his sonnet; yet again, it is not strictly so.
The real subject is that given in the primary title, *Della pittura*

d'amore. Varchi makes this clear in explaining why Love is painted blind or with veiled eyes:

Non è senza meraviglia che il Petrarca dipingendo Amore cosi minutamente in questo luogo, non lo faccia nè cieco nè colla benda agli occhi, come quasi tutti gli altri . . . (p. 492).

It is not without wonder that Petrarch painting Love so minutely in this place did not depict him either blind or with a fillet over his eyes, like almost all others . . .

A single example of the explanations may suffice. Love is painted beautiful because "love is desire of beauty," and as beauty belongs more to celestial love than to terrestrial. Petrarch and other poets praise in the ladies the internal beauty of *bei costumi* (fine customs) more than their corporeal beauty. In some instances alternative explanations are proffered.

The lesson on Dante entitled *Dell'amore* takes the famous verses of the seventeenth canto of the *Purgatorio,* "Nè creator, nè creatura mai . . . ," merely as the starting point for a Neoplatonic statement of the degrees of being. Varchi pays a perhaps excessive tribute to Dante's learning:

. . . Di varietà e di profondità di tutte le dottrine avanza, per giudizio nostro, e con grandissimo vantaggio, tutti gli altri poeti di tutte l'altre lingue . . . (p. 322).[54]

In variety and in profundity of all doctrines he surpasses—in our judgment, by a very great distance—all other poets of all other languages.

Upon the basis of Dante's verses on the universality of love, Varchi describes love as the cause of all creation and conservation, from which all things proceed and to which they return (p. 322). He then expounds the order of the ten *enti* which compose the universe (p. 323 f): (1) prime matter; (2) the four elements, composed of prime matter and substantial form; (3) imperfect mixtures, which lack substantial form; (4) perfect mixtures, which

---

[54] In *Sopra alcune quistioni d'amore,* p. 533, Varchi declares, apropos of a stanza from Petrarch's *canzone Poichè per mio destino,* ". . . Ardirò io dire . . . non trovarsi nè nella greca lingua, nè nella latina altrettanti versi, i quali . . . l'aggiungano" (. . . I shall dare to say . . . that neither in the Greek language nor in the Latin are there verses . . . to equal these).

have such form—for example, metals; (5) plants; (6) brute animals; (7) rational animals; (8) celestial bodies; (9) the souls of the heavens; (10) the being of being, God.

Varchi's eclecticism in temperament and approach is illustrated by his attribution of the statement that God alone understands himself to Aristotle, "who knew everything that a mortal can humanly know"; to Plato "who was divine, and taught Aristotle twenty-three years"; to Socrates "who was the teacher of Plato and the best man in the world"; and to all true philosophers. In discussing "rational animals" he cites the maxim of Hermes Trismegistus "that man is a very great miracle"; for the microcosm man can become all things.[55]

Another treatise which takes the form of a commentary on a sonnet is *Sulla gelosia, Lezione di M. Benedetto Varchi nell' Accademia di Padova sopra un sonetto del Casa e sulla gelosia* (Varchi, *Opere*, II, 568). The title itself indicates that Varchi's intention went beyond comment upon the sonnet of Giovanni della Casa, *Cura, che di timor ti nutri e cresci*. After dividing and discussing the sonnet, Varchi finds that there remain "many fine doubts" (*ibid.*, p. 577) for example, ". . . Se l'amore, intendendo dell'amore, che è disio di bellezza, può essere senza gelosia . . ." (*ibid.*: . . . Whether love—meaning the love which is desire of beauty—can be without jealousy . . .).

He concludes that in carnal love there is always jealousy; and that "the greater the love, the greater will be the jealousy" (*ibid.*, p. 582).

Sopra sette dubbi d'amore is the title of a lecture which Varchi read before the Florentine Academy the first Sunday in June, 1554 (p. 525). Here are the seven doubts (pp. 526–31):

1. What artist may treat of love.

. . . "The metaphysicist will treat of divine love, the physicist, of natural love."

2. Whether the beautiful and the good are the same thing.

They are really not different, except that appetite for beauty is less simple and final than appetite for the good. Platonists—from

---

[55] Pico della Mirandola's *Oration on the dignity of man* is the work best known for propagating these ideas, common in Renaissance writings.

whom Varchi seems here to separate himself—call goodness interior
perfection, beauty external perfection.

3. Whether all beautiful things are also good.

Beautiful things should be good, but all of them are not so. Good
youths rather than the beautiful ones should be loved with honest
love.

4. Why it is that one may love and hate one person more than
another, frequently without knowing the reason.

The stars move occult tendencies in earthly things.

5. Why it is that lovers so desire to be always near their loved
one.

Very subtle spirits generated from the blood issue from the eyes;
their power is known only by him who has experienced it.

6. Why it is that lovers so strongly fear and honor the presence
of the beloved.

7. Why it is that lovers are ashamed to confess that they are in
love.

There are four lessons *Sopra alcune quistioni d'amore* (*On some
questions of love*).

The first lesson is a short summary of Platonic love theory.
Beauty generates love; but from love, the most universal thing (p.
534), alone came all good things (p. 532). The beauty of the soul
is far more worthy than that of the body, and is in turn surpassed
by angelic beauty, proceeding immediately from God. Varchi here
clearly follows Ficino in his definition and classification of love:

. . . La bellezza . . . non è altro che un raggio dello splendore della
luce e bontà di Dio . . . (p. 533).

. . . Beauty . . . is a ray of the splendor of the light and goodness of
God. . . .

E così secondo questa divisione, sono cinque amori nell'uomo, il
demone buono, l'amore contemplativo, l'amore umano, l'amore ferino
e il demone cattivo (p. 534).

And so according to this classification there are five loves in man—
the good demon, contemplative love, human love, feral love, and the
bad demon.

Here he adopts Ficino's own terminology in labelling the five kinds of love, instead of modifying it as in the *Dichiarazione* upon Petrarch's sonnet. However, when he comes to reviewing the literature of love, he prefers Leone Ebreo to the esteemed Ficino,[56] who wrote best on love up to that time.

Pico is also remembered, as is Diacceto, from whose *Panegirico d'Amore* he quotes at length in the second lesson (pp. 541–42). Bembo is lauded more for his eloquence than for his "not little" doctrine. Varchi then passes to the questions about love which are continued through the other three lessons.

In these lessons he proposes twenty questions or doubts about love (pp. 536–60), many of which were discussed by Betussi and quoted by Equicola from the Mantuan Calandra. A listing of them will show that as usual they deal primarily with psychological and moral aspects of human love. Varchi's answers are indicated briefly following the questions.

1. Qual sia più nobile, o l'amante o l'amato (Who is nobler, the lover or the loved one). In vulgar love, the beloved is nobler; in celestial love, the lover.

2. Quale sia più forte e più possente passione, o l'amore o l'odio (Which is a stronger and more powerful passion, love or hate). Love.

3. Se ogni amato necessariamente riama (Whether every loved one necessarily returns love). No, in vulgar love; yes, in celestial love.

4. Se chiunque è amato, è tenuto di dover riamare l'amante (Whether he who is loved is obligated to return the lover's love). Yes, according to Plato.

5. Se nell'amore onesto si sentono passioni (Whether passion is felt in honest love). Yes.

6. Se alcuno può innamorarsi, o amare senza speranza (Whether one can love or fall in love without hope). No.

7. Se amore può essere senza gelosia (Whether love can be without jealousy). No.

[56] See quotation from Varchi on p. 102 of this book.

8. Se alcuno può solo per fama e d'udita innamorarsi (Whether one can fall in love from fame and hearsay alone). No.

9. Se si può amare più d'uno in un tempo medesimo (Whether one can love more than one person at the same time). No; not unless one loves the soul more than the body.

10. Se alcuno può amare più altrui che sè stesso (Whether one can love another more than himself). No.

11. Se alcuno si può innamorare di sè medesimo (Whether one can fall in love with himself). No.

12. Se alcuno amante può, solo che voglia, non amare (Whether any lover can cease to love simply by will power). No.

13. Se l'amore può sanarsi in alcun modo (Whether love can be healed in any way). Yes.

14. Se l'amore può essere regolato dalla ragione (Whether love can be regulated by reason). Love should not be regulated by reason.

15. Se l'amore viene da destino o da elezione (Whether love comes by destiny or by choice). According to philosophy, love comes sometimes from destiny, sometimes from choice.

16. Se i morti possono amare, o essere amati (Whether the dead can love or be loved). The philosophical answer: No.

17. Se l'amore può star fermo in un medesimo stato senza crescere o scemare (Whether love can stand still in the same condition without growing or waning). No; love can grow infinitely.

18. Qual sia maggior cosa e più degna o l'amicizia, o l'amore (Which is a better and more worthy thing, love or friendship). In vulgar love friendship is superior; the contrary appears to be true in virtuous and philosophical love.

19. Chi ama più o i giovani, o gli attempati (Who love more, youths or older people). Older people love better in chaste and sincere love.

20. Se l'amore si può simulare o dissimulare, e quale è più agevole di queste due cose (Whether one can feign or dissemble love, and which is the easier of the two). To feign love is easy; to dissemble it, impossible.

Apropos of the fifth question, Varchi defines love after the manner of Leone Ebreo:

> . . . Amore non è altro che desiderio di godere con unione la cosa o bella, o stimata bella; il che non vuole altro significare, se non che l'amante si trasformi nella cosa amata, con desiderio che ella in lui si trasformi (p. 542).

> . . . Love is the desire of enjoying with union a thing which is either beautiful or judged to be beautiful; which means simply that the lover is transformed into the thing loved with the desire that the latter be transformed into him.

The ladder of Diotima is not to be denied. Mortal beauties may be said to be, philosophically speaking, the means to the bliss of love and knowledge of divine beauties. Through literary and philosophical allusions there transpires the sincerity of personal conviction.

> . . . Dovremmo, mediante l'amore di queste bellezze mortali, le quali amare senza amaro non si possono, a quelle divine sollevarci, nelle quali, come ne insegna il santissimo romito di Lavinello, non solo non si trova dolore nessuno di nessuna maniera, ma tutte le gioie compitamente. E se alcuno mi domandasse se io credo che senza queste bellezze mortali, ciò è non amando nè uomini nè donne, si potessero conoscere le bellezze immortali e salire all'amore divino; gli risponderei, che come cristiano non ho dubbio nessuno di sì . . . Ma come filosofo direi, che . . . niuna via può nè più agevolmente nè meglio introdurci alla cognizione e fruizione delle bellezze invisibili . . . E se bene ancora in cotali amori sono passioni veementissime, sono però tanto lodevoli e da essere desiderate, quanto quelle dell'amor volgare biasimevoli e da dovere essere abborrite (p. 543).

> . . . Through love of these mortal beauties, which can not be loved without bitterness, we should rise to those divine beauties in which, as Lavinello's very holy hermit teaches us, not only is there no sorrow of any kind, but all the joys are found there perfectly. And if someone were to ask me whether I believe that one could know the immortal beauties and rise to divine love without these mortal beauties—that is, loving neither men nor women—I would reply to him that as a Christian I have no doubt of it . . . But as a philosopher I would say that . . . no path can better or more easily introduce us to the knowledge and fruition of the invisible beauties . . . And although there are very

violent passions in such loves, they are nevertheless as praiseworthy and
desirable as those of vulgar love are blameworthy and to be abhorred.

In discussing the eighth question, Varchi insists extravagantly
upon the essential role of the eyes, both active and passive, in the
conception of love.

. . . Non basta . . . il vedere la donna amanda, per dir così, ma
bisogna vederla da vicino; nè è bastante il da vicino vederla, che è di
bisogno il vedere gli occhi di lei; nè questo anco è bastevole che fa di
mestieri il vederli aperti. . . . Nè anco questo è abbastanza, perchè è
necessario vedere la pupilla degli occhi; nè il vedere la pupilla degli
occhi sarebbe sufficiente, se non si riscontrassero quella dell'amante e
quella dell'amanda l'una coll'altra; nè il riscontrarsi insieme le pupille
sarebbe assai; ma conviene ancora ed è forza, che in elle o sia in vero,
o paia all'amante, che sia un certo che di benignità e d'amorevolezza
verso di lui che dimostri, che ella se non accetta, almeno non rifiuta
d'essere amata. E allora finalmente che tutte concorrono queste cose,
nasce e si crea l'amore, e non mai prima (p. 546).

. . . It does not suffice . . . simply to see the woman who is to be
loved, so to speak, but one must see her close by. Nor is it sufficient to
see her close by, for it is necessary to see her eyes; neither is this
sufficient, for one needs must see them open. . . . Not even this is
enough, because it is necessary to see the pupils of her eyes; nor would
seeing the pupils of her eyes be sufficient, if those of the lover and those
of the lady to be loved did not meet each other. Not even the meeting
together of the pupils is enough; but it is yet fitting and indeed essential
that in them there either be, or appear to the lover to be, a certain
benevolence and kindness toward him that shows that even if she does
not accept, at least she does not refuse, to be loved. And when finally
all these things concur love is born and created, and never before.

Apropos of the tenth question, Varchi declares that all human
loves have their "beginning, middle and end" in self-love.

Chi elegge di morire egli perchè un altro viva, ama più sè, che colui
(p. 552).

He who chooses to die himself so that another may live loves himself
more than he loves the other person.

In answering the thirteenth question, he declares that vulgar
love is an infirmity of both mind and body (p. 554).

The discourse *Della bellezza e della grazia* (p. 733) is written in answer to two *dubbi* advanced by Monsignor Leone Orsino, Bishop of Frejus.

Vostra Signoria mi domanda di due dubbi, primieramente se la grazia può stare senza la bellezza: secondariamente, qual più di queste due sia da desiderare o bellezza o la grazia (*ibid.*).

Your Lordship asks me about two doubts: first, whether grace can be without beauty; second, which of these two, beauty or grace, is to be desired.

Varchi answers that while *grazia* may exist without bodily *bellezza*, spiritual *bellezza* is never without *grazia;* hence *bellezza* is to be preferred, as it will necessarily include *grazia* (*ibid.*, pp. 733, 735). Grace is true beauty of soul, which is often combined with bodily beauty and proportion (p. 735). Matter in itself is *bruttissima* (p. 734).

FLAMINIO NOBILI

The *Trattato dell'Amore Humano,* like Pietro Bembo's *Asolani,* is the work of a young man; Flaminio Nobili was only twenty-three when he wrote it. A close friend of Torquato Tasso and of Annibal Caro, he was, like several of the earlier writers of love treatises, a student of both medicine and philosophy. Like Bembo's work, Nobili's treatise combines reminiscences of Dante, Petrarch, and Boccaccio with references to the doctrines of classical philosophy. Platonism is the predominant source of his theories of love and beauty, which can be called Nobili's only in a formal sense, as they lack even the pretense of originality which Varchi maintained. His treatise is theoretical rather than practical (*Trattato dell'Amore Humano,* p. 52 v). His style is stilted in the Boccaccio-like manner of the *Asolani,* the verb often being shunted to the end of the clause. He writes in Tuscan not only because it is pleasant and sweet, but "to be able to avail *himself* of the authority of Messer Francesco Petrarca, who in treating amorous accident left all antiquity very far behind" (*ibid.*, p. 6 r-v). The formal Platonism is modified by Nobili's native skepticism. The love of which he chooses to write "among the other sorts of love, which are many"

(p. 5 v), is that "whereby beautiful and gracious [*gratiose*] ladies are wont to be loved by gentle [*gentili*] and valorous youths"—hence the title, *Treatise on Human Love*.

The eclecticism of the treatise is more openly avowed than in any of the others that we have examined, excepting the early chapters of Equicola's book. Varchi, like Castiglione's Bembo and Guido Cavalcanti, claimed to speak of love from the vantage point of age and experience.

Nobili makes the opposite claim: he who experiences love knows the less of its nature; the author, Nobili, is advantaged by never having been in love (p. 5 v): "Così ò tristo ò lieto ch' egli si sia, la passione gli torce gli occhi, & il fa travedere" (p. 6 r: Thus whether he is sad or happy, the passion twists his eyes and makes him see awry).

Nobili declares that he knows love through other authors. He closes his treatise with the statement: "Questo è quanto ho saputo dell'Amore Humano raccogliore" (p. 57 r: This is what I have been able to collect about human love).

The fundamental Platonism of his "harvest" is evident in the conceptions of love and beauty: "Amore s'intende qual piegamento, & affetione dell'animo nostro verso il bello" (p. 7 r: By love is meant an inclination and affection of our soul toward beauty).

Love takes its origin from beauty. Cicero defined it as "desire of beauty" (p. 12 v) although Diotima, despite the affirmations of all Platonists that Cicero's definition is Plato's, surprisingly declares that love is not the desire of beauty, but "desire of birth in beauty" (p. 14 v). The chief end of amorous desire is to immortalize oneself, to propagate oneself through giving birth (p. 17 v). Man's generation can be either corporeal or spiritual (p. 15 v). For the latter, the "friendly love" of man for youth is more apt than the sensual love of a man for a young lady (p. 16 v). Love usually begins in sense and ascends to the intellect (p. 39 r). The beloved loves her lover as if he were her portrait (p. 40 r). Touch is the vilest of the senses (p. 21 r), and the body is the soul's prison (p. 14 r). ". . . Considering how much pleasure and joy are relished in beholding a mortal beauty and in contemplating the grace and habits of a particular lady, [one] realizes immediately the boundless and infinite happiness there must be in the contemplation and sight of divine beauty . . ." (p. 24 v).

Beauty, a "brief tyranny," is defined in terms of bodily proportion (p. 7 r-v), combined with color and the air of *gentilezza*. It is native to the sense of sight, almost alien in application to the other senses (p. 8 r). Besides the beauty of body there is the beauty of soul; these are the two Veneres, vulgar and celestial, celebrated by Plato (p. 9 v). Beauty of soul may nevertheless appear in the body, especially in the face and eyes. Beauty (*bellezza*) is stationary grace (*gratia stante*); grace (*gratia*), moving beauty (*bellezza moventesi*) (p. 10 v). Woman is loved for beauty; man, for valor, as Dante says in the sonnet, *Amore e 'l cor gentil sono una cosa* (p. 11 v). However, birth "under the same stars" can do a great deal (p. 12 v).

There is a tension, if not a cleavage, between the Platonic doctrines which Nobili repeats from the authors he has read and his own opinions and observations about love. Bembo's Lavinello may conform to the Platonic ideal, but Nobili has never met him in real life.

A me certamente non è mai avvenuto di conoscere alcun Lavinello, il quale si contentasse di goder la bellezza in quel modo, nel quale propriamente si gode la bellezza, dico col vedere, coll'udire, col pensare . . . (p. 17 r).

It certainly never happened to me to meet any Lavinello who was satisfied with enjoying beauty in the way that beauty is properly enjoyed, that is to say, by seeing, hearing and thinking. . . .

He feels sure that love in human experience cannot, nor should, exclude sexuality. He therefore defends his picture of "human love," sanctioned by society and nature, from imputations of sin and bestiality.

Hora se un Giovane essendosi messo ad amare una bella, & ben costumata Giovinetta, & conveniente al grado suo s'ingegna di ottenerla per Moglie, & in questa guisa divenir posseditore dell'animo & del corpo di lei, non violando le leggi, anzi obedienza prestando alla Natura, veramente humano & ragionevole Amante si dirà, ne in questo Amore sarà peccato, massimamente se le Regole della temperanza si serveranno; la qual temperanza non vieta mica, che a tempo, & luogo non si prenda piacere col tatto, purche non si offendano le leggi. Per la qual cosa può apparire, quanto s'ingannino coloro, che ogni desio di congiungnersi chiamano bestiale, & ferino . . . (p. 22 r-v).

Now if a young man, having begun to love a beautiful and well-bred young girl, suitable to his rank, endeavors to obtain her for his wife and in this way becomes the possessor of her soul and body, not violating the laws but on the contrary obeying nature, truly it will be called a human and reasonable love. Nor will there be sin in this love, especially if the rules of temperance are observed. Such temperance does not at all prohibit their taking pleasure in touch at the proper time and place, provided that the laws are not transgressed. The foregoing shows how much they are deceived who call every desire of union bestial and ferine. . . .

Petrarch himself, "of whom it would be wickedness [*sceleratezza*] to think that he loved bestially," exhibits the most intense desire (p. 23 r).[57]

In short, human love is "that which is reasonable and honest." Either the *amata* must be one's wife, or only her soul and the sight of her must be enjoyed. Nobili's concept is more antithetical to courtly love than to Platonic love. He arrives at the following synthetic definition:

Amore humano . . . è gagliardo piegamento dell'appetito, & della volontà nostra, escitato da conosciuta bellezza, & risolventesi in desiderio di generare nel bello, ò di acquistar la gratia della Donna amata (p. 31 r).

Human love . . . is a vigorous inclination of our appetite and will, excited by known beauty and issuing in desire to generate in beauty or to acquire the favor of the beloved woman.

Youth is a poor subject for divine love (p. 24 v). Feminine beauty is a less effective incentive to the ascent of the *scala coeli* than the contemplation of celestial movements and eternal beauties described by Bembo in the speech of the hermit, by Dante in the "last cantos" of *Paradise,* and by Plato himself.

A questo Divino Amore non sò già quanto necessaria scala sia la bellezza donnesca; percioche il considerare i miracolosi, & pur ordinati effetti della Natura, i movimenti stabili del Cielo, il vigor della luce, la perfettione dell'universo, mi pare molto più sicura strada per condurci

---

[57] Both Petrarch and Bembo are quoted.

alla cognition della somma Bellezza, che il perdersi, & star fisso in un volto . . . (p. 25 r-v).[58]

I don't know how necessary a ladder feminine beauty may be to this divine love; since considering the miraculous and yet ordered effects of nature, the stable movements of the sky, the vigor of light, the perfection of the universe seems to me a much surer road to the knowledge of the highest beauty than losing oneself and remaining fixed upon a countenance . . .

Finally, Nobili says that love makes man temperate, and that in mature age the sight of a beloved woman can make him yearn for divine visions, as Petrarch thought (p. 50 v). He who lives without the gentle passion of love is either stupid or far removed from any humanity (p. 49 v).

FRANCESCO DE' VIERI

In 1580 Francesco de' Vieri wrote a discourse which, although not strictly speaking a *trattato d'amore*, has many points in common with the literature under consideration. It belongs to the same genre as Benedetto Varchi's lessons on verses of Petrarch and Dante, and like them was prepared for delivery to the Florentine Academy. However, the author tells us in the dedicatory letter to Count Ulisse Bentivogli that infirmity and unspecified affairs prevented him from reading his lesson to the Academy.[59] Ostensibly the lesson is a commentary on Petrarch's sonnet, *In qual parte del ciel, in quale idea*, which finds the ideas themselves inadequate models for the beauty of Laura's *viso leggiadro* (1. 3: lovely face), *chiome d'oro* (1. 6: golden hair), *vertuti* (1. 7: virtues), *occhi* (1. 10), for the sweetness of her sighs, her words, her laughter (ll. 13–14). De' Vieri states his purpose as follows:

. . . Ho pensato di compiacervi con la nobilità, & grandezza del soggetto, . . . che saranno l'Idee delle cose, che si contengono nella mente di Dio, & le grazie, & le bellezze di M. Laura: onde . . . s'harà

[58] Nobili seems here to have missed the point of Diotima's discourse, which proposes not at all "to lose oneself and be fixed upon a countenance."

[59] *Lezzione di M. Francesco de' Vieri fiorentino, detto il Verino Secondo. Per recitarla nell'Accademia Fiorentina, . . . l'Anno 1580. Dove si ragiona delle idee, et delle bellezze*, p. 4.

più profonda . . . intelligenza di quel . . . Sonetto del nostro M. Francesco Petrarca . . . (De' Vieri, *Lezzione,* p. 8).

. . . I have thought to please you with the nobility and greatness of the subject, . . . which will be the Ideas of things, which are contained in the mind of God, and the graces and beauties of Madonna Laura, whence . . . one may derive a more profound . . . understanding of that . . . sonnet of Messer Francesco Petrarca. . . .

However, as in Varchi's readings, the focus is on general concepts much more than on the interpretation of the text at hand. The *ragionamento* is divided into three parts: (1) ideas; (2) the beauties of Madonna Laura—"only so much however, as pertains to the understanding of this sonnet"; and (3) the exposition of several words in the text and the solving of a few doubts. What makes the discourse almost a treatise on love is the identification of or rather the lack of distinction between beauty and love; so that the latter also is brought into discussion.

The first part of the treatise provides the philosophical basis for the more literary considerations of the second and third parts. The author quotes from Dante and Averroes in picturing a universe of which God is the center and the source of participation. His approach is even more reconciliatory than that of most of his eclectic predecessors in the field; he declares that his exposition is in accordance with Plato, Aristotle, and Petrarch. However, he shows more philosophic verve than the majority of the *trattatisti.*

Ideas are *notizie,* "incorruptible and eternal substances," only partially analogous to a sculptor's idea of his sculpture (*ibid.,* p. 10). The ideas in God's mind are eternal and are not distinguished as to universal and particular, like the artisan's idea (pp. 10–11). Although Aristotle denies the ideas, he denies them only in their "false sense" as "immediate principle agents and outside the divine essence" (p. 18). De' Vieri holds that the ideas are in God's mind not only according to Christian theologians and Plato, but according to Aristotle as well (p. 15 f.). There are ideas of all things created by God (p. 21); however, there are not ideas of man-made things or accidents or monsters (p. 22); nor of genera, for the genus is never found outside its species. Ideas are the divine essence itself, not absolutely, but in so far as they are similitudes or reasons of its creatures (p. 24).

His definition of beauty is Platonic rather than Plotinian. He not only defines beauty as "a certain proportion and grace which results from a plurality of things," but states that a single thing or element cannot be called beautiful (p. 26). He considers the following definition as superior to his first definition:

[La bellezza] è un fiore, & una grazia, ò splendore di più bontà, & perfezzioni unite, che è ardentissimamente disiderata (*ibid.*).

[Beauty] is a flower and a grace or splendor of a number of combined goodnesses and perfections, which is desired most ardently.

Infinite beauty and goodness are equated with God; they deserve to be loved with very ardent and even infinite love (*ibid.*, p. 27). Beauty must be seen either physically or mentally before one can fall in love (p. 27). However, the concepts of beauty and love are so closely associated in de' Vieri's mind that they are unconsciously interchanged, as in some other treatises. For example, De' Vieri in one passage compares Ficino's three kinds of "love," mental, visual, and auditory, with his own enumeration of two kinds of beauty, of body and soul, derived from Aristotle and Plato (p. 28).[60]

Many of the doubts which de' Vieri takes up in the third part of his treatise are related specifically to Petrarch's sonnet. For example, how can Laura's face, a particular, have been in some part of the heavens and in some idea? If her charms tend to cause Petrarch's "death," how can they be praised as good? (pp. 33–34). The more general *dubbi* are equally trivial. If there are three loves, bestial, human, and divine, why are there but two Veneres? Why is beauty called the mother of love and not the father? Why is beauty called by a feminine name and love by a masculine name, when the former is perfect and the latter imperfect, conjoined with poverty or lack? (p. 29). The conclusion of the *ragionamento* is that Petrarch "has celebrated the beauties and graces of his Madonna Laura with no less loftiness of concepts and beauty of order than

[60] In fairness to the author it must be remembered that in his dedication, p. 4, de' Vieri says that he has not only been unable to deliver his speech, but "even to review it and polish it."

majesty and grace of words" (p. 36). De' Vieri ends by thanking God for a sonnet which so well exhibits His goodness and beauties (p. 38).[61]

TORQUATO TASSO

Torquato's writings on love and on related subjects, such as beauty and jealousy, were written over a span of at least fifteen years, from the *Conclusioni amorose* in 1570 to *Il forestiero napoletano* (*The foreigner from Naples*) in 1585. The dates of some of them, such as *Il Minturno* and the *Discorso sopra due questioni amorose,* are uncertain. There are philosophical motives in some of these writings, more Platonic than Aristotelian, but in tone they are much more like the mid-century dialogues of Betussi and Speroni than like the philosophically oriented pieces of Ficino, Leone, and Diacceto. Lively conversations reflecting contemporary customs and attitudes towards social and moral matters give the works something of the sociological interest inherent in the works of Sansovino and Gottifredi. The earliest of these works, the *Conclusioni amorose,* is a compendium of the century of Platonic love literature which preceded it. In later works, such as *Il cavalier amante,* the superficial spirituality of Platonic dilettantes is replaced by a sober skepticism toward the demi-spiritual love discussed in literary and courtly circles. The lucid prose, terse and yet animated, is a welcome change from the affected and involved prose of some other essayists.

The *Conclusioni amorose* was written by the young Tasso for the ill-fated marriage of Princess Lucrezia d'Este and Prince Francesco Maria della Rovere, which took place January 28, 1570. It was published January 11 and publicly disputed on January 18 and February 6 in the Academy of Ferrara. It truly consists of "gleanings of gleanings," repeating ideas which had been stated and reiterated throughout the century of Platonism that began with Ficino's *Commentary* on the *Symposium.* However, many of the "conclusions" long antedate Ficino, for they are common to Provençal and early Tuscan literature. Tasso drew most heavily upon

---

[61] De' Vieri is unconscious of the irony.

Flaminio Nobili's *Trattato dell'amore humano,* which he studied
and annotated, and which itself was an avowed *raccolta* of the
"best" analyses of love. An excerpt of the most pertinent conclusions will perhaps be more appropriate than an analysis of ideas
already examined in several other authors, and will serve as a summary of the problems discussed in the entire body of literature from
which the conclusions are culled.

I. La bellezza essere splendore de la divinità, il quale penetra e riluce
per l'universo in una parte più chiaramente, e meno in un'altra.

II. La bellezza, o vero il bello, come lo splendore del sole, essere del
bene inseparabile; e tutto ciò ch' è bello esser buono; e tutto ciò ch' è
buono, esser bello.

III. La bellezza allettare tutte le cose, ne le quali risplende, e rapirle
a sè con impeto di amoroso desiderio.

IV. Il bene non destare amore sotto la forma del bene ma solo sotto la
piacevole imagine del bello.

V. La bellezza che sotto il nome di Venere è significata da gli antichi
esser padre non madre d'Amore; ciò è, cagion produttrice, non materiale: difendersi nondimeno.

VI. Venere, o presa per la bellezza o per l'anima, come prendono
alcuni, potersi dire padre d'Amore.

VII. Il piacere o 'l compiacimento non essere amore, ma principio e
compagno d'amore.

VIII. Amore essere desiderio d'unione per compiacimento di bellezza.

IX. Amore essere il vincolo e legame de l'atto e de la potenza, o di
Dio e de la materia, che vogliam dire.

X. Amore esser proprietà di quel ch' è, per cui si fanno, si conservano,
si rendono perfette tutte le cose, così naturali come artificiali e civili.

XI. Ciascuna natura che opera, o sia conoscente o priva di cognizione,
operar sempre per amore e nissuna mai per odio.

XII. L'odio non esser contrario d'amore, ma seguace d'amore.

XIII. Amor esser non solo da l'inferiore al superiore, e da l'eguale a
l'eguale, ma anco dal superiore a l'inferiore;[62] onde potersi porre in Dio,
senza notar in lui difetto.

XIV. Amor tanto esser più nobile, quanto governato da la ragione.

XV. Tre essere i generi d'amore, sotto ai quali tutti gli amori si
riducono.

XVI. L'amore umano abbracciare in sè tutti gli amori, ch' a tutti gli
enti si convengono: onde propriamente nominarsi amore, ed innamorato
chi ama secondo tutte le seguenti conclusioni.

[62] For Ficino's description of such threefold love, see his *Opera omnia,* II,
1328 *f.*

XVII. A l'amore umano convenirsi in particolare quella definizione che si è data a l'Amore in universale; cioè, che sia desiderio d'unione per compiacimento di bellezza: potersi nondimeno affermare, senza contradizione ch' egli sia un rivolgimento di tutti gli appetiti in un oggetto solo.

XVIII. Amore non presuppore l'elezione, nè però seguire che si conceda il destino; ma presuppore necessariamente somiglianza fra l'amante e l'amata.

XIX. La bellezza de l'animo per sè sola non destare amore; e vana esser l'opinione di coloro, che credono potersi amare l'animo o la virtù solamente.

XX. Amor giunger perfezione a la donna; nè però negarsi ch'ella per se stessa non sia cosa perfettissima.

XXI. L'uomo in sua natura amar più intensamente e stabilmente che la donna.

XXII. Amore esser più ne l'amata che ne l'amante.

XXIII. La donna amata non sempre riamar colui che l'ama; e con tutto ciò affermarsi senza contradizione che l'amata sempre ami l'amante.

XXV. Nessuna amata esser, o poter esser ingrata. Nissuno amore asseguir mai il suo fine.

XXVII. Ogni piacere amoroso esser accompagnato da dolore, nè darsi ne gli amati alcuna pura e sincera allegrezza.

XXVIII. Gli occhi esser quelli che più godono, e quelli di cui più si gode ne l'amore.

XXIX. Gli occhi esser principio e fine d'amore.

XXXI. La felicità o 'l sommo diletto de l'amante esser riposto nel servir l'amata, non nel signoreggiarla.

XXXVI. Veri essere i miracoli d'amore, che menzogne de' poeti giudica il vulgo; veri, dico, secondo il più esatto modo di verità; cioè, che l'amante divenga la cosa amata, e che gli amanti siano non due, ma uno.

XLI. Non darsi dolore in amore, in cui non sia più il dolce che l'amaro.

XLII. Ogni cosa esser temuta da gli amanti, e quelle medesime ancora che più sono da loro desiderate.

XLVI. La gelosia esser segno certissimo d'ardentissimo amore, ed accrescer l'amore; nè può negarsi, ch' ella non distrugga l'amore.

XLVIII. Se più si meriti, o servendo o non servendo l'amata.

L. Se più si goda, o de' furti fatti a l'amata o de' doni ricevuti da lei.

I. Beauty is the splendor of the divinity, which penetrates and shines throughout the universe more clearly in one part and less in another.

II. Beauty, or the beautiful, like the splendor of the sun, is inseparable from the good; all that is beautiful is good, and all that is good is beautiful.

III. Beauty allures all the things in which it shines and transports them to itself with the impetus of amorous desire.

IV. The good does not awaken love under the form of good, but only under the pleasant image of the beautiful.

V. The beauty which the ancients signified by the name of Venus is the father, not the mother, of love—that is, productive cause, not material. Nevertheless it can be defended.

VI. Venus, taken either as beauty or as the soul, as some take it, can be called the father of love.

VII. Pleasure or satisfaction is not love, but the beginning and companion of love.

VIII. Love is desire of union for the contentment of beauty.

IX. Love is the link and bond of act and potency, or of God and matter, however we wish to say it.

X. Love is a property of that which is, by which all things, the natural as well as the artificial and civil, are conserved and rendered perfect.

XI. Everything that acts either knowingly or without cognition always acts from love and never from hate.

XII. Hate is not the opposite of love, but a follower of love.

XIII. Love is not only of the superior by the inferior and of the equal by the equal, but also of the inferior by the superior; whence it may be posited of God, without attributing a defect to him.

XIV. The more love is governed by reason the nobler it is.

XV. There are three kinds of love, to which all loves may be reduced.

XVI. Human love embraces in itself all the loves which are suitable for all beings—whence he who loves according to all the following conclusions may properly be called "enamored" and the word "love" may properly be applied.

XVII. The definition given to love in the universal—the desire of union for contentment of beauty—is particularly fitting to human love. It can nevertheless be affirmed without contradiction that it is a turning of all the appetites to one object alone.

XVIII. Love does not presuppose choice; yet it does not follow that it is a matter of destiny. But love necessarily presupposes a likeness between the lover and the beloved.

XIX. Beauty of soul by itself alone does not arouse love; and vain is the opinion of those who believe that one can love the soul or virtue only.

XX. Love adds perfection to woman; yet we do not deny that per se she is a most perfect thing.

XXI. Man by his nature loves more intensely and stably than woman.

XXII. Love is more in the beloved than in the lover.

XXIII. The loved woman does not always return the love to him who loves her; and nevertheless it may be affirmed without contradiction that the loved woman always loves the lover.

XXV. No *amata* [loved lady] is or can be ungrateful. No love ever attains its end.

XXVII. Every amorous pleasure is accompanied by sorrow, nor is there any pure and sincere joy in loved ones.

XXVIII. It is the eyes which enjoy most and which are most enjoyed in love.

XXIX. The eyes are the beginning and end of love.

XXXI. The lover's happiness or greatest delight lies in serving the *amata,* not in governing her.

XXXVI. The miracles of love are true, though the common people judge them poets' lies—true, I say, in the most exact manner of truth; that is to say, that the lover becomes the thing loved, and that lovers are not two, but one.

XLI. There is no pain in love in which there is not more sweetness than bitterness.

XLII. All things are feared by lovers, including the very ones that they most desire.

XLVI. Jealousy is a very sure sign of most ardent love, and it increases love; yet it cannot be denied that it destroys love.

XLVIII. Whether one is more deserving in serving or in not serving his beloved.

L. Whether one enjoys more his thefts from the loved one or the gifts received from her.

Il cavalier amante e la gentildonna amata (*The loving gentleman and the beloved gentlewoman*), written in 1580, is a polite quarrel between two disputants stemming from a lady's refusal to dance. Among the questions raised and answered are the questions of whether a love which begins by choice can also end by choice (*I dialoghi amorosi,* p. 18) and whether the judicious lady should give her love "to lovers or to those who are not lovers" (p. 27).

His answer to the first question is affirmative; to the second he answers that "favors" are to be granted to nonlovers rather than to lovers—a distant echo of Socrates' first and "false" answer in the *Phaedrus.* The atmosphere of the dialogue is similar to that of the treatises of Betussi, of Tullia d'Aragona, and of Varchi. The Platonism, however, is missing. Here love is no longer desire of beauty or desire of engendering beauty in beauty, but a biological "desire of embracing." Tasso in the words of the *cavalier amante* staidly criticizes the denial of the senses to which some writers have pretended.

> . . . Vorrei che tra noi rimanessimo d'accordo, quel che fosse amore: perciochè alcuni d'amor parlano, come s'essi fossero non uomini ma intelligenzie, i quali altro che l'animo non mostrano d'amare; e se pur de gli occhi o de la bocca de la sua donna ragionano alcuna volta, in modo che paia che di questi obietti ancora si compiacciano, non passano nondimeno più oltre; nè gli altri sentimenti del corpo chiamano a parte de' diletti d'amore. Ma io per me credo che l'uomo, che è animal composto di sentimento e di ragione, voglia ne l'amore appagare così i sentimenti tutti come la ragione; onde direi che l'amor fosse desiderio d'abbraciamento (p. 26).[63]

> . . . I should wish for us to agree between ourselves about what love may be, since some speak of love as if they were not men but intelligences, who appear to love nothing but the soul. And if they yet discuss their ladies' eyes or mouths sometimes, so that they seem even to take pleasure in these objects, they none the less go no further, nor do they call up the other feelings of the body for the delights of love. But for my part I believe that man, who is the animal composed of sense and reason, wishes to satisfy all the senses as well as the reason; whence I should say that love is a desire of embracing.

La Molza o vero de l'amore (1583) is formally distinguished from other dialogues on love by being written in the first person, the author being one of the interlocutors. Tasso here examines a series of definitions and descriptions of love by "Orpheus," classical "physicians" and "natural philosophers," several characters in the Platonic dialogues, Lucretius, Plotinus, St. Augustine, St. Thomas, Dante, Egidio Colonna, Petrarch, and Bembo. He classifies them in six genera according to their respective emphases on desire, infirmity, virtue, act, will, and pleasure (p. 39).

He attributes (pp. 40–41) to St. Thomas and Egidio Colonna a separation of affections into three degrees: *compiacimento* (liking), *desiderio* (desire), *diletto* (delight). Upon them he models a pro-

---

[63] Tasso qualifies his definition of love by saying that "not every desire of embracing is love." The lover is "colui che de gli abbraciamenti è cupido, per compiacimento ch' abbia d'alcuna particolare bellezza" (he who is desirous of embracing because of the liking that he has for some particular beauty).

gression of three "ages" of love: love in swaddling bands, *la prima piacenza;* love who has drunk the milk of hope and has grown wings, *desiderio;* and love which possesses its object and is placated by pleasure (p. 42). Virtue itself is but "order of love." Love which is directed toward the first good is charity, the first theological virtue. The dialogue is not a Platonic *trattato d'amore.* Its method, historical review, is reminiscent of Equicola's.

In his *Discorso del Maritarsi* (1585), Tasso writes to his cousin Ercole Tasso that marriage is necessary for "just and legitimate generation"; and that beauty of soul, which is chastity, is reflected in the beauty of the body, especially in the face and eyes (p. 121).

Platonic elements are more abundant in *Il Minturno o vero de la bellezza,* a dialogue of uncertain date, than in the other dialogues on related subjects. There is a trace of misogyny in the bitterness of its antimaterialism. Authentic beauty is spiritual and divine; it cannot be found in the vain and shadowy objects of sense in which men seek it. The discovery of its nature is reserved for the intellect, "exercised in the contemplation of forms separated from this . . . filth of matter"; not even the "more spiritual" senses of sight and hearing can attain it (p. 76). Beauty is profitable and useful, the father of good (p. 73); it is loved for itself (p. 75). Beauty is always accompanied by chastity (*onestà*); if Helen was lewd, she was not beautiful (p. 73). Beauty is not proportion, for simple things such as colors and light are very beautiful. The things which "wretched mortals" commonly judge beautiful—especially so-called feminine beauty—"are frauds and deceits of the things of nature, shadows of light, phantasms [*larve*] and simulacra of beauty (p. 79). Beauty, like the virtues, is inborn in the soul; ugliness is an alien derivation from the contagion of body (p. 81). We are as foolish as Narcissus to seek beauty in the empty images which are worldly members. Such "pleasant objects" are to be avoided by the eyes of the body; true beauty may be found only with the mind's eyes.

Tasso wrote two dialogues on jealousy. The first was a *Discorso della gelosia* delivered in 1577; the second, entitled *Il forestiero napoletano o vero de la gelosia,* was written in 1585. The former begins with a disclaimer of philosophy and a claim, oratorical and traditional, that the author spoke from experience.

Ascoltate dunque, pietose donne, non quello che le carte socratiche e peripatetiche m'insegnano; ma quanto, nelle scole d'amore, affettuoso amante ne discorre (p. 85).

Listen then, compassionate ladies, not to that which Socratic and Peripatetic books teach me, but to what an affectionate lover says of it in the schools of love.

He then, like Varchi, who made a similar declaration, proceeds to utter commonplaces about beauty, love and jealousy. Beauty generates love by inclination to the good; jealousy by the flight from evil (p. 86). The material cause of jealousy is the cooling of the blood around the heart (p. 88). Jealousy and desperation are born from love (p. 91). The Socratic person loves abstract beauty without jealousy (p. 98). God is beauty itself (p. 97).

Il forestiero napoletano, a dialogue, defines jealousy as "pain at another's good" (p. 49) and explains how it may be a moral virtue.

. . . Per la quale temendo l'amante di perder la grazia de la sua donna temerà in conseguenza di far cosa, per cui la perda meritamente: laonde d'intemperato diverrà temperato, d'avaro liberale, di timido forte, di vile magnanimo, ed in questo modo la gelosia sarà cagione che l'animo s'addorni di tutte le virtu . . . , (p. 56).

. . . Because of which [jealousy] the lover fearing to lose the favor of his lady will consequently fear to do anything for which he might deservedly lose her: whence he will change from intemperate to temperate, from miserly to generous, from timid to strong, from vile to honorable, and in this way jealousy will be the cause of the soul's adorning itself with all the virtues . . .

ANNIBALE ROMEI

The *Discorsi* of Annibale Romei celebrates the court of Alfonso II d'Este at Ferrara; it is dedicated to Lucrezia d'Este, Duchess of Urbino. Written and published in 1585, the year in which Bruno's *Eroici furori* was published, it professes to describe conversations held at the court retreat at Mesola during the autumn of 1584, in hopes that "gentle" readers may derive utility and beauty from them (*I discorsi,* p. 3).

Only the speeches of the first two days, on beauty and on human love respectively, are directly related to the *trattati d'amore.* The work as a whole belongs to the same genre as Castiglione's *Cortegi-ano*. In the remaining days the following topics are discussed: third day, *Dell'onore* (*Of honor*); fourth day, *Del duello; Del modo di far pace e accomodar le querele* (*On the duel; of the way to make peace and settle quarrels*); fifth day, *Della nobiltà* (*Of nobility*); sixth day, *Delle ricchezze* (*Of riches*); seventh day, *Della prece-denza dell'arme o delle lettere* (*On the precedence of arms or of letters*).

On the first day, in a circle of *dame* and *cavalieri*, a speech on beauty is requested of the Platonist Francesco Patrizzi. Following his discourse there is a further discussion of beauty in which Gio-vanni Battista Guarini, the author of the *Pastor fido*, and Signora Tarquinia Molza, familiar to us from Torquato Tasso's dialogue on love in which she has the title role, are introduced. The author undertakes to discuss the beauty of the universe, corporeal sensible beauty, artificial beauty, intellectual beauty, essential divine beauty, and the beauty of the human body. Patrizzi's, or rather Romei's, definition of beauty is based upon proportion and color. Beauty is created by God to arouse love. As desire cannot be caused by good-ness without proportion, so cannot love be caused by the beautiful without proportion (*ibid.*, p. 30). There are two kinds of beauty, sensible and intelligible.

[La bellezza] non è altro ch' una graziosissima qualità che nell'uni-verso risplende, nascente da proporzione o da colori o dall'un e l'altro insieme, dal sommo Creatore non per altro prodotta, che per accendere con maraviglia e diletto amore in tutte quelle anime che comprender la possono (p. 10).

[Beauty] is a very gracious quality that shines in the universe, born of proportion or colors or of both together, produced by the highest Creator expressly to kindle love with wonder and delight in all those souls which can apprehend beauty.

To Guarini's statement that Plotinus objected to the definition of beauty as proportion, not finding it applicable to color, light and sound, Patrizzi replies that beauty is a quality and must exist in a subject (p. 23). Proportion in divine beauty is the idea of the universe, present in the divine intellect, more beautiful than in the world itself, where it is deformed by matter. Beauty is born from form, ugliness from matter (p. 26).

> . . . Il divino Plotino diffinisce la bellezza . . . il fior della forma vincente la materia (*ibid.*).

> . . . The divine Plotinus defines beauty . . . as the flower of form subduing matter.

True, essential beauty is found in the first intellect or God, creator of all beautiful things (p. 16). This beauty, too, "consists in color and proportion, although in a supereminent way" (p. 17).

Poetical and oratorical beauty are intelligible artificial [*artificiata*] beauty. The beauty of the human soul is found in the intellect; it is the lowest kind of intelligible beauty (p. 14). Human beauty surpasses all other beauty in the inferior world (p. 19). *Grazia* is seen in the sweet (*soavi*) movements of the body. The beauty of the human face depends upon four things: proportioned features, color, air, and grace. Only in the human species is the female more beautiful than the male (p. 20); for beauty, as Anacreon said, is the proper value (*fregio*) of woman. The function of feminine beauty is to excite in men the desire to generate in beauty (pp. 20–21).[64] However, this position, which seems to take at face value Signor Morello's objection to Pietro Bembo's discourse in *The courtier,* is apparently contradicted at the end of Patrizzi's oration by the following Platonic declaration to the queen of the day, which may be quoted as an example of the oratorical style in which the treatise is written:

> Mi resta, serenissima Reina, per concludere questo mio discorso, dir all'Altezza vostra, che non per altro è stata dal sommo Creatore prodotta l'umana bellezza, tra tutte le bellezze sensibili in grado eccellentissimo, se non per accendere quell'onesto e santo amor divino che unisce l'umana creatura al suo Creatore; perchè mirando l'uomo l'umana bellezza, tutto pien di stupore, alza la mente a contemplar la vera ed essenzial bellezza . . . (p. 22).

> To conclude this discourse of mine, most serene Queen, it remains for me to say to Your Highness that human beauty, most excellent in rank among all the sensible beauties, was produced by the highest

[64] Cf. Second discourse, p. 46.

Creator for no other reason than to kindle that honest and holy divine love that unites the human creature with his Creator; for man, looking at human beauty, all full of wonder, elevates his mind to the contemplation of true and essential beauty . . .

Underlying Romei's concept of beauty is the adopted view of the sensible world and the intelligible world, of which the human soul is the lowest order. The world soul acts as an unerring intelligence (p. 12). The angelic intellects, forever in the act of understanding, are so beautiful that they are incapable of any ugliness (p. 16). The human intellect, on the other hand, is liable to become ugly by debasing itself to the darkness of sensuous pleasures. The Neoplatonic metaphor of light is recurrent in Patrizzi's speech. The human intellect is exposed to divine light. Like the sun, which is conceived as the first thing visible, seen and seeing, the first intellect by its essential light is the first intelligible, both understood and understanding (p. 18).

Human love is the subject of the second day's discourse and discussion by wish of the queen of the day, who is dissatisfied with Petrarch's descriptions of young winged love (Trionfo d'Amore, Chap. 1): "Ei nacque d'ozio e di lascivia umana" (He was born of human lust and idleness). Here human love is conceived, somewhat as by Leone Ebreo, as including man's love of God; so that divine love is also considered in Guarino's speech. Like Varchi and Tasso, he prefaces his words with the declaration that he has dedicated his life to love from his early years. Leaving aside universal love, which is "rather the inclination of every created thing to its proper good, than true love," he defines love as follows:

Dico . . . che amor . . . è . . . una gagliardissima perturbazione dell'animo umano eccitata da conosciuta bellezza per una occulta conformità di natura, che ha lo amante con la cosa amata, risolvendosi in desiderio d'unirsi col bello con amor reciproco (Romei, *I discorsi*, p. 39).

I say . . . that love . . . is . . . a very strong perturbation of the human soul excited by known beauty through an occult conformity of nature which the lover has with the thing beloved, resolving itself in a desire to unite with the beautiful in mutual love.

He cites Plato, Aristotle, and Petrarch as authorities.

There are three kinds of human love, which basically correspond to the kinds of love posited by Ficino. The first, which is "similar to heavenly love born of the celestial Venus," is divine love, the divine madness of Plato, here deprived of its virility.

[Il divin amante] lontano da ogni atto brutto, solo di veder la sua bella e cara amata si appaga, la cui bellezza contemplando come imagine della divinità, da quella innalza la mente alla vera bellezza (*ibid.*, p. 45).[65]

[The divine lover] far from every ugly act is satisfied only by seeing his dearly loved and beautiful lady, contemplating whose beauty as an image of the divinity he raises his mind to true beauty.

La seconda specie, senza punto macchiar i casti pensieri, solo in mirare, ragionare e conversare colla sua amata, ed esser da quella di pari amore amato, gioisce (p. 45).

The second kind enjoys only looking, discussing, and conversing with the beloved lady, without in any way sullying one's chaste thoughts.

To the second kind of lover, who remains on the same moral plane without ascending to essential beauty, "it appears that the kiss is granted *per mercede*," the kiss as in the *Courtier* being rather a joining of souls than of bodies. The third kind is like that which Nobili called human love. It is of both soul and body, "but in a licit and honest way"; its institution is marriage, its purpose reproduction.

After delivering his speech, Guarini answers a series of doubts raised by other characters present. Almost all of them were previously discussed by Varchi, who frequently answered them differently; they deal with questions such as destiny, separation, jealousy, possession, desire, object, and duration. Romei repeatedly quotes verses from Petrarch, frequently only to disagree with them. To the question whether love is good or bad he replies that it is "very excellent; indeed, necessary to good and blessed living," excepting of course feral love, which "is truly bad and . . . deprives us of liberty" (p. 59). The nonlover is "a vulgar man and altogether insipid" (p. 61). In answering whether the *amata* is constrained to

---

[65] Cf. p. 59, where divine love is defined as "desiderio d'unirsi col bello, come vero simulacro della divinità . . ." (desire of uniting with the beautiful as a true image of the divinity).

return love, Romei refutes the famous verse from Dante, *Amor, ch' a nullo amato amar perdona* (*Inferno*, V, l. 103: Love, which exempts no loved one from loving), with appropriate questions from Petrarch and Ariosto. To various other doubts he answers that men love more fervently than women (Romei, *I discorsi*, p. 67), that it is possible to love only one person at a time (*ibid.*, p. 72), that one cannot love oneself,[66] and that unreturned love can continue a long time if it is nourished by hope, as in Petrarch's case.

[66] Here his opinion is diametrically opposed to that of Varchi, as expressed in *Opere*, p. 552.

CHAPTER III

De gli eroici furori

THERE are undeniable contrasts between poetry and philosophy: the poet's endeavor to give lyrical and imaginative expression to his thoughts and emotions seems to have little to do with the philosopher's effort to logically order facts into an understandable pattern. Yet the two fields are not altogether separate. Behind the poetry of any school or period, and even of any individual poet, there is a conceptual, cultural, and psychological framework which when clearly formulated can best be described as "philosophical." On the other hand, many philosophers have given literary or poetic expression to their thoughts and feelings. Giordano Bruno's *Eroici furori* combines philosophy with poetry. Bruno in his invocation calls upon the Muses to inspire in him "profound doctrine" (*De gli eroici furori*, I, i, 338, in *Opere italiane*, vol. II).

The *Eroici furori* is a book in two parts of five dialogues each. In each dialogue except the last, two interlocutors discuss certain sonnets by "the Nolan." The subject of the sonnets and of the discussion is love—more specifically, the heroic lover's pursuit of his divine object. In the five dialogues of the first part the chief expository role is given to the poet Tansillo, the other character, Cicada, asking most of the questions and generally being limited to modifications or minor extensions of Tansillo's statements. In the first two dialogues of the second part their roles are taken over by Maricondo and Cesarino, respectively. In the third dialogue Liberio is the explainer, Laodonio the questioner; in the fourth dialogue they are in turn replaced by Severino and Minutolo. Spampanato and Fiorentino, also a Bruno scholar and editor, have identified some of the characters, and it appears that Bruno intended each one to represent a real person. Yet for practical purposes the interlocutors are but two. In the final dialogue, however, their roles are somewhat changed: there is a narrator, Laodomia, and a listener, Giulia, who does not speak until near the end of the dialogue. They perhaps represent two girls known to Bruno when he was a youth in Nola.

Formally the *Eroici furori* parallels the *Vita Nuova* in that the author is not only poet and commentator, but also the protagonist of his poems. There is, however, no evidence that Bruno wrote any of the sonnets or other poems that appear in the *Eroici furori* prior to writing the prose commentary, except for the sonnet, *Amor, per cui tant'alto il ver discerno,* prefixed to the dialogue *De la causa, principio e uno,* which reappears without comment in the first dialogue of the *Eroici furori* (p. 345). Furthermore, there is relatively little narrative in the prose passages of the *Eroici furori* except for the autobiographical allusions of the final dialogue. Two themes which Dante's *Vita Nuova* inherited from Guinizelli and Cavalcanti—the lover's praise of the object of his love (his lady) and the severe effects of love upon the lover—are paramount in the *Eroici furori,* as is also the *stilnuovo* ethical motive of the lover-poet striving to be worthy of that object, in Bruno's dialogue not a lady, but the divine principle. These motives were transmitted to Bruno's poetry by Petrarch and the Petrarchists. However, since in the *Vita Nuova* the lover's lady is divine, not only metaphorically but symbolically, as well, the conflict between carnal and religious love, which ultimately meant recantation in the poetry of the troubadour, the *stilnuovo* school, and Petrarch, is avoided. In the *Vita Nuova,* as in the *Eroici furori,* love is not only transformation, but also transfiguration: ". . . ond'io mi cangio in figura d'altrui." [1]

In content the *Eroici furori* is more similar to parts of the *Convivio* than to the *Vita Nuova.* In the *Convivio* love, carefully considered, is "spiritual union of the soul with the thing loved," allegorized in the second and third tractates into a philosophical study which bears some resemblance to the intellectual love of the

---

[1] *Vita Nuova,* Chapter xiv, line 12 of the sonnet, *Con l'altre donne mia vista gabbate.* Cf. the first sonnet of the *Eroici furori,* quoted on p. 209 of this book.

Eroici furori. Like Bruno's dialogue, and like the *Divine Comedy* itself, the *Convivio* has an overall Neoplatonic coloring, derived in large part from the *Liber de causis,* to which Dante makes frequent reference in the *Convivio.*[2]

Dante interprets allegorically *canzoni* written to an apparently real lady, whereas Bruno applies motives current in love lyrics directly to his object, obviating the necessity for allegorical interpretation. In both, however, the metaphors of love convey the message that in philosophy there is salvation or self-realization. Hear Dante's comment on two lines of the first *canzone* of the *Convivio, Voi che 'ntendendo il terzo ciel movete:*

> . . . Chi veder vuol la salute,
> faccia che li occhi d'esta donna miri, . . .
> (ll. 11–12 of the second stanza.)

Let him who wishes to see salvation look at the eyes of this woman.

O dolcissimi e ineffabili sembianti, e rubatori subitani de la mente umana, che ne le mostrazioni de li occhi de la Filosofia apparite, quando essa con li suoi drudi ragiona! Veramente in voi è la salute, per la quale si fa beato chi vi guarda, e salvo da la morte de la ignoranza e da li vizii (*Convivio,* II, xv).

O sweetest, ineffable sights, sudden robbers of the human mind, which appear in the demonstrations of the eyes of Philosophy, when she converses with her friends! In you truly is the salvation by which he who looks at you becomes blessed and is saved from the death of ignorance and from vices.

Bruno recognizes the non-allegorical nature of his uses of common love symbols. He states in the preface to the *Eroici furori* that, although less replete with "occult sentiment" than Solomon's *Canticles,* the *Eroici furori* is akin to that book as interpreted by "the mystics and Cabalistic doctors," in that the language of common love is used to describe divine passions (Bruno, *Eroici furori,* "Argument," p. 314). Bruno refrained from entitling his dialogue *Cantica* not only because he feared the censure of "certain Pharisees" for usurping a sacred title for his "natural and physical discourse," but also because of the "great dissimilarity" between the

---

[2] Tractate III, Chapters 2 (three times), 6 (twice), and 7; Tractate IV, Chapter 21.

Song of Songs and the *Eroici furori* in the former's manifest use of allegorical figures.

The *Eroici furori* is formally similar to the commentaries of Dante, Lorenzo de' Medici, and Girolamo Benivieni upon their own verses in that it also is a commentary by an author upon his own sonnets. However, it alone of all the commentaries upon verses which we have examined is written in dialogue form, with two interlocutors carefully analyzing each sonnet. The phrase-by-phrase commentary of the sonnets forms only a part of the dialogues, as the discussion intermittently ranges over the wider implications of heroic passion and of the other concepts under consideration. The sonnets themselves are quite repetitive. The doctrinal content, if extracted, would take up no more than a few pages. Considerable attention is given to the formal and stylistic aspects of the dialogues. Phrases mentioned in the sonnets are not used as in Dante's *Convivio* as a pretense for the discussion of matters superfluous to an understanding of the verses. Bruno undertook in the *Eroici furori* to compose a kind of *canzoniere* to heroic love of an ineffable metaphysical object, modelled upon the *canzonieri* of the Petrarchists, addressed to their respective liege ladies. Although he is his own commentator, he does not narrate the events, external or psychological, which led to the composition of individual sonnets.

After our consideration of love treatises, two observations about the *Eroici furori* are in order: (1) that it is a Platonic love treatise; (2) that it goes beyond the bounds of the typical Platonic love treatise. The theme of these treatises—that by love of ideal beauty and goodness man realizes his higher calling and the divine principle within him—is the thesis of the *Eroici furori*. Indeed, the *Eroici furori* is distinguished by the very fervor and utter sincerity with which this faith is propounded. Philosophical problems, such as the relation of intellect and will, are given greater attention than in the conventional love treatises. Bruno's use of allegory and personal allusion in the final dialogue of the *Eroici furori* serves further to differentiate his work from the category of commentary and elaboration upon the classical Platonic writings. Astrological and medical considerations about love, as well as the "practical" questions of human love, are largely omitted, while on the other hand there are several characteristics of the *Eroici furori* which are not found in other love treatises—for example, the extreme misogyny of the Preface; the identification of Petrarchan love with "bestial" love; the acceptance of the doctrine of transmigration; the new post-Copernican cosmology which Bruno developed in other works, but refers to in the *Eroici furori*. Furthermore, Bruno's prose is more virile and less affected than that of most of the *trattatisti d'amore*.

The pervasive thematic similarity between the *Eroici furori* and prior Platonic love treatises is pointed up by a myriad of minor congruencies. Although his love is intellectual and divine, Bruno devotes a great part of the *Eroici furori* to the consideration of its sensuous effects, a stock theme of love treatises and lyric love poetry. The *Eroici furori* manifests the same snobbish tendency of many dialogues to despise vulgar love because it is practiced by vulgar people. Like almost all writers of Platonic love treatises Bruno calls man a microcosm (*ibid.*, II, iii, 476). Love is symbolized by fire, because it converts into itself that with which it comes into contact (I, i, 340). Love is born from beauty (I, i, 338); it enters through the eyes (I, i, 345; I, iv, 383); it is a god (I, iv, 377), a torment (I, iii, 366), an ardent desire for the unpossessed (II, iii, 483); it is bittersweet. A true love can have but one object (I, i, 339; II, i, 454). Jealousy is the inevitable and poisonous accompaniment of love and sometimes kills it (I, i, 341–43). Sexual love is justified only for reproduction and has no emotional or spiritual value (I, ii, 357). The lover strives to be virtuous in order to be worthy of his love (I, i, 343; II, i, 434), in whose presence he is timid or humble; and if he loves circumspectly in his youth he will surely do so in his old age as well (I, i, 343–44). He dies in himself and lives in his beloved. He is subject to antitheses of emotion—such as cold hopes and warm desires ("Argument," 318)—and of situation, in his present martyrdom and hope of future reward (I, ii, 355). The flesh is a prison (I, iii, 366); the soul is united with the body by a spiritual tie. Spiritual beauty is reflected in bodily beauty (I, ii, 357), which is an incitement to the discovery of divine beauty (II, v, 518).

The ladder of Diotima, the Neoplatonic ontological hierarchy, metaphors of light and fire—the list is long indeed of major motives common to the *Eroici furori* and to earlier love treatises. Bruno's dialogue also evinces the same fondness of interpreting the classical myths of love's parentage, its capriciousness and changefulness, its blindness, and so forth. There are occasional *dubbi*, although by and large not the traditional ones.

Bruno, as we shall see in our analysis of specific topics of the *Eroici furori*, took over Ficino's classification of the kinds of love, his dualistic concept of the human soul, the doctrine of the infinity of intellect and will, and the belief, shared by many intervening Neoplatonists, in an ancient and continuous tradition of Platonistic writings by Hermes Trismegistus, Zoroaster, Orpheus, Pythagoras, and Dionysius the Areopagite.

The closest stylistic precedent of the *Eroici furori* and of Bruno's dialogues generally is the *Dialoghi d'amore* of Leone Ebreo. In their philosophical discussions Filone expounds doctrines and clarifies Sofia's doubts in a way that points clearly toward the procedure of Bruno's conversers. The hybrid language also inescapably reminds one of Bruno's mixture of learned and colloquial speech.[3] The doctrinal similarities to Bruno's works are also very numerous. It is of course difficult, as in the comparisons of Bruno and Spinoza, to decide what to attribute to direct influence of the one upon the other, and what to common sources and outlook. It may be objected that Bruno nowhere mentions Leone Ebreo,[4] as he does, for example, Nicholas of Cusa. However, he mentions Ficino by name only once,[5] though he occasionally attributes to Plotinus what are actually quotations from Ficino; and fails to mention by name Pico and the host of love essayists. These facts are largely explained by his preference for the exalted company of ancient authors. Our purpose is not so much to establish evidence of the direct influence of these writers upon Bruno as to show that the *Eroici furori* is so closely related to the tradition of Platonic love treatises that it cannot be properly understood apart from that tradition.

[3] This quality in Leone's dialogue may be partially attributable to a possible unknown editor of Leone's works.

[4] The Leo Hebraeus whom Bruno mentions in the *De immenso,* Book III, chap. 10, in *Opera latine conscripta,* I, 395, is the French Jewish philosopher and astronomer, Levi ben Gerson (1288–1344).

[5] *De monade,* in *Opera latine conscripta,* I, ii, 408.

Despite the contrasts of tone between the love literature of scholastically oriented writers such as Dante and Dino del Garbo, literary theorizers like Lorenzo de' Medici, philosophically minded humanists such as Ficino and Pico, and courtly writers of the sort of Bembo and Castiglione, the theories and attitudes expressed show a surprising degree of uniformity. Both poet and physician call love an illness; the man of letters does not hesitate to describe love scientifically; the professed man of the world may end his treatise in a soaring eulogy of religion. A given writer may choose to discuss only one kind of love, but none disputes that there is an animal love and a divine love, and that intermediate between the two is a human love racked by its tendencies toward the conflicting extremes. Love is so popular a theme that philosophers—Leone Ebreo and Giordano Bruno, for example—use it as a literary and linguistic instrument for the expression of a whole body of metaphysics.

Bruno best defines and describes heroic love in the third dialogue of Part I (p. 360).

Questi furori de quali noi raggioniamo . . . non son oblio, ma una memoria; non son negligenze di se stesso, ma amori e brame del bello e buono con cui si procure farsi perfetto con transformarsi ed assomigliarsi a quello. Non è un raptamento sotto le leggi d'un fato indegno, con gli lacci de ferine affezioni; ma un impeto razionale che siegue l'apprension intellettuale del buono e bello che conosce, a cui vorrebbe conformandosi primente piacere; di sorte che della nobiltà e luce di quello viene ad accendersi ed investirsi de qualitade e condizione per cui appaia illustre e degno.

These passions which we are discussing . . . are not a forgetting, but a memory; they are not negligence of oneself, but love and desire of the beautiful and good through which one tries to perfect himself by resembling it and transforming himself into it. It is not a rapture under the laws of an unworthy fate with the snares of feral affections; but a rational impetus that pursues the intellectual apprehension of the good and beautiful which it knows, which it would likewise please by conforming to it. In this way it comes to be kindled and imbued with a quality and condition that make it appear illustrious and worthy.

The emotional characteristics and the results of heroic passion are described at great length in the sonnets of the *Eroici furori;*

but its pith and substance lie in its intellectuality. It is a "rational impetus," which seeks the intellectual apprehension of its dual goal, the good and the beautiful.

Heroic love's intellectualism and consequent high ethical motivation constitute its antithesis to "vulgar love," a contrast which is one of the most strongly emphasized motives of the *Eroici furori*. Love is to sensuality as knowledge is to ignorance. The Preface declares (p. 314):

Voglio finalmente dire, che questi Furori eroici ottegnono suggetto ed oggetto eroico, e però non ponno . . . cadere in stima d'amori volgari e naturaleschi . . .

Finally I want to say that these heroic passions have a heroic subject and object; therefore they cannot . . . be considered vulgar and natural loves.

The intention of the *Eroici furori* is "to achieve divine contemplation" ("Argument," p. 317). Only in love does man learn the highest truths. Love opens and clarifies the intellect in a miraculous way (I, i, 345). Common persons are satisfied by the vulgar philosophy that deals with superficial causes; the heroic lover will never rest in his effort to penetrate the created world to its hidden essence. Without the stimulus of cognition the affections would be impotent ("Argument," p. 319); but without the incessant passion for union with the divinity man would never realize his capacity for knowledge. Love and intellection are two operationally related facets of man's response to the divinity in the universe. Love's progress is measured by the degree of intelligence to which one has attained at a given stage of the Platonic ascent (I, iv, 390). The multitude of the ideas which he contemplates incites the lover to know the excellence of their unique source. His enthusiasm is linked inseparably with his thought.

La moltitudine delle specie ed idee particolari . . . mostrano l'eccellenza della marca dell'unico fonte di quelle, mediante le quali vien incitato l'affetto verso alto ("Argument," p. 320).

The multitude of the particular ideas and species . . . shows the excellence of the stamp of their only source, through which the affection is urged upward.

We have seen that the majority of Renaissance essayists who wrote on love held vulgar love in low esteem. In considering the love of man for woman as sheerly carnal Bruno agreed with long-standing ecclesiastical and scholastic opinion. However, the extreme misogyny of the Preface to the *Eroici furori* is nowhere paralleled in the Platonic love treatises. Woman is *cosa senza fede, priva d'ogni costanza, destituta d'ogni ingegno, vacua d'ogni merito, senza riconoscenza e gratitudine alcuna, dove non può capir più senso, intelletto e bontade, che trovarsi possa in una statua o imagine depinta al muro* (a faithless thing, totally lacking constancy, destitute of all wit, without any merit, lacking any gratitude or thankfulness, where there can be no more sense, intellect, and goodness than can be found in a statue or image painted on the wall); full of *superbia, arroganza, protervia, orgoglio, ira, sdegno, falsitade, libidine, avarizia, ingratitudine ed altri crimi exiziali* ("Argument," p. 310: conceit, arrogance, stubbornness, haughtiness, anger, scorn, falseness, lust, greed, ingratitude, and other pernicious faults). She is *quella estrema ingiuria e torto di natura, che con una superficie, un'ombra, un fantasma, un sogno, un Circeo incantesimo ordinato al serviggio della generazione, ne inganna in specie di bellezza* ("Argument," p. 311: that extreme injury and wrong of nature that with an exterior, a shadow, a phantasm, a dream, a Circean enchantment ordained to the service of procreation, deceives us under the similitude of beauty).

However, in his typical style of conscious self-contradiction, provoked and demanded by his pre-Baroque artistic mentality, Bruno immediately counters ("Argument," p. 312) by calling sexual love *quel più dolce pomo che può produr l'orto del nostro terrestre paradiso* (that sweetest apple which the garden of our earthly paradise can produce) and the "holy institution of nature," established by "divine providence." He is no "enemy of reproduction"; he does not "hate the sun." No proposal of "realms and beatitudes" has ever made him wish to be castrated.

What is the key to this contradiction? The real target of Bruno's apparent diatribe against women is not "vulgar love" at all—which is justified in several passages ("Argument," p. 312)—but the refined and studied love celebrated by Petrarch and the countless Petrarchists of Bruno's century:

Che spettacolo, o Dio buono!, più vile ed ignobile può presentarsi ad un occhio di terso sentimento, che un uomo cogitabundo, afflitto, tormentato, triste, maninconioso, per dovenir or freddo, or caldo, or fervente, or tremante, or pallido, or rosso, or in mina di perplesso, or in atto di risoluto . . . ? ("Argument," p. 309).

What spectacle—O good God!—more vile and ignoble can be presented to an eye of lucid sentience, than a man who is worried, afflicted, tormented, sad, melancholy, cold one minute, hot the next, now fervent, now trembling, now pale, now red, now with a perplexed air, now appearing resolute . . . ?

Socrates had called love a tyranny. How base and ugly, says Bruno, is the man who devotes the better part of his time to forming public monuments to the tortures he has suffered *sotto la tirannide d'una indegna, imbecille, stolta e sozza sporcaria* (*ibid.*: under the tyranny of an unworthy, imbecile, foolish, and loathsome filth).[6]

Earlier Platonic writers on love had occasionally been embarrassed by Petrarch's more sensual expressions:

Con lei foss'io da che si parte il sole,
E non ci vedess' altri che le stelle,
Solo una notte! e mai non fosse l'alba . . .[7]

Would that I were with her from the setting of the sun, and that none saw us but the stars, one sole night, and it were never dawn.

Disturbing also was Petrarch's admission of guilt and of the conflict between his love of Laura and the love of God:

Questi m'ha fatto men amare Dio
Ch'i' non deveva, e men curar me stesso.[8]

She has made me love God less than I should have, and take less care of myself.

---

[6] Cf. Flaminio Nobili, *Trattato dell'amore humano*, p. 46 v, where Nobili says that philosophy teaches us that it is a very bad thing for man to debase himself by becoming the serf (*mancipio*) of a *feminella*.

[7] *Canzone, A qualunque animale alberga in terra*, ll. 31–33.

[8] *Canzone, Quell'antiquo mio dolce empio signore*, ll. 31–32. See Nobili, *Trattato dell'Amore Humano*, p. 48r.

In the main, however, they had identified his love of Laura with the moral or conversational love given an approved intermediate classification by Ficino. They rightly recognized Petrarch's frequent allusion to the moral elevation worked in him by Laura as the stronger tone of the *Canzoniere*. Bruno breaks completely with these writers when he identifies Petrarch's love with the lower, "bestial" kind of love in Ficino's classification: Petrarch's *Canzoniere* expresses *gli affetti d'un ostinato amor volgare, animale e bestiale* (*Eroici furori*, "Argument," p. 316: the effects of an obstinate, vulgar, animal, and bestial love). This identification was inconsistent with Bruno's categorization of the species of love, which is basically that which the other Platonists had taken from Ficino's interpretation of the *Symposium*. In none of the *trattati* is there a passage containing the violent misogyny and scathing anti-Petrarchism of the Preface to the *Eroici furori*. In none of them has the condemnation of vulgar love so broad a base as to include Petrarchan love in the attack.

In sum, Bruno tells us in the Preface that his *Eroici furori* is to be understood in terms of its antithesis to the studied sensual love of the Petrarchists which he, breaking with the traditional attitudes of Platonizing writers on love, calls vulgar and bestial love.

Ficino describes thus the three loves intermediate between the good demon or *eterno amore di vedere la bellezza divina* (eternal love of seeing divine beauty) and the so-called bad demon—really good, according to Ficino—or *occulto stimolo a generar figliuoli* (occult stimulus to beget children):

> Di qui nascono quelli tre amori: Perchè noi siamo generati & allevati con inclinazione a l'una delle tre vite: cio è, o a la vita contemplativa, o attiva, o voluttuosa. Se noi siamo fatti inchinevoli a la contemplativa, subito per lo aspetto della forma corporale, ci inalziamo a la considera-zione della spirituale & divina. Se a la voluttuosa, subito da 'l vedere caschiamo nella concupiscenzia del Tatto. Se a la attiva & morale, noi solamente perseveriamo in quella dilettazione del vedere & conversare (Ficino, *Sopra lo amore*, VI, viii, 149–50).

From this those three loves are born: because we are created and brought up with an inclination toward one of the three lives—that is, either the contemplative life or the active or the voluptuous. If we are made with a tendency to the contemplative life, we quickly rise through the aspect of corporeal form to the consideration of spiritual and divine form. If to the voluptuous life, we quickly fall from seeing to the concupiscence of touch. If to the active and moral, we only persevere in that delectation of seeing and conversing.

Bruno repeats this classification almost verbatim as follows:

Sai bene che come il rapto platonico è di tre specie, de quali l'uno tende alla vita contemplativa o speculativa, l'altro a l'attiva morale, l'altro a l'ociosa e voluptuaria; cossì son tre specie d'amori, de quali l'uno dall'aspetto della forma corporale s'inalza alla considerazione della spirituale e divina; l'altro solamente persevera nella delettazion del vedere e conversare; l'altro dal vedere va a precipitarsi nella concupiscenza del toccare (*Eroici furori*, I, ii, 356).[9]

You well know that as the Platonic *raptus* is of three kinds, one of which tends to the contemplative or speculative life, another to the active, moral life, and the other to the idle and voluptuous life; so are there three kinds of love, one of which rises from the aspect of corporeal form to the consideration of spiritual and divine form; another only perseveres in the delectation of seeing and conversing; and the other throws itself into the concupiscence of touching.

Bruno adds that there are other kinds of love compounded of the first kind and the second, the first and the third, or all three together; according to whether the affections of the *furioso* are directed more toward the spiritual object, more toward the corporeal object, or equally toward both. Those who try to harvest the fruits of corporeal beauty have a barbarous mind (I, ii, 356–57). The lover who delights in the aspect of spiritual beauty and grace which shines in the beauty of the body is frequently checked from seeking a physical relationship by the fear of losing through his presumption the friendship which he enjoys. Such love, however, is worthy of conservation, provided that great care is taken to avoid the degradation resulting from a base and unworthy object (357).

Vulgar love is the forge of Vulcan. The God within us will punish us for any disorderly love (I, v, 415). The body is a prison which deprives the soul of its liberty, a veil which blinds the sight, a tyrant (II, i, 443).

Love of the body has its justification, however, in "making the race"; but says Bruno, *Mi par cosa da porco o da cavallo di tormen-*

[9] The sense of "touch" was a conventional euphemism for sexual intercourse.

tarvisi su . . . (I, ii, 357: To torment oneself about it seems to me the act of a pig or a horse . . .). The *animo generoso* (generous soul) will not pay undue tribute to a vile and ignoble object (I, ii, 358). ". . . Let that which is Caesar's be given to Caesar, and that which is God's be rendered to God" ("Argument," p. 313). Vulgar love is further justified when it provides the impetus for the love of intellectual beauty. Love of bodily beauty by persons who are "well disposed" not only does not hold them back from greater undertakings, but on the contrary "prepares their wings" for the latter (II, i, 434). Lesser beauties derive from higher ones and by the former we accede to the latter by degrees (435).

Queste, se non son Dio, son cose divine, sono imagini sue vive: nelle quali non si sente offeso, se si vede adorare . . . (*ibid.*).

These, if they are not God, are divine things; they are his living images; if he sees himself being adored in them, he does not feel offended. . . .

It is the spiritual beauty of souls, derived from the highest divine beauty, which shines in beautiful bodies. The well-ordered affection will love bodily beauty only as an indication of the beauty of the soul. Beauty consists in "a certain harmony and consonance of members and colors": Bruno in this definition follows Plato, not Plotinus.[10] He also repeats the Platonic theory that one person becomes enamored of another because of the affinity of his spirit with that which he sees reflected in the beauty of his beloved. He omits, however, the usual astrological explanation that the affinity of loving souls derives from their birth under the same sign of the Zodiac.

Tutti gli amori se sono eroici . . . hanno per oggetto la divinità, tendeno alla divina bellezza, la quale prima si comunica all'anime e risplende in quelle; e da quelle poi o, per dir meglio, per quelle poi si comunica alli corpi; onde è che l'affetto ben formato ama gli corpi o la corporal bellezza, per quel che è indice della bellezza del spirito. Anzi quello che m'innamora del corpo è una certa spiritualità che veggiamo in esso, la qual si chiama bellezza; la qual non consiste nelle dimensioni maggiori o minori, non nelli determinati colori o forme, ma in certa

[10] This definition is Ficino's first definition of beauty in his *Sopra lo amore o ver' Convito di Platone.*

armonia e consonanza de membri e colori. Questa mostra certa sensibile affinità col spirito a gli sensi più acuti e penetrativi; onde sèguita che tali più facilmente ed intensamente s'innamorano . . . (I, iii, 363–64).

All loves if they are heroic . . . have the divinity as their object and tend toward divine beauty, which first communicates itself to souls and shines in them; and then from them, or better, through them, communicates itself to bodies; whence it is that the well-formed affection loves bodies or bodily beauty for that which is an index of the beauty of the spirit. Indeed, that which enamors me of the body is a certain spirituality that we see in it which is called beauty and which does not consist in greater or lesser dimensions, in specific colors or forms, but in a certain harmony and consonance of members and colors. This harmony shows to the most acute and penetrating senses a certain sensible affinity to spirit; whence it follows that such persons fall in love more easily and intensely. . . .

The beautiful body has the power of exciting love, but not of binding the lover, unless assisted by the graces of the spirit, honesty, gratitude, courtesy, sagacity (I, iii, 364). Love is born at the precise time that the original sensuous attraction is intellectualized, and goodness and beauty are no longer seen as visible particulars, but as cogitable concepts (I, iv, 384).

Bruno's considerations on each of the three kinds of love follow Ficino and his disciples in their Platonic course. His *eroico furore* is readily identifiable with the divine love expounded by the *trattatisti*. It is characteristically contemplative. Although purely intellectual, it may nevertheless have its roots in sensual love, not only because divine love is capable of combination with sensual love (I, ii, 356), but also because in the Diotiman ladder of love which Bruno twice repeats divine love has its roots in sensual love. There are, however, substantial differences between Bruno's and others' understanding of divine love. The Nolan philosopher had a new and grander conception of its object, and hence of its ethical consequences. The nearest approach in the *trattati* to Bruno's *eroico furore* is the *furore divino,* likewise of Platonic inspiration, of Marsilio Ficino.

Ma quella spezie di furore la quale Dio ci inspira, innalza l'uomo sopra lo uomo: et in Dio lo converte (Ficino, *Sopra lo amore,* VII, xiii, 238).

But that kind of passion that God inspires in us raises man above man and changes him into God.

Plato in the *Phaedrus* called love a kind of divine madness—an appellation which inspired Bruno's title, *De gli eroici furori*. Socrates there recants the speech in which he has just said that the beloved should prefer the nonlover to the lover on the grounds of the latter's madness, for madness is not simply an evil. There is also a madness which is God-given, the source of man's greatest happiness. This divine madness is of four kinds. First there is prophecy, superior to the human art of divination as, by the testimony of the ancients, madness is superior to sanity. A second kind of madness, which is needed to make men whole from plagues or ancient wrath, is the rite of purification. Again, there is the divine frenzy of poetry whereby the Muses enter and take possession of a "tender and virgin soul." The poetry of the same and uninspired writer, on the other hand, is worth little in comparison with that of the madman.

Socrates declares that he could recount many other noble deeds deriving from divine madness. Therefore, he says, in taking up the fourth kind of madness, let no one frighten us by saying that sane and prudent love is to be preferred to passionate love. Socrates, for his part, will prove that the madness of love is the greatest of heaven's blessings. Socrates' "proof" consists in the great myth of the soul, the ceaselessly self-moving, and therefore immortal, principle which sustains all creation. Its true form only the gods could define; but Socrates can describe it in the figure of a charioteer, reason, who drives a pair of winged horses, the noble steed of spirit or disciplined emotion and the ignoble and unruly steed of unbridled emotion or appetite. The soul's wings grow strong upon beauty, wisdom, and goodness; the opposites of these qualities cause the soul to lose its wings and gravitate to the earth. The gods themselves feast their eyes upon the real being of justice, temperance, knowledge, and the other changeless ideas. The human soul tries desperately to follow in the train of his god and strains to the utmost to see ideas but, weighted down by the vice of the bad horse which the charioteer can scarcely control, it plunges earthward. The lover whose soul in heaven glimpsed the essence of beauty finds the image of celestial beauty here on earth: for of ideas only beauty has a visible counterpart. Beholding it, his wings moisten and he warms to an uneasy excitement. The true lover tries to mold his beloved in the image of his own patron god; the beloved, unaware, sees himself reflected in his lover. The passionate horse cannot be restrained. But if the charioteer and the disciplined horse can establish order, enslaving the vicious elements and freeing the virtuous forces in the soul, philosophy will prevail over the lower life of ambition, and the soul will begin its return to celestial reality.

The *furore* of Bruno's heroic enthusiast is of a different sort from the *furor divinus* of the *Phaedrus*. The Nolan's "madness" is a "rational impetus" (*Eroici furori*, I, iii, 360) which, banishing every vestige of sense, follows ever the upward path of intellection and soars to the stars. The madness of love in the *Phaedrus*, although divinely inspired, is after all directed toward a fellow human being rather than toward God. Plato's love is transformed into philosophy when the passionate steed is overcome by reason and discipline. Bruno's *eroico furore* is from the beginning distinguished by its intellectuality.

Bruno declares that there are "several species of *furori*, all of which may be reduced to two kinds" (I, iii, 359):

. . . Altri non mostrano che cecità, stupidità ed impeto irrazionale che tende al ferino insensato; altri consisteno in certa divina abstrazione per cui dovegnono alcuni megliori, in fatto, che uomini ordinarii (*ibid.*).

. . . Some show only blindness, stupidity, and an irrational impulse that tends toward senseless animality; others consist in a certain divine abstraction by which some in fact become better than ordinary men.

The latter are subdivided into two species: those who, being inhabited by gods or divine spirits, say and work remarkable things without understanding them; and a second group described in these colorful phrases:

Altri, per essere avezzi o abili alla contemplazione, e per aver innato un spirito lucido ed intellettuale, da uno interno stimolo e fervor naturale, suscitato dall'amor della divinitate, della giustizia, della veritade, della gloria, dal fuoco del desio e soffio dell'intenzione, acuiscono gli sensi; e nel solfro della cogitativa facultade accendono il lume razionale con cui veggono più che ordinariamente: e questi non vegnono, al fine, a parlar ed operar come vasi ed instrumenti, ma come principali artefici ed efficienti (*ibid.*, I, iii, 359–60).

Others, because they are accustomed to or able in contemplation and because they have innately a lucid and intellectual spirit, moved by an internal stimulus and natural fervor, excited by love of the divinity, of justice, of truth, of glory, and by the fire of desire fanned by the under-standing, whet their senses; and in the sulphur of the cogitative faculty they kindle the rational light by which they see more than ordinarily. These persons do not come, finally, to speak and act as vessels and instruments, but as principal builders and doers.

Bruno's preference is obviously for the latter, despite his state-ment that the former have dignity, power, and efficacy in them-selves "because they have the divinity"; whereas the latter are more worthy (*degni*), more powerful and efficacious, and are themselves divine. Such language sounds like sophistry. It is however, based upon the real distinction between possession of an attribute by the passive reception of it from an external source and the meritorious possession of it as an intrinsic characteristic. Leone Ebreo used similar subtle distinctions between adjective and substantive forms of the same word.

As a rule, says Bruno of the first category of divinely impassioned persons, undisciplined and ignorant persons are chosen as instru-ments of the divinity. Being void of any spirit and sense of their own, the divine sense and spirit may the more readily take posses-sion and clearly manifest to the multitude of men that such *furiosi* *speak* and act according to the dictates of a superior intelligence. They "are worthy as the ass that carries the sacraments"—and we know from the *Cabala del Cavallo Pegaseo* Bruno's estimation of that dignity. The divinely passionate men in the second category are worthy "as a sacred thing"; in them is seen the excellence of their own humanity (I, iii, 360).

Bruno's attitude toward the ignorant *furioso* is reminiscent of Plato's treatment of divinely inspired poetic madness in the *Ion*, where Socrates' respect for the rhapsode's inspiration is strongly tinged with irony. The rhapsode is inspired by the poet whom he interprets, who in turn is inspired by God. When Ion performs, he cries and his hair stands on end. The "envious" Socrates concludes from these symptoms that the performing rhapsode is mad, even as the poet who composes his beautiful poems not as works of art, but because he is inspired and possessed.

In the fourth dialogue of the second part (p. 499), Bruno returns to the theme of two kinds of madness—one, which is divine, tending upward, farther than most people can ascend, and the other leading down into insanity. The former is called insane because its subject "knows too much" (I, iv, 381). Both groups have in common an extraordinary sense which makes them mad (*pazzi*). Bruno apparently agrees with the common opinion that genius is akin to insanity.

Although the "heroic passion" of Bruno's dialogue differs essentially from the divine madness of love in Plato's *Phaedrus* and the divine poetic madness of the *Phaedrus* and the *Ion,* we find a brief reflection of the Platonic myth and theory of reminiscence in the statement that "these *furori* . . . are not forgetfulness, but a memory" (I, iii, 360). Bruno does not amplify this declaration, but he surely did not make such a statement without having in mind the Platonic theory.

The ascent to divine love and knowledge is described by Bruno in the familiar language of the *Symposium,* repeated in all Platonic love treatises, whether with the literary brilliance of a Castiglione or in the dull stereotyped version of many subsequent authors. Here, then is the first of the Diotiman passages which are to be found in Bruno:

La bellezza che si vede ne gli corpi, è una cosa accidentale ed umbratile, e come l'altre che sono assorbite, alterate e guaste per la mutazione del suggetto, il quale sovente da bello si fa brutto, senza che alterazion veruna si faccia ne l'anima. La raggion dunque apprende il più vero bello per conversione a quello che fa la beltade nel corpo, e viene a formarlo bello; e questa è l'anima che l'ha talmente fabricato e infigurato. Appresso l'intelletto s'inalza più, ed apprende bene che l'anima è incomparabilmente bella sopra la bellezza che possa esser ne gli corpi; ma non si persuade che sia bella da per sè e primitivamente: atteso che non accaderebbe quella differenza che si vede nel geno de le anime; onde altre son savie, amabili e belle; altre stolte, odiose e brutte. Bisogna dunque alzarsi a quello intelletto superiore il quale da per sè è bello e da per sè è buono. Questo è quell'unico e supremo capitano, qual solo, messo alla presenza de gli occhi de militanti pensieri, le illustra, incoraggia, rinforza e rende vittoriosi sul dispreggio d'ogni altra bellezza e ripudio di qualsivogli'altro bene. Questa dunque è la presenza che fa superar ogni difficultà e vincere ogni violenza (I, v, 403).

The beauty seen in bodies is an accidental and shadowy thing, like other things that are absorbed, changed, and spoiled by the mutation of their subject, which often changes from beautiful to ugly without any alteration being made in the soul. The reason then apprehends a truer beauty by turning toward that which imparts beauty to the body and shapes it in beauty—the soul which has thus built and fashioned it. Next the intellect rises higher and clearly comprehends that the soul is incomparably more beautiful than the beauty which can be in bodies. But the intellect does not believe that the soul is beautiful in itself and fundamentally: otherwise that difference which one sees in the quality of souls would not occur, whereby some are wise, lovable, and beautiful, others foolish, hateful, and ugly. It is therefore necessary to rise to that superior intellect which in itself is beautiful and in itself is good. This is that unique, supreme captain who, standing alone before the eyes of the militant thoughts, enlightens, encourages, and strengthens them and renders them victorious through the scorn of every other beauty and the rejection of any other good. This then is the presence which causes every difficulty to be overcome and every violence to be conquered.

The successive objects of the intellect are bodily beauty (accidental, inconstant, and shadowy); the more beautiful soul which informs the beautiful body; and, following the realization that although the soul's beauty is incomparably greater than that of any body, it is not yet the primary beauty, the "superior intellect" which in itself is beautiful and good. Like other Platonists from Plotinus onward, Bruno omits from the hierarchy Socrates' "beautiful laws and institutions." To his highest object Bruno applies the figure which he used in the sonnet *Chiama per suon di tromba il capitano* (I, i, 339) of a captain rallying his militant thoughts. It is no accident that he here adopts the figure which in that sonnet describes the will: for the conclusion and character of the ascensive process is not primarily intellectual or aesthetic, but moral, although couched in the language of beauty and knowledge. The presence of the "supreme captain" of the intellect will enable the subject "to overcome every difficulty and defeat every violence" in the progressive repudiation of all beautiful and good things except the highest one.

Here is Bruno's second rendition of Diotima's ladder:

. . . Quantunque un rimagna fisso su una corporal bellezza e culto esterno, può onorevolmente e degnamente trattenirsi; purchè dalla bellezza materiale, la quale è un raggio e splendor della forma ed atto spirituale, di cui è vestigio ed ombra, vegna ad inalzarsi alla considerazion e culto della divina bellezza, luce e maestade; di maniera che da queste cose visibili vegna a magnificar il core verso quelle che son tanto più eccellenti in sè e grate a l'animo ripurgato, quanto son più rimosse da la materia e senso. Oimè, dirà, se una bellezza umbratile, fosca, corrente, depinta nella superficie de la materia corporale, tanto mi piace e tanto mi commuove l'affetto, m'imprime nel spirito non so che riverenza di maestade, mi si cattiva e tanto dolcemente mi lega e mi s'attira, ch'io non trovo cosa che mi venga messa avanti da gli sensi che tanto m'appaghe; che sarà di quello che sustanzialmente, originalmente, primitivamente è bello? che sarà de l'anima mia, dell'intelletto divino, della regola de la natura? Conviene dunque, che la contemplazione di questo vestigio di luce mi amene mediante la ripurgazion de l'animo mio all'imitazione, conformità e participazione di quella più degna ed alta, in cui mi transforme ed a cui mi unisca; perchè son certo che la natura che mi ha messa questa bellezza avanti gli occhi, e mi ha dotato di senso interiore, per cui posso argumentar bellezza più profonda ed incomparabilmente maggiore, voglia ch'io da qua basso vegna promosso a l'altezza ed eminenza di specie più eccellenti (II, i, 433–44).

Although one be attached to a bodily beauty and exterior cult, he may abide honorably and worthily, provided that from material beauty, which is a ray and splendor of spiritual form and act (of which it is the vestige and shadow), he rise to the consideration and cult of divine beauty, light, and majesty. Thus from these visible things he may exalt his heart to those things which, the further they are removed from matter and sense, the more excellent they are in themselves and the more pleasing to the cleansed soul. Alas, he will say, if a shadowy, cloudy, fleeting beauty painted upon the surface of a body so pleases me and moves my affection, impresses in my spirit I know not what reverence of majesty, captures me and so sweetly draws me to it, that I find nothing which is presented to me by the senses that so satisfies me; what will happen with that which is substantially, originally, and fundamentally beautiful? What will happen to my soul? What of the divine intellect and the rule of nature? It is fitting therefore for the contemplation of this vestige of light to lead me through the cleansing of my soul to the imitation of, conformity with, and participation in that worthier and higher light, into which I would transform myself and to which I would be united. Because I am certain that the nature which has put this beauty before my eyes and has given me the interior sense by which I can infer a more profound and incomparably greater beauty wants me to be elevated from down here to the height and eminence of more excellent species.

Again Bruno's intent is ethical. When the philosopher knows divine beauty, he will love it; and loving it, he will transform himself so as to unite with it. This is the theme of the *Eroici furori* from the first sonnet to the closing lines of the last dialogue.

This passage reaffirms the sensual origin of love. Bruno continues by saying that his true god (*nume*) will surely feel no contempt if the lover honors and worships him *in vestigio ed imagine*, provided that his affection be orderly and aim higher. Indeed, he may be unable to understand this god "in his own essence and substance" (II, i, 434).

The passage quoted above is less specific than the earlier passage, the author being content to identify the beginning and end of the progression without naming all the intermediate stages. The central ideal is the process of purgation whereby the soul removes itself ever further from "matter and sense" until it realizes a complete transformation and unity with "divine beauty, light, and majesty."

The rhetorical question in the passage quoted above, "Alas, . . . if a shadowy, cloudy, fleeting beauty painted upon the surface of a body so pleases me . . . what will happen with that which is substantially, originally, and fundamentally beautiful?" is perhaps the most familiar landmark in the numerous treatises which repeat the ladder of Diotima. The extent to which such works were stereotyped—and Bruno here fails to distinguish his expression from that of other *trattatisti*—is shown by the following quotations from several authors of what is in substance the same question.

Leone Ebreo:

Che se la bellezza corporea, che è ombra de la spirituale, diletta tanto chi la vede che se l'usurpa e converte in sè e gli leva la libertà e la voglia di quella: che farà quella bellezza intellettuale lucidissima, de la quale la corporea è solamente ombra e immagine, a quelli che son degni di verderla?" (*Dialoghi d'amore*, pp. 318–19).

For if the corporeal beauty which is a shadow of spiritual beauty so delights whoever sees it that it usurps him and converts him into itself, and takes away his liberty and desire; what will that clearest intellectual beauty do, of which corporeal beauty is only a shadow and image, to those who are worthy of seeing it?

Pietro Bembo:

E quando, agli atti d'una semplice donnicciuola, che qui empie il numero dell'altre, ripensando, prendi e ricevi sodisfacimento, quale sodisfacimento pensi tu che riceverebbe il tuo animo, se egli, da queste caliggini col pensiero levandosi e puro e innocente a quelli candori passando, le grandi opere del signore, che là su regge, mirasse e rimirasse intentamente e ad esso con casto affetto offeresse i suoi disii? (*Gli asolani*, p. 156).

And when thinking on the acts of a simple little woman (who here stands for all of them) you take and receive such satisfaction, what satisfaction do you think your soul would receive if it were to rise from these mists with its thought and pass pure and innocent to those splendors—the great works of the Lord who reigns up there—and look and again look intently and offer its desires to him with chaste affection?

Baldassare Castiglione:

Se adunque le bellezze, che tutto dì con questi nostri tenebrosi occhi vedemo nei corpi corruttibili, che non son però altro che sogni ed ombre tenuissime di bellezza, ci paion tanto belle e graziose, che in noi spesso accendon foco ardentissimo, e con tanto diletto, che reputiamo niuna felicità potersi agguagliar a quella che talor sentemo per un sol sguardo che ci venga dall'amata vista d'una donna: che felice maraviglia, che beato stupore pensiamo noi che sia quello, che occupa le anime che pervengono alla visione della bellezza divina! che dolce fiamma, che incendio suave creder si dee che sia quello, che nasce dal fonte della suprema e vera bellezza! etc. (*Il libro del Cortegiano*, IV, lxix, 495).

If then the beauties which we see every day with these shadowy eyes of ours in corruptible bodies, which however are only dreams and very tenuous shadows of beauty, seem to us so beautiful and lovely that they often kindle a very ardent fire in us—and with such delight that we deem no other felicity capable of equaling that which we sometimes feel from a single glance coming to us from the beloved sight of a woman—what happy wonder, what blessed bewilderment we may imagine is that which fills the souls that arrive at the vision of divine beauty! What a sweet flame, what a pleasing fire must we believe is that which emerges from the fount of the true, supreme beauty! Etc.

Benedetto Varchi:

Ora se le bellezze corporali che vere bellezze non sono, ma simulacri e sembianze, o più tosto ombre di bellezze, cagionano negli alti cuori e spiriti generosi cotanti effetti, ed hanno quaggiuso cotali privilegi, che avemo da credere, altissimi ed ingegnosissimi ascoltatori, che abbiano in sè e producano in noi le bellezze dell'anime, le quali tanto più degne sono e più perfette di quelle dei corpi, quanto le terrene cose e transitorie delle celesti e sempiterne men perfette e men degne sono? Che poi delle bellezze angeliche? le quali sole come da Dio, ottimo e grandissimo, immediate procedenti, sono le vere e proprie bellezze. Oh felici dunque . . . (*Sopra alcune quistioni d'amore*, p. 532).

Now if bodily beauties, which are not true beauties but images and semblances or rather shadows of beauties, cause such effects in high hearts and generous spirits and have such privileges down here, what are we to believe, my honored and most able listeners, that the beauties of souls may have in themselves and produce in us, seeing that they are worthier and more perfect than the beauties of bodies to the degree that earthly and transitory things are less perfect and less worthy than things celestial and everlasting? What then of angelic beauties, which alone issuing immediately from God, the best and greatest, are true and proper beauties? Oh, happy then . . .

In the *Symposium* itself the "bodily beauty" which is rejected is that of *pulchri pueri adolescentesque* (*Omnia D. Platonis Opera Tralatione Marsilij Ficini*, p. 251: handsome boys and adolescents). There follows the exclamation which was to be taken up by a veritable chorus of Renaissance writers:

Quam felix illud spectaculum fore putamus, si cui contigerit, ut ipsum pulchrum intueatur, syncerum, integrum, purum, simplex, non humanis carnibus, coloribus, non alijs mortalibus nugis contaminatum, sed ipsum secundum se pulchrum divinum inspiciat. (*ibid.*).

Let us consider how happy a sight it would be to gaze upon beauty itself, unadulterated, whole, pure, simple, not contaminated by human flesh, colors, or other mortal trumpery; but to behold divine beauty in itself.

The end of the philosophical enterprise is unity with God; more than that, it is transformation into God (*Eroici furori*, "Argument," p. 318). The chief means to this end is contemplation, which at first is extremely difficult; but the higher the soul rises, the easier is its flight (*ibid.*, II, i, 451). Bruno, like St. Augustine, Dante, and Ficino, compares the love for God with the inclination of the elements:

. . . Ogni parte de corpi e detti elementi quanto più s'avvicina al suo luogo naturale, tanto con maggior impeto e forza va, sin tanto che al fine (o voglia o non) bisogna che vi pervegna. Qualmente dunque veggiamo nelle parti de corpi a gli proprii corpi, cossì doviamo giudicare de le cose intellettive verso gli proprii oggetti . . . (*ibid.*).

Every part of bodies and said elements, the nearer it comes to its natural place, the greater the impetus and force with which it goes, until finally whether it wishes or not it needs must arrive there. Thus as we see [the attraction] of parts of bodies toward their own bodies, so must we judge of intellectual things toward their own objects . . .

Contemplation of the "magnificent and heroic" object attenuates or annuls the perception of lesser things. Negatively, the philosopher renounces his ties to the world of sense; positively, he ascends from particular beauties to universal beauty—and beyond. By a process of contraction, which Bruno explains in the *Explicatio triginta sigillorum*, the soul so anesthetizes the body that it feels neither pain nor pleasure, does not fear death, and may altogether leave the body (*ibid.*, II, i, 446). In this state of *raptus* the lover sees his object. "To see the divinity is to be seen by it" (*ibid.*). Here immortality is a quality of life, attainable in this world.

Cesarino. Vuol dire quella morte de amanti che procede da somma gioia, chiamata da cabalisti *mors osculi*? la qual medesima è vita eterna, che l'uomo può aver in disposizione in questo tempo ed in effetto nell'eternità?
Maricondo. Cossì è (*ibid.*, II, i, 448).

Cesarino. Does he refer to that death of lovers which comes from supreme joy, called by the Cabalists *mors osculi*—which itself is eternal life, which man can have in some measure in this life and in full in eternity?
Maricondo. Yes.

Having achieved his goal of knowing divine beauty, the heroic lover can never again love anything else; neither can he desist from loving his object.

. . . È impossibile che uno possa voltarsi ad amar altra cosa, quando una volta ha compreso nel concetto la bellezza divina; ed è impossibile che possa far di non amarla . . . (II, i, 454).[11]

[11] A frequent statement in the literature of vulgar love is that he who truly loves someone will always love that person.

. . . It is impossible for a person to turn to loving something else when once he has understood the concept of divine beauty; and it is impossible for him not to love it. . . .

All heroic loves, declares Bruno, have as their object the divinity (I, iii, 363), or divine beauty (I, i, 344, and elsewhere). However, he frequently warns us, the ultimate nature of the highest principle remains obscured to us in this life by reason of the human soul's native impotence. He frequently praises negative theology and Socratic ignorance, both of which, however, he attacked in the *Cabala del cavallo pegaseo*. On the other hand, he asserts in several passages that God pervades all the universe and can be known by introspection because he is within us. Some critics of Bruno have objected that he was unable to decide for either the transcendent or the immanent aspect of the First Principle. To say that he was acutely aware of both aspects is not to tax him with a contradiction.

Divine beauty is the sole object capable of drawing to itself the heroic lover, who becomes its subject and captive (I, i, 344). The lover's goal—man's greatest perfection—is union with God. He burns with a single, all-consuming flame, for love like fire converts other elements into itself. There is but one paradise, one "first and last good, because other goods are only participants in truth and essence (I, i, 340). The "principal lesson" which love teaches men is to contemplate divine beauty *in ombra* (in a shadowy fashion), when they cannot do so *in specchio* (as in a mirror); "and like Penelope's suitors to entertain the maidservants when they are unable to converse with the mistress" (I, iii, 362).

The following sonnet and the author's comments on it are illuminating in regard to the duality of the heroic lover's object:

> Bench' a tanti martir mi fai suggetto,
> Pur ti ringrazio, e assai ti deggio, Amore,
> Che con sì nobil piaga apriste il petto,
> E tal impadroniste del mio core,
>   Per cui fia ver, ch'un divo e viv' oggetto,
> De Dio più bella imago 'n terra adore;
> Pensi chi vuol ch' il mio destino sia rio,
> Ch' uccid' in speme e fa viv' in desio.
>   Pascomi in alta impresa;
> E bench' il fin bramato non consegua,

E 'n tanto studio l'alma si dilegua;
　　Basta che sia sì nobilment' accesa;
　　Basta ch'alto mi tolsi,
E da l'ignobil numero mi sciolsi.
　　　　　　　　　　　　(I, iii, 365–66)

Although you make me subject to so many torments, yet do I thank you, and a great deal do I owe you, Love, who opened my breast with such a noble wound and so became master of my heart,
　　that in truth it adores a divine and living object, the most beautiful image of God on earth. Let him who wishes think my destiny evil, which kills me in hope and makes me live in desire.
　　I take delight in high enterprise; and if my soul does not attain the coveted goal and loses itself in such zeal,
　　it suffices that it burns so nobly; it is enough that I went so high and freed myself from the vile number.

The "divine and living object" of the sonnet is "the highest intelligible species of the divinity that he [the lover] has been able to form." This object is not the "final, last, and most perfect" object, the divinity itself, but only the likeness (*similitudine*) of God which we are able to know *in questo stato* (in this life).[12] The intellect must be content with the umbra of divine beauty which we see in its effects and works until in the supernal world we are permitted to look with purer eyes upon the real presence of divine beauty (I, iii, 367). The *ignobil numero* (vile number) is "the body and sensual cognition" (I, iii, 370).

Despite the limitation in this life of the intellect's ability to comprehend its object, heroic love can be consummated on earth in the Platonic *raptus* which Leone Ebreo called "copulation." Having formed the highest possible concept of God, the intellect, "conjoined to that light itself becomes light, and in consequence is made a god: because it contracts in itself the divinity, being itself in God by the effort [*intenzione*] with which it penetrates the divinity (to the extent that it is possible), and God being in it, inasmuch as after having penetrated the divinity the intellect comes to conceive it and (to the extent that it is possible) to receive and comprehend it in its concept" (I, iii, 367).

The closing tercet of the sonnet is interpreted by the author to

---

[12] The qualification *in questo stato* is constantly reiterated.

mean that the soul, if now incapable of ultimate knowledge, should console itself in experiencing the greatest glory possible to man in this life (I, iii, 368). The idea or "intelligible species" is the means by which the philosopher is able to unite with the divine mind (*ibid.*). Such cognition will never be perfect to the extent that the highest object can be understood, but to the extent that our intellect can understand: it will suffice, says Bruno, for the philosopher to see divine beauty to the limits of his own horizon (I, iii, 369).

Basta che tutti corrano; assai è ch' ognun faccia il suo possibile; perchè l'eroico ingegno si contenta più tosto di cascar o mancar degnamente e nell'alte imprese, dove mostre la dignità del suo ingegno, che riuscir a perfezione in cose men nobili e basse (*ibid.*).

It is enough for all to strive; it is a great deal for each to do his best; because the heroic mind is better satisfied falling or failing worthily in high undertakings, where it may show the worth of its genius, than in succeeding perfectly in lower, less noble things.

If Bruno restricts the limits of love and knowledge "in this life," he never limits the philosopher's aspirations. The heroic spirit, he says in the first dialogue of the second part (II, i, 434), will ever aspire to more excellent and magnificent objects "until he sees himself elevated to the desire of divine beauty in itself, without similitude, figure, image, and species, if it be possible; and more, if he knows how to accomplish such." The impetus of the philosopher's love may indeed carry him beyond the knowledge of the ideas to a union—in exaltation if not in knowledge—with the Plotinian superessential entity which is the source of ideas and all that is ontologically subsequent to them. Bruno so tells us in his commentary upon the sonnet, *Che la bogliente Puglia o Libia mieta*:

Ma dove l'affetto intiero è tutto convertito a Dio, cioè all'idea de le idee, dal lume de cose intelligibili la mente viene exaltata alla unità superessenziale, è tutta amore, tutta una, non viene ad sentirsi sollecitata da diversi oggetti che la distraano, ma è una sola piaga, nella quale concorre tutto l'affetto . . . (II, i, 459).

But where the whole affection is turned to God, that is, to the idea of ideas, the mind becomes exalted by the light of intelligible things to superessential unity, is all love, all one. It does not find itself importuned by diverse objects that distract it, but is one sole wound in which the whole affection gathers. . . .

As in Plotinus (*Ennead* V, 3, 17), the vision of truth is a sudden occurrence.

. . . La divina verità . . . non proviene con misura di moto e tempo, come accade nelle scienzie fisiche . . . ; ma subito e repentinamente . . . (*Eroici fuori*, II, iv, 499).

. . . Divine truth . . . does not come in measured movement and time as happens in the physical sciences . . . ; but suddenly and immediately. . . .

This "supernatural" illumination is reserved to only a few persons. It may operate like Christian grace in an ignorant subject who has not sought it; but the divine mind is revealed in a "different way" to those who seek it, and to them only. Here, although the preparatory study takes time and effort, the apprehension of divine truth is an instantaneous act, to which Bruno applies the Plotinian terms of "immediate conversion" (II, iv, 502) and "immediate vision" (II, iv, 503).

Certo non niego che al disporsi bisogna tempo, discorso, studio e fatica, ma, come diciamo che la alterazione si fa in tempo e la generazione in instante . . . cossì accade proporzionalmente al proposito (II, iv, 500).

Certainly I do not deny that the preparation requires time, study, zeal, and effort, but just as we say that alteration is accomplished in time and generation in an instant . . . so does it happen analogously in this case.

Bruno's distinction between the immanent and transcendent aspects of the divinity reflects his adherence to the Plotinian theory of divine emanation. Ultimately, Plotinus is the main source of the philosophic structure of the *Eroici furori*. The transcendent and immanent manifestations of God which are described in the *Eroici furori* correspond respectively to the first and third hypostases of the Plotinian hierarchy. Although Bruno gives little specific emphasis to ideas in the *Eroici furori*, he attributes to "second intelligences" or ideas an intermediate position in the godhead both in the downward path of the generation of worldly things (II, i, 452) and in the upward path of intelligence, where they grant what access we have to the God who is perhaps unknowable "in this life" (I, iii, 368). In the following excerpt these divine manifestations are personified, as Diana and Apollo respectively, after the fashion of the closing *canzone* of the *Eroici furori*, where they become Oceanus and Jupiter.

> . . . Diana, che è l'ordine di seconde intelligenze che riportano il splendor ricevuto dalla prima, per comunicarlo a gli altri che son privi de più aperta visione; . . . [il] nume più principale, Apollo, che con il proprio e non improntato splendore manda le sue saette, cioè gli suoi raggi, da parti innumerabili, tali e tante che son tutte le specie delle cose; le quali son indicatrici della divina bontà, intelligenza, beltade e sapienza . . . (II, i, 452).

> . . . Diana, who is the order of second intelligences which take the splendor received from the first intelligence in order to communicate it to others who are deprived of more open vision; . . . [the] chiefer god, Apollo, who with his own underived splendor sends his arrows, that is, his rays, into innumerable places, such and so many that they are all the species of things, which are indicators of divine goodness, intelligence, beauty, and wisdom. . . .

In the opening sonnet of the second dialogue in Part Two the huntress Diana, "the splendor of intelligible species" (II, ii, 464) wounds with her grace and beauty the protagonist of the sonnets, the heroic *furioso,* who is happy to surrender to such a consort. The arrows which wound his heart, Bruno elsewhere explains (II, i, 458), are "the innumerable individuals and species of things, in which there shines the splendor of divine beauty, according to their degrees, and whence the affection is heated for the proposed and understood good" (II, i, 458–59). The Diana of the above-mentioned sonnet (II, ii, 463) is contrasted, as in the first dialogue of the second part (II, i, 452), to the supreme Apollo:

> Però a nessun pare possibile de vedere il sole, l'universale Apolline e luce absoluta per specie suprema ed eccellentissima; ma sì bene la sua ombra, la sua Diana, il mondo, l'universo, la natura che è nelle cose, la luce che è nell'opacità della materia, cioè quella in quanto splende nelle tenebre (II, ii, 472).

Thus to none does it seem possible to see the sun, the universal Apollo and absolute light, as the supreme and most excellent species; but rather his shadow, his Diana, the world, the universe, the nature which is in things, the light which is in the opacity of matter, that is, the [absolute] light as it shines in the shadows.

This is certainly a key passage for the understanding of Bruno's philosophy. The knowable object of Bruno's philosophy is the natural universe, his concept of which he expounds in the dialogue *De l'infinito, universo e mondi*. This knowable world he describes as a monad which is the image of the divine monad or "true essence of the being of all things." The one is related to the other as the generator to the generated.

Questa è la Diana, quello uno che è l'istesso ente, quello ente che è l'istesso vero, quello vero che è la natura comprensibile, in cui influisce il sole ed il splendor della natura superiore, secondo che la unità è destinta nella generata e generante, o producente e prodotta (II, ii, 473).

This is that Diana, that one which is being itself, that being which is truth itself, that truth which is comprehensible nature, in which is the influence of the sun and the splendor of the superior nature, according as unity is distinguishable into the generated and the generating or producer and product.

The allegorical ode in the final dialogue of the *Eroici furori* contrasts the visible *due più vaghe al mondo stelle*—presumably the stars previously identified as beauty and goodness, or perhaps goodness and truth—with the entity which is hidden in darkest shadow even from the most ardent seeker:

> . . . Allor, s'avvien ch' aspergan le man belle
> Chiunque a lor per remedio s'avicina,
> Provar potrete la virtù divina
> Ch' a mirabil contento
> Cangiando il rio tormento,
> Vedrete due più vaghe al mondo stelle.
>   Tra tanto alcun di voi non si contriste,
> Quantunque a lungo in tenebre profonde
> Quant' è sul firmamento se gli asconde;
> Perchè cotanto bene
> Per quantunque gran pene
> Mai degnamente avverà che s'acquiste. . . .
>   (II, v, 513)

. . . Then if it happens that the beautiful hands wash whoever goes to them to be cured, you can experience the divine virtue, for, your cruel torment changing to marvelous contentment, you will see the two most beautiful stars in the world.

Let none of you meanwhile become sad, however long all that is in the firmament remains hidden from you. For it will never happen that so great a good will be sufficiently possessed, no matter through what great pain. . . .

The allegorical narrative which follows this ode describes the philosopher's object as "the image of the greatest good on earth" (II, v, 515). This natural good is represented in the final *Canzone de gl'illuminati* by Oceanus, the suprarational truth by Jupiter.[13] Their dialogue is as follows:

—Non oltre invidio, o Giove, al firmamento,
Dice il padre Ocean col ciglio altero,
Se tanto son contento
Per quel che godo nel proprio impero.—
   —Che superbia è la tua? Giove risponde;
A le ricchezze tue che cosa è gionta?
O dio de le insan' onde,
Perchè il tuo folle ardir tanto surmonta?—
   —Hai, disse il dio de l'acqui, in tuo potere
Il fiammeggiante ciel, dov' è l'ardente
Zona, in cui l'eminente
Coro de tuoi pianeti puoi vedere.
   Tra quelli tutt'il mondo admira il sole,
Qual ti so dir che tanto non risplende,
Quanto lei che mi rende
Più glorioso dio de la gran mole.
   Ed io comprendo nel mio vasto seno,
Tra gli altri, quel paese ove il felice
Tamesi veder lice
Ch' ha di più vaghe ninfe il coro ameno;
   Tra quelle ottegno tal fra tutte belle,
Per far del mar più che del ciel amante
Te, Giove altitonante,
Cui tanto il sol non splende tra le stelle.—
   Giove responde:—O dio d'ondosi mari,
Ch' altro si trove più di me beato,
Non lo permetta il fato;
Ma miei tesori e tuoi corrano al pari.
   Vagl' il sol tra tue ninfe per costei;
E per vigor de leggi sempiterne,

[13] This interpretation was originated by Giovanni Gentile.

De le dimore alterne,
Costei vaglia per sol tra gli astri miei.

(II, v, 517–18)

"No longer, O Jupiter, do I envy the firmament," says Father Ocean with raised brow, "for I am very happy about that which I enjoy in my own dominion."

"What pride is yours?" answers Jupiter. "What is added to your riches? O god of the senseless waves, why does your mad daring reach so high?"

"You have in your power," said the god of waters, "the flaming sky, where the burning zone is located in which you can see the eminent chorus of your planets.

"Among them the whole world admires the sun, which I can tell you does not shine as bright as she who renders me the most glorious god of the great mass.

"And I contain in my breast that country among all others where the happy Thames may be seen, which has a pleasing chorus of the most lovely nymphs.

"Among them I have one so beautiful among all as to make you, O thundering Jupiter, more fond of the sea than of the sky, for not even the sun shines so among the stars."

Jupiter replies, "O god of the tossing seas, fate does not allow another to be more blessed than I. But let my treasures and yours contend equally.

"Let the sun take her place among your nymphs; and by the power of the eternal laws of alternating abodes, let her take the place of the sun among my stars."

In sum, the philosopher's knowable object, even though it is not identical with the ultimate cause of the universe, is exalted to a position of equality with that hidden principle. This "object" is fully capable of satisfying the subject of heroic love.

The reference to England is in harmony with the allegorical narrative of this final dialogue, which is replete with autobiographical allusions. Bruno was in England when he published the *Eroici furori*. One is justified in seeing in "she who renders me the most glorious god" the same object of Bruno's homage with which the *Eroici furori* begins—Queen Elizabeth. It is nothing uncommon in medieval and Renaissance allegory for a single figure to have a multiple significance.

In at least three passages of the *Eroici furori* Bruno emphasizes the immanent aspect of God without mentioning the transcendent God which he elsewhere posits as the object of negative theology. In the light of the passages we have just considered it would seem appropriate to bear in mind the transcendent aspect of the divinity when reading these words: "Dio è vicino, è nosco, è dentro di noi" (I, v, 415: God is near, he is with us, he is inside us).

Dio, la divina bellezza e splendore riluce ed è in tutte le cose; però non mi pare errore d'admirarlo in tutte le cose, secondo il modo che si comunica a quelle (II, i, 435).

God, divine beauty and splendor, shines and dwells in all things. Therefore it does not seem wrong to me to admire him in all things according to the manner in which he is present in them.

. . . Dio è vicino, con sè [con l'erocio amante] e dentro di sè più ch' egli medesimo esser non si possa; come quello ch' è anima de le anime, vita de le vite, essenza de le essenze . . . (II, i, 442).

. . . God is near, with him [the heroic lover] and inside him more than he himself can be; for he is that which is the soul of souls, life of lives, essence of essences. . . .

The divinity is not only in people but is just as intimately present in all that is to be seen, "high or low" (*ibid.*).

The object of the heroic lover's affection generically is the divinity. Specifically it is usually called divine beauty. The Platonistic identification of the beautiful and the good which man loves with the goodness and truth which he knows produces frequent references to the "two lights" (II, ii, 472) or "twin splendor" ("Argument," p. 325) of goodness and beauty. There are also a few more or less express references to the hero's object as a triad of beauty, goodness, and truth. These various ways of considering the object of love are illustrated by the following quotations.

Beauty:

> . . . l'oggetto . . . ,
> L'alta bellezza, . . .
> Ogni ben mi presenta . . .
> (I, i, 340)

. . . the object . . . ,
the high beauty, . . .
Gives me every good . . .

Tutti gli amori . . . eroici . . . tendeno alla divina bellezza. . . .

(I, iii, 363)

All heroic . . . loves . . . tend to divine beauty. . . .

Goodness and truth:

Cossì si descrive il discorso de l'amor eroico, per quanto tende al proprio oggetto, ch' è il sommo bene, e l'eroico intelletto che giongersi studia al proprio oggetto, che è il primo vero o la verità absoluta (I, iv, 374).

Thus may one describe the course of heroic love when it tends toward its proper object, which is the highest good, and of the heroic intellect that strives toward its proper object, which is the first truth or absolute truth.

. . . Perchè quelle luci che facea presente l'intelletto agente illuminatore e sole d'intelligenza, ebbero facile entrata per le sue luci: quella della verità per la porta de la potenza intellettiva; quella della bontà per la porta della potenza appetitiva al core, cioè alla sustanza del generale affetto (II, i, 453).

. . . Because those lights which were rendered present by the active intellect, the illuminator and sun of intelligence, gained easy entrance through his [the *furioso*'s] lights—that of truth through the door of the intellective power; that of goodness through the door of the appetitive power to the heart, that is, to the substance of affection in general.

Beauty, goodness, and truth:[14]

. . . Qual forma megliore e più eccellente può presentarsi che di quella bellezza, bontà e verità, la quale è il fonte d'ogni altra verità, bontà, beltade? (II, i, 454).

. . . What better form can present itself than that beauty, goodness, and truth which are the source of every other truth, goodness, beauty?

. . . Questo fuoco è l'ardente desio de le cose divine, questa saetta è l'impression del raggio della beltade della superna luce, questi lacci son le specie del vero che uniscono la nostra mente alla prima verità, e le specie del bene che ne fanno uniti e gionti al primo e sommo bene (I, iii, 363).

. . . This fire is the ardent desire of divine things, this arrow is the impression of the ray of beauty of the supernal light, these snares are the

[14] We also find these three concepts enumerated among the triads of the *De monade,* in *Opera latine conscripta,* I, ii, 359.

species of truth which unite our mind to the first truth and the species of good which unite and join us to the first and highest good.

The soul's progression to God (which in the last analysis is a return) is described in the dualistic terms of intellect and will, which Platonizing philosophers of the Renaissance inherited from medieval theological discussions. An entire dialogue, the third of the second part, is devoted specifically to that consideration, as Bruno tells us in the Argument:

> Là si fa dubio, se l'intelletto o generalmente la potenza conoscitiva, o pur l'atto della cognizione sia maggior de la volontà o generalmente della potenza appetitiva, o pur de l'affetto: se non si può amare più che intendere, e tutto quello ch' in certo modo si desidera, in certo modo ancora si conosce, e per il roverso; onde è consueto di chiamar l'appetito cognizione . . . ("Argument," p. 321).

There it is debated whether the intellect (or the cognitive power in general or yet the act of cognition) is greater than the will (or generally the appetitive power or the affection)—whether one cannot love more than he understands, and whether all that one in some way desires he must in some way know, and vice versa; whence it is customary to call the appetite cognition . . .

Bruno is interested in the dualism of intellect and will as it applies to man. Much of the theological discussion of the subject had dealt with their relationship and interaction within the Trinity. Both areas are fields of subtle reasoning. Bruno's discussion is complicated by the fact that not only the will, but the intellect as well, is identified with love. Hence a discussion of the relation of intellect to will does not resolve itself, as might appear at first sight, into a discussion of the relation between knowledge and love.

Intellect and will interact in mutual stimulation (*ibid.*); they also act upon each other as limiting factors, for neither can outstrip the other in scaling the ladder of love which leads to the knowledge of the infinite. Intellect and will, cognition and love, are not so much separate faculties in the heroic lover as parallel currents in the same basic response to the divine principle in the cosmos, so closely related as to be effectively inseparable in their operation.

Bruno generally attributes chronological precedence to the intellect. We do not desire unknown things (I, iv, 384). The will, on the other hand, is more insistent.

. . . L'operazion de l'intelletto precede l'operazion della voluntade; ma questa è più vigorosa ed efficace che quella . . . (I, iv, 375).

. . . The operation of the intellect precedes the operation of the will; but the latter is more vigorous and active than the former. . . .

. . . Con l'intelletto speculativo prima si vede il bello e buono, poi la voluntà l'appetisce, ed appresso l'intelletto industrioso lo procura, sèguita e cerca (II, iii, 484).

. . . With the speculative intellect one first sees the beautiful and good, then the will desires it, and next the industrious intellect pursues and seeks it.

However, although cognition precedes volition, it is love (here identified with will) which first moves the intellect to precede it "as a lantern" (I, iv, 375).

In the first dialogue of the second part the intellect and the "intellective will" are pictured as the two wings on which the soul rises to its dual object of goodness and beauty:

L'ascenso procede nell'anima dalla facultà ed appulso ch' è nell'ali, che son l'intelletto ed intellettiva volontade, per le quali essa naturalmente si riferisce ed ha la sua mira a Dio, . . . cossì come ogni cosa naturalmente ha impeto verso il suo principio regressivamente, e progressivamente verso il suo fine e perfezione, come ben disse Empedocle (*ibid.*, II, i, 449).[15]

The ascent proceeds in the soul from the faculty and tendency that are in the wings, which are the intellect and the intellective will, by which the soul naturally directs itself and aims toward God; . . . as everything has a natural impulse toward its source regressively and progressively toward its end and perfection, as Empedocles well said.

All authors of Platonic love treatises attributed to vision the primacy among the senses and an analogical relation to intellection;

[15] Ficino frequently spoke of will and intellect as the wings of the soul. In the preface to *De Christiana religione,* in *Opera omnia,* p. 1, he writes as follows: "Nam cum animus (ut Platoni nostro placet) duabus tantum alis, id est, intellectu & voluntate possit ad coelestem patrem, & patriam reuolare, ac philosophus intellectu maxime, sacerdos uoluntate nitatur, & intellectus uoluntatem illuminet, uoluntas intellectum accendat . . ." (As the soul (in the opinion of our Plato) can fly back as though with two wings—intellect and will—to its celestial father and fatherland; and the philosopher flies especially with the intellect, the priest with the will, and the intellect enlightens the will, while the will kindles the intellect . . .).

and traditionally the heart was the seat of the affections and of the will. Hence it was quite natural for Bruno to express the interaction of intellect and will in the third dialogue of the second part by a series of eight sonnets with alternating *proposte* and *risposte* of the eyes to the heart and of the heart to the eyes ("Argument," p. 321).

A striking precedent for the central image of these sonnets, if not their actual source, is the *canzone* of the first book of the *Asolani* (pp. 27–28), which declares in repetition of the prose passage which precedes it that only the counteraction of two modes of death —by tears and by the fire of love—preserve the life of the unhappy lover Perottino.

> Voi mi poneste in foco
> > Per farmi anzi 'l mio dì, Donna, perire;
> > E perchè questo mal vi parea poco,
> > Col pianto raddoppiaste il mio languire.
> > Or io vi vo' ben dire:
> > Levate l'un martire,
> > Che di due morti i' non posso morire.
> Però che da l'ardore
> > L'umor che ven dagli occhi mi difende
> > E, che 'l gran pianto non distempre il core,
> > Face la fiamma, che l'asciuga e 'ncende.
> > . . . Vostra voglia infinita[16]
> > Sana la sua ferita,
> > Ond, io rimagno in dolorosa vita.
> > > (Bembo, *Gli Asolani*, p. 27)

You put me into the fire to make me perish, Lady, before my day; and because this hurt seemed slight to you, you doubled my languor with weeping. Now I wish to tell you clearly, remove one martyrdom, for I cannot die two deaths.

Since the moisture which comes from my eyes protects me from the burning, and the flame keeps the great weeping from dissolving my heart by drying and kindling it.

. . . Your infinite desire heals its wound, whence I remain in dolorous life.

Bruno adds to the image of the mutually negating causes of death the metaphorical meaning whereby the eyes signify the lover's intellect and the heart, his will. The idea of infinity, men-

---

[16] A desire "Veder in polve questa carne ardita" (To see this audacious flesh in dust).

tioned casually by Bembo, is specifically attributed to these internal antagonists.

The eight sonnets of Bruno proceed as follows:

1. The heart attributes to the eyes the great fire with which it burns.

2. The eyes in turn charge the heart with causing them to become eternal rivers of tears.

3. The heart replies to the eyes: How can my immortal flame be the cause of your tears? Why rather do I not cook you? Do you believe that by resisting one contrary, the other acquires force?

4. The eyes reply to the proposition of the heart in the first sonnet: Your passion confuses you. We contain the seed of the seas; all Neptune could be recovered from us.

5. The heart asks, Where is this flood of yours that does not appear to the senses?

6. The eyes ask, How is it that you do not go up in flame to the sun? Not even a spark is seen to issue from your chest.

7. The heart replies, Foolish is he who looks only to sense instead of to reason: my fire cannot fly upward, and the infinite conflagration is not seen, because the eyes have placed the sea over it, and one infinite does not exceed the other. How, eyes, can we escape this evil fate and discover ourselves to the beautiful god [*bel nume*] that he may take pity?

8. The eyes reply to the heart's question, Alas, the infinite vigor of the fiery heart denies an exit to the watery element. Afflicted heart, who can cry our unhappy love, if the greater our hurt [*male*], the less its power to appear?

When Bruno, in commenting on the first of these sonnets, says, *Per ministerio de gli occhi, vien infiammato il core* (*Eroici furori*, II, iii, 476: Through the action of the eyes the heart is set aflame), he is following the psychology of Provençal and Tuscan lyric poetry, according to which love enters the heart through the eyes. Consistently he adopts the language of "vulgar love" to describe the heroic passion. In his sonnets, however, that idiom becomes metaphorical: sight is knowledge, the desirous heart is will. The tearful eyes symbolize the difficulty experienced by the lover because of his separation from his object (II, iii, 484).

The lover's object has made him a "rebel to his own soul" (II, iii, 476). Will and intellect are infinite potencies checking each other from act. Two finite forces could not cancel each other indefinitely, for there is no exact equality in natural things (II, iii, 482).

The intention of the sonnets is paradoxical in relation to their content. In their *tenzone* the heart and the eyes lament their mutual negation. Yet the net effect intended by Bruno, as evidenced by his statements both in the Argument[17] and in the prose commentary upon the sonnets, is positive:

Gli occhi apprendono le specie e le proponeno al core, il core le brama ed il suo bramare presenta a gli occhi: quelli concepeno la luce, la diffondeno ed accendeno il fuoco in questo; questo, scaldato ed acceso, invia il suo amore a quelli, perchè lo digeriscano (II, iii, 484).

The eyes apprehend the species and propose them to the heart, the heart covets them and presents its desire to the eyes. The latter receive the light, diffuse it, and kindle the fire in the heart, which warmed and burning sends its love to the eyes so that they may assimilate it.

When the heroic lover reaches the point at which he can no longer comprehend "divine orders and counsels," he forces himself onward by an act of sheer will (I, iii, 361). Beyond the ken of conceptual thought there lies the infinite and unfathomable cause of all being. The proper object of his speculation is the infinite but knowable God-permeated universe, as Bruno reveals in the last dialogue. However, the door is always left open to an even higher intuitive knowledge which possibly can be realized by a suprarational effort of the will. Ultimately, Bruno is a voluntarist. This intuitive or suprarational knowledge is quite similar to that described by Leone Ebreo in the *Dialoghi d'amore,* where the "pure divine intellect" can show the ideal essences to a meritorious and well-trained reason in "unique and abstract cognition."

Volition and intellection are infinite, as is their object; hence they cannot end in a state of rest. The object does not satiate or bore the philosopher, who by infinite study always has it and always seeks it. Heroic happiness is an activity; its end is "motion and apprehension," not quiet and comprehension (II, iii, 484). Were not the

[17] See p. 197 of this book for quotation from *Eroici furori*, Argument, p. 321.

highest good and the affective impulse toward it infinite, the result could be less than good: for too much food can be poison (II, iii, 483). The divine lover is never satiated without appetite, nor yet has he appetite without being in some way satiated (II, iii, 484). Such felicity begins in this life (II, iii, 483).

The infinite or unlimited action of the intellect and the will is determined by the infinity of their object. Neither faculty can be satisfied by a finite entity, because their object is infinity itself. The highest good, which is infinite, communicates itself infinitely to things according to the receptive capacity of each. No finite good can satisfy the will; beyond any such entity it will desire and seek a higher species. The maximum of an inferior species is the minimum of the superior species and, although the forms are not infinite, their modes receive in infinite variety the being communicated by the infinite good.

. . . Perchè essendo infinito l'oggetto de la mente, ed a l'intelletto non essendo definito oggetto proposto, non può essere la volontade appagata de finito bene; ma se oltre a quello si ritrova altro, il brama, il cerca, perchè (come è detto commune) il summo della specie inferiore è infimo e principio della specie superiore, o si prendano gli gradi secondo le forme le quali non possiamo stimar che siano infinite, o secondo gli modi e raggioni di quelle, nella qual maniera, per essere infinito il sommo bene, infinitamente credemo che si comunica secondo la condizione delle cose alle quali si diffonde. Però non è specie definita a l'universo (parlo secondo la figura e mole), non è specie definita a l'intelletto, non è definita la specie de l'affetto (II, iii, 482).

. . . For as the object of the mind is infinite, and no finite object is proposed to the intellect, the will cannot be satisfied by a finite good; but if beyond such a good it finds another, it desires it and seeks it, because (as is common knowledge) the highest of the inferior species is the lowest and the beginning of the superior species, whether the ranks be taken according to the forms, which we cannot judge to be infinite, or according to the modes and reasons of the forms, in which case, since the highest good is infinite, we believe that it communicates itself infinitely according to the condition of the things to which it diffuses itself. Therefore there is no finite species for the universe (I speak of its figure and mass), no finite species for the intellect, and there is no finite species for the affection.

Bruno's reasoning about the infinity of intellect and will is identical with that of Ficino:

Voluntas solius infiniti boni possessione potest impleri. . . . Quia vero vis quaeque eo solo contenta esse potest in quo integra obiecti sui ratio reperitur, sequitar ut intellectus et voluntas solo Deo satiari possint, in quo solo est integra veritatis bonitatisque ratio. Et quia ille ab aliis veris semper discurrit ad alia, haec ab aliis bonis fertur in alia, satis constat quietem his ex eo solo obtingere posse quod talia cuncta complectitur (Ficino, *Opera omnia*, p. 236).

The will can be satisfied only by the possession of the infinite good. . . . Indeed, since each faculty can be contented only by that in which the whole nature of its object is found, it follows that both the intellect and the will can be satisfied only by God, in whom alone is the whole nature of truth and goodness. And since the intellect always runs from one truth to another, and the will is led from one good to another, it is quite clear that these faculties can attain the state of rest only through that which embraces all such truths and goods.

According to both writers, the philosopher proceeds from one object of knowledge and volition to another in a restless progression. The satisfaction found in each successive object is greater or less according to the object's rank in the hierarchy of being, but it is never complete. The ultimate object in every particular cognition or affection is the infinite, or God, in whom only the infinite movement of the mind can find its consummation.

Bruno, in the passage quoted above, deduces the infinity of intellect and will from the infinity of the *sommo bene* infinitely communicated to things according to their "modes and reasons." The near-identity of Bruno's speculation with that of Ficino is pointed up by the similarity of wording:

[Potest] bonitas rebus innumerabilibus per infinitos modos communicari. Si voluntas eousque affectat bonum quousque intellectus offert, hic autem offert infinitum bonum et infinita bona, sequitur ut totidem voluntas affectet (*ibid.*).

Goodness [can be] communicated to innumerable things in infinite ways. If the will desires the good to the extent that the latter offers infinite good and infinite goods, it follows that the will desires the same.

Actually, there is no end to Bruno's intellectual love: for the infinite, if it could be comprehended, would not be infinite. The *quies* mentioned by Ficino (*ibid.*) is denied by Bruno. "Indi hanno la sazietà come in moto ed apprensione, non come in quiete e com-

prensione . . ." (*Eroici furori*, II, iii, 484: Thereby they are satisfied as in motion and apprehension, not as in quiet and comprehension . . .). The intellect's understanding of the infinite is
discursive; it is in the nature of potency and aptitude, lacking the
perfection of act. The infinite, precisely because it is infinite, must
be infinitely pursued.

. . . Non è cosa naturale nè conveniente che l'infinito sia compreso,
nè esso può donarsi finito, perciochè non sarrebe infinito; ma è conveniente e naturale che l'infinito, per essere infinito, sia infinitamente perseguitato, in quel modo di persecuzione il quale non ha raggion di moto fisico, ma di certo moto metafisico; ed il quale non è da
imperfetto al perfetto, ma va circuendo per gli gradi della perfezione,
per giongere a quel centro infinito, il quale non è formato nè forma (I,
iv, 380).

. . . It is neither natural nor fitting for the infinite to be comprehended, nor can it be taken as finite, since then it would not be
infinite. But it is fitting and natural for the infinite, since it is infinite,
to be infinitely pursued in that manner of pursuit which is not
physical motion, but a sort of metaphysical motion; and which is not
from imperfect to perfect, but which goes circling through the degrees
of perfection to reach that infinite center, which is neither formed nor
form.

Bruno's description of "metaphysical motion" is another way of
saying that the intellective process is without end: circular movement is the image of perpetuity. Infinite pursuit implies that the
center of the circle cannot be reached; in that case the intellect continues circling through the degrees of perfection. Metaphysical
motion is said to be not from imperfect to perfect, but through the
degrees of perfection, because to every being the highest good imparts its goodness to the extent of the recipient's capacity.[18]

The end of metaphysical endeavor is intellectual felicity, a kind
of qualitative immortality in which the soul "drinks from the foun-

[18] Bertrando Spaventa, in "La dottrina della conoscenza di Giordano Bruno," in
Saggi di critica, pp. 252–55, offers a different interpretation of this passage. He
sees in Bruno's metaphysical motion, "circuendo per li gradi della perfezione"
(circling through the degrees of perfection), the return of the spirit into itself;
hence the procedure, not from finite to finite or finite to infinite, but from
infinite to infinite. The eternal rhythm or process of the spirit is from itself,
through itself, to itself.

tain of eternal life." The beautiful and the good are not understood exhaustively, but only to the extent of the individual soul's capacity, which becomes ever more inebriated by the nectar of which it drinks.

In questo dunque che l'intelletto concepe la luce, il bene, il bello, per quanto s'estende l'orizonte della sua capacità, e l'anima che beve del nettare divino e de la fonte de vita eterna, per quanto comporta il vase proprio; si vede che la luce è oltre la circuferenza del suo orizonte, dove può andar sempre più e più penetrando; ed il nettare e fonte d'acqua viva è infinitamente fecondo, onde possa sempre oltre ed oltre inebriarsi (II, iii, 482–83).

Since the intellect conceives the light, the good, the beautiful, as far as the horizon of its capacity extends, and the soul drinks of the divine nectar of the fount of eternal life as much as its vessel permits, it is clear that the light is beyond the circumference of the soul's horizon, which it can always penetrate farther and farther; and the nectar and fount of living water are infinitely fecund, so that the soul can always become more and more inebriated.

Bruno being in agreement with Leone Ebreo[19] that God is understood by each individual according to his capacity, it is difficult to see why he felt it necessary to say with Ficino that the intellect infinitely pursues the divinity. His concept of two modes of infinity, though phrased in paradoxical terms, clarifies his position. The intellect is infinite in its potency; its object is unqualifiedly infinite. The human intellect, although of finite nature and act, is said to have infinite potency because it is eternal; there is no limit to its happiness. Its only real infinity is that of its object; in itself the intellect is finite. The potency of the intellect is "finitely infinite"; its object is "infinitely infinite" (I, v, 421).

The *Eroici furori* describes the process by which the heroic lover, or philosopher, comes to know his exalted object. The end—happiness—which the subject of this love seeks is found in his satisfaction by his object.

[19] Leone Ebreo, *Dialoghi d'amore*, p. 234. "[In Dio, amore] dice volontà di bonificar le sue creature e tutto l'universo, e di crescere la lor perfezione quanto la lor natura sarà capace . . ." ([In God, love] means the will to make his creatures and all the universe good and to increase their perfection as far as their nature is capable . . .").

L'oggetto contenta il suggetto, che non si pasce d'altro, altro non cerca, non s'occupa in altro e per quello bandisce ogni altro pensiero (I, i, 342).

The object satisfies the subject, who wants no other nourishment, seeks nothing else, does not busy himself with anything else, and for that object bans every other thought.

The figure of Acteon is adapted from Greek myth to illustrate the philosophic quest of the heroic lover. Upon seeing the resplendent beauty of the nude Diana, he is changed into a deer. The meaning of this myth is that when the lover beholds and receives the divine beauty and goodness of his object—the hunter's prey— he is transformed into his beloved.

The *furori eroici* are so called because both their subject and their object are heroical ("Argument," p. 314). The subject, in a general sense, is the lover who aspires to the knowledge of divine beauty and goodness, hence a Platonic lover. Specifically, however, there is no doubt but that he is Giordano Bruno. From the first sonnet there are autobiographical references to Bruno's tribulations and aspirations.[20] The various interlocutors of the dialogues refer interchangeably now to the *furioso* of the sonnets, now to "the Nolan," their author. Finally, in the fourth and fifth dialogues of the second part, the subject is pluralized into nine blind men, the blindness of each representing a different cause of the difficulty of knowing the object. Again the autobiographical allusions of the final dialogue, more numerous than in the previous dialogues, identify the subject as "the Nolan."

The nine kinds of blindness, representing so many examples of the disproportion between the subject of heroic love and its object, are as follows:

1. Native blindness.

[20] E.g., *Eroici furori*, II, i, 452–53. ". . . Il presente furioso mostra aver durato sei lustri, nel discorso de quali non era venuto a quella purità di concetto, che potesse farsi capace abitazione delle specie peregrine, che offrendosi a tutte ugualmente batteno sempre alla porta de l'intelligenza" (. . . The present *furioso* shows that he spent thirty years in the course of which he had not attained that purity of concept that would have made him a fit habitation of the alien species, which offering themselves equally to all always knock at the door of the intelligence).

2. Jealousy—in the lover of "truth and beauty," anger toward "those who wish to adulterate, devastate, and corrupt it."

3. The sudden appearance of the object in its blinding light.

4. Excessive looking at the light, which renders the subject blind to lesser lights—contemplation of the unity which "steals" the subject from the multitude.

5. Ceaseless tears, signifying the disproportionateness of the means available to the subject.

6. Dryness of the eyes, likewise from tears, symbolizing "the lack of real intellectual nourishment." How can man, whose body is subject to the alteration or "otherness" of motion, know that which is "immobility, substance, entity, and truth"?

7. Consumption of the eyes by flame from the heart—the outstripping of the intellect by the will; also its hindrance by sectarianism.

8. Piercing by a burning arrow. The act of union with the object or its species "defeats, alters, and corrupts the power of apprehension, which is suppressed by the weight and falls under the impetus of that presence."

9. Dejection of spirit. The ninth blind man from fear of offending the object of his love has suppressed not only his sight, but also the faculty of speech. His muteness and blindness signify "the occult divine judgment which has given to men this study and thought of investigating, in such manner that he can never arrive higher than the cognition of his own blindness and ignorance." Hence "the negative theology of Pythagoras and Dionysius is celebrated above the demonstrative theology of Aristotle and the scholastic doctors." [21]

The myth of the nine blind men is inspired by Marco Antonio Epicuro's *Dialogo di tre ciechi,* or *Cecaria.* Bruno's borrowings from that work are studied in detail by Spampanato in *Bruno e Nola,* and the most salient of them are noted by Gentile in his edition of Bruno's dialogues.

There is no systematic ethics in the *Eroici furori.* There are,

[21] The nine blind men are described in *Eroici furori,* II, iv, 486–98, and interpreted in pp. 498–506 and in the Argument, p. 322.

however, specific and implied ethical ideas in the dialogue, which are much more closely related to the ethical tone of the Platonic love treatises of other authors than to Bruno's other writings. The "heroic" ethic of the *Eroici furori* is one of purification of the soul in order to enable the lover to become worthy of his object and—more important—capable of understanding it. Bruno's theories of cognition are therefore inseparable from his moral philosophy.

This ethical conception is devoid of social content. Bruno expresses nothing but contempt for the *volgo* or multitude, from which the heroical lover will withdraw intellectually if not physically. Indeed, a psychological counterpart—or component—of Bruno's heroic love is his fierce antipathy toward those things and persons which he finds vulgar, earthbound, pretentious, unimaginative.

Certo, nessuno ama veramente il vero e buono che non sia iracondo contra la moltitudine . . . (II, iv, 499).

Certainly, no one truly loves the true and good who is not angry toward the multitude . . .

Perchè la mente aspira al splendor divino, fugge il consorzio de la turba, si ritira dalla commune opinione (II, i, 441).

Because the mind aspires to divine splendor, it flees the company of the crowd and withdraws from common opinion.

For the common herd the established religion not only suffices, but is necessary to restrain it from vice and crime by the fear of hell.

. . . La moltitudine . . . se a gran pena può essere refrenata da vizii e spronata ad atti virtuosi per la fede de pene sempiterne, che sarebbe se la si persuadesse qualche più leggiera condizione in premiar gli eroici ed umani gesti, e castigare gli delitti e sceleragini? ("Argument," p. 324).

If . . . the multitude . . . can with great difficulty be restrained from vices and spurred to virtuous acts by the belief in eternal punishment, what would happen if it should be convinced of some lighter condition in rewarding heroic and human deeds and in punishing crimes and wickedness?

Bruno therefore has no quarrel with theologians and statesmen (*ibid.*). The philosophy of "natural reason" is to be reserved for the "few, good and wise" (*ibid.*).

The kernel of the ascensive process is precisely the transformation of the lover. The strong ethical import of heroic love is evident from Bruno's best definition of the concept:

> Questi furori de quali noi raggioniamo . . . son . . . amori e brame del bello e buono con cui si procure farsi perfetto con transformarsi ed assomigliarsi a quello (I, iii, 360).

These passions which we are discussing . . . are . . . loves and desires of the beautiful and good by which one tries to become perfect through transforming himself to resemble it.

The aspirational enthusiasm of such a love and the personal concept of ethics which it carries are nowhere better expressed than in the book's opening sonnet:

> Muse, che tante volte ributtai,
> Importune correte a' miei dolori,
> Per consolarmi sole ne' miei guai
> Con tai versi, tai rime e tai furori,
> Con quali ad altri vi mostraste mai,
> Che de mirti si vantan ed allori;
> Or sia appo voi mia aura, àncora e porto,
> Se non mi lice altrov' ir a diporto.
> O monte, o dive, o fonte,
> Ov' abito, converso e mi nodrisco;
> Dove quieto imparo ed imbellisco;
> Alzo, avvivo, orno il cor, il spirto e fronte,
> Morte, cipressi, inferni
> Cangiate in vita, in lauri, in astri eterni.
>
> (I, i, 332–33)

Muses whom I so often rejected, you run unseasonably to my sorrows, alone, to console me in my grief with such verses, such rimes, and such passions

As you never showed others who boast of myrtle and laurel. Now may my breeze, anchor, and harbor be with you if I am not permitted to go elsewhere for recreation.

O mount, O goddesses, O fountain where I live, commune, and find nourishment, where I quietly learn and gain beauty,

I raise, quicken, and adorn my heart, spirit, and brow; change death, cypresses, and hell into life, into laurels, into eternal stars.

The two concluding lines of this sonnet are a prayer that he may be *immortale, . . . poeta, . . . illustre* (I, i, 338).

Love is primarily a rational search for the divinity; but this search cannot succeed without a moral transformation of the searcher, which ends in his own transformation into a god. The purification of the soul is indispensable to the knowledge of the *Deus in rebus* which the philosopher seeks, for, without a purgation of the inactive and vegetative tendencies in one's disposition, the higher levels of intellectual life will forever remain beyond reach. Realizing the finiteness of his bodily existence, the philosopher will naturally deny his selfish desires and pleasures in order to be united with the infinite. This quest necessarily entails a kind of ascetic exaltation. The ascent of the ladder of Diotima is a progressive abandonment of the senses for an intellectual life that cares nothing for the pains and pleasures of the world and the derisive attitude of the ignorant crowd who will call it madness. The morality of the *Eroici furori,* in contrast to that of the *Spaccio della Bestia Trionfante,* is at least as ascetic as that of any of the *trattati d'amore* which we have examined. Divine love has almost lost its sensual base.

Sensual love is not in itself base or evil; but the failure to see beauty imaginatively in the light of its ascendant possibilities and the soul's deepest wants is a contradiction of man's real nature, of his inherent celestial origin. Man by his very essence is rational. Carnal love is a turning away from man's proper good, a denial of his higher nature, a fatal reversion to animality ordained by our *madrigna natura* ("Argument," p. 311: stepmother nature).

Exalted knowledge necessarily comports moral betterment. As Plato said in the *Phaedrus,* and as Platonists generally maintained, moral purification is a prerequisite of higher knowledge. All through the *Eroici furori* there pulses the driving desire of man to raise himself, to be better than he commonly is, to realize the noble potentialities within him. The goal of the heroic lover is intellectual; but the natural result of its attainment is an ethical response which harmonizes the philosopher's thoughts and actions with the "symmetry" of divine law. This idea Bruno expresses in a beautiful prose passage in the third dialogue of Part I:

> Ma [il furore eroico] è un calor acceso dal sole intelligenziale ne l'anima e impeto divino che gl'impronta l'ali; onde più e più avvicinandosi al sole intelligenziale, rigettando la ruggine de le umane cure, dovien un oro probato e puro, ha sentimento della divina ed interna armonia, concorda gli suoi pensieri e gesti con la simmetria della legge insita in tutte le cose (I, iii, 361).

> But [the heroic passion] is a heat kindled in the soul by the intelligential sun; a divine impulse which readies the wings of the soul. Whence approaching ever nearer to the intelligential sun, casting off the rust of human cares, the soul becomes a proven and pure gold, experiences divine and internal harmony, attunes its thoughts and deeds to the symmetry of law innate in all things.

The ethic of the *Eroici furori*, negatively, is detachment from all secondary goods; positively, it is the intellectual and emotional intensification of one's relation to the infinite. Man is held back in this "generous undertaking" by the "affections of the senses" (I, iv, 381). Again and again (II, i, 441–42) Bruno tells us that he who would know God must withdraw from the multitude and search within himself. Borrowing a figure from lyricists and essayists of "vulgar love," he says that the heroic lover's soul will leave his body to effect his unity with the divine principle, the body remaining in such a condition that it feels neither the love nor hate, neither the pain nor pleasure, of mortal things. With all the Platonizing humanists and philosophers who preceded him in Italy, he calls the body a prison which would deprive the soul of its liberty (II, i, 443).

The ethic of purification is an immediate consequence of the soul's awakening to its higher destiny. Love furnishes the motive power for the philosopher's conversion to God. In the ascent of the ladder of Diotima, the soul rises through successively higher degrees of understanding and love. Reason is strengthened by the intellect against the downward pull of sense. Negatively, the lover advances by denying the inferior or sensual desires of his soul; positively, by applying himself to the *specie superiori* and turning all his will and affection toward God (I, v, 402–3).

The coincidence of ethics and epistemology in the *Eroici furori* is nowhere better illustrated than by the three methods of "conversion" of the soul to God which Bruno borrows from Ficino:

> Con tre preparazioni che nota il contemplativo Plotino nel libro *Della bellezza intelligibile;* de le quali la prima è proporsi de conformarsi d'una similitudine divina, divertendo la vista da cose che sono infra la propria perfezione, e commune alle specie uguali ed inferiori; secondo è l'applicarsi con tutta l'intenzione ed attenzione alle specie superiori; terzo il cattivar tutta la voluntade ed affetto a Dio (I, v, 402–3).

> By three preparations which the contemplative Plotinus notes in his book *On intelligible beauty.* First, to try to conform to a divine likeness, diverting the eye from things which are beneath one's own perfection or common to equal and inferior species; second, to apply all one's intention and attention to the superior species; and third, to submit all one's will and affection to God.

As Tocco and Gentile pointed out, the passage which Bruno had in mind was Ficino's commentary on Plotinus' book (*Ennead* V, 8, 11), which reads as follows:

> Deo fruiturus debet per communem Dei notionem atque fidem se ipsum in primis divina quadam similitudine conformare deinde tota ad deum cogitationis intentione contendere: tertio tota deum solum voluntate ardenter amare.

> God is to be enjoyed by the combined knowledge of and faith in God; first by conforming to a certain divine likeness, then by striving toward God with total intention of thought, and thirdly, by loving ardently God only with all one's will.

Love does not work its conversion of the philosopher's soul without producing externally visible effects, principally those which Dino del Garbo emphasized in his learned commentary on Cavalcanti's ode, which reappeared in Ficino's commentary on the *Symposium,* and which were given copious lyrical expression in the sonnets of Petrarch and his followers. The lover is a soul in torment, torn by the inner conflict between his desires and the possibilities of realizing them, which manifests itself in the physical symptoms of alterations of color, temperature, and tears with laughter, reflecting the emotional alterations of hope and despair, determination and vacillation, exaltation and humility. It is these very effects which Bruno in the preface to the *Eroici furori* ridicules as manifestations of folly. He can unblushingly describe the same effects in the lover of his sonnets because the intellectual passion of which he writes is called "love" by a kind of metaphor. The language of love and that of knowledge traditionally are intermingled: one speaks of carnal knowledge and of ideal and intellectual love.

The inner conflict in Cavalcanti's lover derived from the contradiction between the fantasy of feminine beauty cherished by his intellect and the reality of the sensual passion aroused in him by a real woman. In Petrarch's love there was the unresolved conflict between sensual love of Laura and religious love of God, as well as the conventional conflicts or alternations of hope of affection and fear of losing it, pleasure in his lady's presence and pain in her absence, joy in her signs of favor, remorse following her expressions of disapproval.

The tragedy of love, inevitable according to Cavalcanti's *Canzone,* is potentially present in the concept of heroic love. From the *doi appolsi* (*Eroici furori,* I, iii, 371: two impulses) of the soul arises the terrible inner conflict in the lover which is the dominating motive in many of Bruno's sonnets. It is only the intervention of the heroic, if not superhuman, will that saves man from the vulgarizing pull of the senses which would carry him to oblivion. The author of the *Eroici furori,* however, is according to his own conception himself a heroic lover, fired with unrestrainable enthusiasm for his object. Hence the moral tone of the dialogue is one of optimism, in contrast to that of Cavalcanti's ode.

The effects of love alleged by poets, medical commentators, and essayists on love alike in their descriptions of the sensual lover are continually attributed by Bruno to the heroic lover, occasionally with philosophical interpretations. The lover is elevated by intellectual desire, downcast toward hell by its sensual opposite (I, ii, 354). As in Leone Ebreo's "honest" love, in the heroic passion ardent and insatiable desire is laudable. The lover is sustained by hope of future reward, but presently suffers persistent torment. Although he sees his folly, he delights in it and cannot be happy without it (I, ii, 355)—a condition which Bruno contrasts with "brutal" love, which enjoys the present (I, ii, 350). Jealousy, as most of the *trattatisti* proclaimed, is the inseparable accompaniment of love. Bruno defines it, in relation to heroical love, as "a zeal of the lover for the beloved thing," which can be understood only by him who has experienced it (I, i, 341). Jealousy, as the treatise writers agree, is "the daughter of love from which it derives, companion of the latter with which it always goes together," love's sign and necessary consequence. Yet it poisons all that is beautiful and good in love (I, i, 342), and frequently kills love outright by engendering scorn (I, i, 343).

Here are other adaptations to heroic love of sentences upon the effects of "human" love by the treatise-writers whom we have examined:

. . . Ogni amante, ch'è disunito e separato da la cosa amata . . . si trova in cordoglio e pena, si crucia e si tormenta: . . . perchè è privo di quella fruizione la quale otterrebbe se fusse gionto a quel termine al qual tende. Non dole per il desio che l'avviva, ma per la difficultà del studio ch'il martora (I, iii, 366).

. . . Every lover who is disunited or separated from the object of his love . . . is in anguish and pain, and racks and torments himself . . . because he is deprived of that enjoyment which he would obtain if he had arrived at that end to which he tends. He does not suffer from the desire which quickens him but from the difficulty of the endeavor which torments him.

È certo, che chi è avezzo nella gioventù d'amar circonspettamente, amarà vecchio senza straviare (I, i, 343-44).

It is certain that he who is accustomed in his youth to loving circumspectly will love as an old man without getting out of bounds.

Love in the heroic soul encourages the emulation of virtues and greatness because of the desire to please and become worthy of the beloved thing (I, i, 343).

It is not love that is blind, but the subject of love: similarly, nocturnal birds are blinded by the presence of the sun (*ibid.*, I, i, 344).[22]

The lover languishes and suffers and refrains from declaring the full extent of his desires, lest he offend his beloved. Only the hope

[22] Romei adopts the same simile from the apocryphal Book II of Aristotle's *Metaphysics.*

of future reward enables him to endure his present martyrdom.
This timidity is the subject of the pastoral dialogue in sonnet form
which is found in the second dialogue of the first part of the *Eroici
furori*. Its sense is given by the following excerpts:

> Pastore . . . Amor . . . Fere . . . Con gli occhi . . .
> . . . Spero . . . Mercè . . . Da chi sì mi martora nott'e dì.
> Filenio . . . Sei folle . . . Vaneggi . . .
> Pastore . . . Temo il suo sdegno, più che miei tormenti (I, ii, 354–
> 55).

> Shepherd . . . Love . . . wounds . . . with its eyes . . .
> . . . I hope . . . to be rewarded . . . by the one who
> torments me so night and day.
> Filenio . . . You are mad . . . you rave . . .
> Shepherd . . . I fear disdain more than my torments.

Ficino spoke of the fear of rejection in connection with the intermediate, conversational love; other *trattatisti* seconded the idea
when they wrote of "human love." The translation of this effect
from the sphere of human love to that of divine love is quite explicit in Bruno. The pastoral dialogue is interpreted as a metaphor
of heroic love:

> Sarebbe dunque un vituperio grande ad un animo generoso, se d'un
> sporco, vile, bardo ed ignobile ingegno (quantunque sotto eccellente
> figura venesse ricuoperto) dica: *Temo il suo sdegno più ch'il mio tor-
> mento* (I, ii, 358).

It would be a great shame for a generous soul to say of a dirty, vile,
stupid, and ignoble mind (however excellent the body which housed
it), "I fear its disdain more than my torment."

Analysts of the medical aspect of love, whether Platonic commentators on the *Symposium* or Aristotelian commentators on
Cavalcanti's *Canzone*, described love as a sickness of which the
symptoms were melancholy, loss of appetite and vigor, insomnia,
infected blood, alternate depression and exaltation, and restlessness.
Bruno again in this field translates effects traditionally predicated
of vulgar love to his heroic lover.

> . . . Il spirito affetto di tal furore viene da profondi pensieri distratto,
> martellato da cure urgenti, scaldato da ferventi desii, insoffiato da spesse
> occasioni. Onde trovandosi l'anima suspesa, necessariamente viene ad
> essere men diligente ed operosa al governo del corpo per gli atti della

potenza vegetativa. Quindi il corpo è macilento, mal nodrito, estenuato, ha difetto de sangue, copia di malancolici [sic] umori, li quali se non saranno instrumenti de l'anima disciplinata o pure d'un spirito chiaro e lucido, menano ad insania, stoltizia e furor brutale; o al meno a certa poca cura di sè e dispreggio de l'esser proprio, il qual vien significato da Platone per gli piedi discalzi (I, v, 416).[23]

. . . The spirit affected by such passion is distracted by deep thoughts, hammered by urgent cares, heated by fervent desires, importuned by many circumstances. The soul being suspended, it necessarily becomes less diligent and active in governing the body and the acts of the vegetative power. Consequently the body is lean, undernourished, and weak, has poor blood, and is full of melancholy humors, which, if they do not become instruments of a disciplined soul or a clear and lucid spirit, lead to insanity, stupidity, and bestial passion, or at least to a certain self-neglect or scorn of one's own being, which Plato signifies by Love's bare feet.

The most severe of love's effects described by Guinizelli and Cavalcanti in verse and by Cavalcanti's commentators in prose is the metaphorical "death" wherein the lover achieves a state of suspended animation with regard to the everyday concerns of life. This concept, too, finds its counterpart in the heroic lover's *raptus* or ecstasy which Bruno takes over from other Platonists.

Qua se per virtù di contemplazione ascende o è rapita sopra l'orizonte de gli affetti naturali, onde con più puro occhio apprenda la differenza de l'una e l'altra vita, allora vinta da gli alti pensieri, come morta al corpo, aspira ad alto; e benchè viva nel corpo, vi vegeta come morta, e vi è presente in atto de animazione, ed absente in atto d'operazioni . . . (I, iv, 389–90).

If by virtue of contemplation the soul rises or is transported above the horizon of the natural affections so that with purer eye it sees the difference between one life and the other, then vanquished by high thoughts, as though dead in the body, it aspires to higher things; and though it may live in the body, it is present there in the act of animation and absent in the act of operations. . . .

The possibility of such a state of "death," here caused not by the passion for a lady, as in *stilnuovo* poets, but by heroic passion for divine knowledge, as in Marsilio Ficino and Leone Ebreo, is inherent in the relation of body to soul: the body is as though dead

[23] Cf. Plato, *Symposium*, 203 c-d.

to the soul, its source of life and perfection, and the soul is as though dead to the superior intelligence which illuminates the intellect (II, iii, 484).

The origin of the lover's travail and internal dissension is in the very nature of his soul. One entity, it is subject to the contrary attractions of sense and intelligibility, of eternity and temporality, of corporeity and spirituality. As Ficino and Pico said, the soul is located on the horizon of the corporeal world and the spiritual world; like the sun's ray, it touches both the earth and its parent star (I, iv, 388).[24] In this concept as well as in other considerations about the soul Bruno largely follows the Florentine *alter Plato*. In describing the two knots which bind the soul to the body he paraphrases Ficino's commentary on Plotinus' *Enneads,* as Gentile points out (I, iii, 370, note 2). He identifies his source as "the Platonists"; in the *Eroici furori* he comes no closer to explicit citation of Ficino or any other Renaissance Platonist.

Dicono gli platonici due sorte de nodi con gli quali l'anima è legata al corpo. L'uno è certo atto vivifico che da l'anima come un raggio scende nel corpo; l'altro è certa qualità vitale che da quell'atto risulta nel corpo (I, iii, 370).

The Platonists posit two kinds of knots by which the soul is bound to the body. One is a certain vivifying act which descends like a ray from the soul into the body; the other is a certain vital quality which results from that act in the body.

Ficino's commentary on Plotinus (*Ennead* IV, 4, 19) reads as follows:

Duobus quasi nodis anima cum corpo devincitur: unus quidem vergit ad animam, id est vivificus eius actus emicans erga corpus: alter vero declinat ad corpus, id est qualitas ipsa quasi vitalis per hunc actum infusa corpori.

The soul is bound to the body as though by two knots: one indeed is directed toward the soul, that is, its vivifying act springing toward the body; the other, however, declines to the body—the vital quality itself, as it were, instilled in the body by that act.

Sicut ex sole micat lumen, . . . sic ab anima nostra emicat vivificus actus (Commentary on *Ennead* IV, 4, 18).

[24] Cf. Ficino, *Opera omnia*, I, 657–58 and 119.

As light shines from the sun, . . . so from our soul springs the vivifying act.

An important characteristic of the soul is its mobility. Bruno
calls it a "most noble moving number" (*Eroici furori*, I, iii, 370–
71). From its central position as the least entity in the scale of
spiritual things it naturally descends into the body and rises again
into the divine hierarchy. There are three kinds of souls or intelligences:

. . . Son tre gradi d'intelligenze: perchè son altre nelle quali l'intellettuale supera l'animale, quali dicono essere l'intelligenze celesti;
altre nelle quali l'animale supera l'intellettuale, quali son l'intelligenze
umane; altre sono nelle quali l'uno e l'altro si portano ugualmente, come
quelle de demoni o eroi (I, iv, 388).

. . . There are three degrees of intelligences, because there are some
in which the intellectual surpasses the animal, which are called celestial
intelligences; others in which the animal surpasses the intellectual,
which are human intelligences; and others in which both are equal,
as in demons or heroes.

Bruno here gives us a specific reason why his lover is called
"heroic": only in demons or heroes does force of intellect equal the
animal drive.

Of the soul's two inherent tendencies the mundane proclivity
here seems at least as strong as the spiritual, perhaps stronger.
There is no theological reference to original sin; the soul is subject
to an inherent duality. The ascensive tendency in Brunian love is
not Dante's natural and serene elevation of the redeemed soul, but
a dynamic impetus resulting from heroic effort. Nevertheless, the
origin of the soul in Bruno's doctrine is the divinity, working
through the world soul. Hence man's soul experiences a feeling
of ill-being and restlessness in its vestment of flesh, which causes
it to cry out,

Lasciami vita corporale, e non m'impacciar ch'io rimonti al mio più
natio albergo, al mio sole . . . (I, iv, 390).

Leave me, bodily life, and do not keep me from remounting to my
more native abode, to my sun. . . .

Only the spiritual potency works for the good of the soul. In the last analysis the soul's origin determines its natural home, in relation to which the world man lives in is an "enemy country."

Essendo dunque che nella essenza unica de l'anima se ritrovano questi doi geni de potenze, secondo che è ordinata ed al proprio e l'altrui bene, accade che si depinga con un paio d'ali, mediante le quali è potente verso l'oggetto delle prime ed immateriali potenze; e con un greve sasso, per cui è atta ed efficace verso gli oggetti delle seconde e materiali potenze. Là onde procede che l'affetto intiero del furioso sia ancipite, diviso, travaglioso e messo in facilità de inchinare più al basso, che di forzarsi ad alto: atteso che l'anima si trova nel paese basso e nemico, ed ottiene la ragione lontana dal suo albergo più naturale, dove le sue forze son più sceme (II, i, 450).[25]

There being in the one essence of the soul these two kinds of potencies, selfish and altruistic, it happens that it is painted with a pair of wings by which it is potent [i.e., can fly] toward the object of the first and immaterial powers; and with a heavy stone by which it is apt and efficacious [i.e., can fall] toward the objects of the second, material powers. Hence the whole affection of the *furioso* is split, divided, troubled, and more easily inclined downward than impelled upward, since the soul finds itself in low, enemy country and holds the reason far from its more natural abode, where its powers are diminished.

. . . L'anima fa gli doi progressi d'ascenso e descenso, per la cura ch'ha di sè e de la materia; per quel ch'è mossa dal proprio appetito del bene, e per quel ch'è spinta da la providenza del fato (I, iv, 390. Cf. I, iii, 371).

. . . The soul follows two paths, of ascent and descent, according to the care that it has for itself and for matter: the one which is motivated by its own desire of the good and the other along which it is driven by the providence of fate.

The reader who is surprised to find "the providence of fate" in opposition to the "appetite for the good" may identify the former with the "occult" inclination of the soul toward "generation, as to a sort of lesser good," which Bruno mentions in the third dialogue of Part I (I, iii, 372).

Each particular soul is part of the world soul. The soul alone is the substance which is really man; it governs and controls the body

[25] Ficino compares the soul to a stone in *Opera omnia*, I, 304.

as the skipper pilots his ship. The soul turns and moves about God, as the body about the soul (I, iii, 367). Soul is the body's intrinsic form and its extrinsic framer (*ibid.*).

One Platonic theme which was abandoned by Christianizing love treatise writers is the transmigration which Plato attributed to souls in the great myth of the *Phaedrus*. Although Ficino mentions transmigration as a Platonic doctrine, as a Christian he cannot believe it, and says with Pico that it must be understood allegorically. For Bruno the doctrine of transmigration is a cosmic extension of the concept of the soul's mobility in response to its two contrary impulses. Bruno makes reference to the theory of metempsychosis in the *Eroici furori* (I, iv, 391, and I, v, 405), but does not give it the full importance which it has in the *Spaccio della Bestia Trionfante* and in his testimony before the Venetian Inquisition.

It is ironic, though logical, that Bruno's tirade against Petrarch should be prefixed to the *Eroici furori;* for the sonnets of the ten dialogues are undeniably Petrarchian in their derivation. It was natural for Bruno to choose, perhaps unconsciously, the idiom of the despised master of Vaucluse, as the means for expressing his exalted passion. Nor was there in his mind any question of inconsistency: he never denies that he is a lover. On the contrary, the heroic enthusiast is the greatest of lovers; only the object of his love is different from Petrarch's. Petrarchism was so pervasive among sonnet writers of the *Cinquecento* that scarcely any of them escaped its strong influence. Michelangelo is perhaps the only sixteenth-century sonneteer of stature in whom Dante's presence is as strongly felt as that of Petrarch. Bruno himself explains that heroic love is formally similar to "baser passions":

Ecco dunque, per venir al proposito, come questo furor eroico, che si chiarisce nella presente parte, è differente dagli altri furori più bassi, non come virtù dal vizio, ma come un vizio ch'è in un suggetto più divino o divinamente, da un vizio ch'è in un suggetto più ferino o ferinamente: di maniera che la differenza è secondo gli suggetti e modi differenti, e non secondo la forma de l'esser vizio (I, ii, 352).

Here then, to come to the point, is how this heroic passion, which is clarified in this section, is different from other, lower passions, not as a virtue is different from a vice, but as a vice which is in a more divine subject (or more divinely) differs from a vice which is in a more bestial subject (or more bestially). Thus the difference is according to the different subjects or modes and not according to the form of being a vice.

Like Petrarch's love for Laura, Bruno's passion is characteristically bittersweet. He longs for an end that is almost unattainable; but his torment is a pleasure. He constantly pursues with great heat of affection an object which encourages him but flees and is ever beyond his grasp. The effect of his passion is to disrupt his constitution.

> Che tenti più, dolce nemico, Amore?
> Qual studio a me ferir oltre ti muove,
> Or ch'una piaga è fatto tutto il cuore?
>   (II, i, 458)

What more do you attempt, sweet enemy, Love? What zeal moves you to injure me further, now that all my heart is made one wound?

. . . [L'anima è] dolente non già per vera discontentezza, ma con affetto di certo amoroso martire . . . (I, iv, 379).

. . . [The soul is] sorrowful not because of true discontent, but with affection of a certain amorous suffering. . . .

Bruno overworks the antitheses which Petrarch and other lyricists and essayists of love attributed to the lover. He devotes the second dialogue of Part I to the topic of love's contrarieties, internal and external. Naturally his expression is baroque in the extreme.

> Io che porto d'amor l'alto vessillo,
> Gelate ho spene e gli desir cuocenti:
> A un tempo triemo, agghiaccio, ardo e sfavillo,
> Son muto, e colmo il ciel de strida ardenti:
>   Dal cor scintillo, e dagli occhi acqua stillo;
> E vivo e muoio, e fo riso e lamenti:
> Son vive l'acqui, e l'incendio non more,
> Chè a gli occhi ho Teti, ed ho Vulcan al core.
>   Altr'amo, odio me stesso;
> Ma s'io m'impiumo, altri si cangia in sasso;
> Poggi' altr' al cielo, s'io mi ripogno al basso;
>   Sempre altri fugge, s'io seguir non cesso;

S'io chiamo, non risponde;
E quant'io cerco più, più mi s'asconde.

(I, ii, 348)

I, who carry high the standard of love, have frozen hopes and burning desires: at the same time I tremble and freeze, burn and spark, I am mute and fill heaven with ardent cries.

From the heart I sparkle and from my eyes I shed water; I live and I die, laugh and lament. The waters live and the fire does not die, for in my eyes I have Thetis and in my heart, Vulcan.

I love another, I hate myself; if I fledge, that other one changes into stone; the other mounts to the sky if I dwell low.

The other always flees, if I do not cease to follow, and if I call, does not reply; and the more I seek, the more that other one hides from me.

Many of the figures are taken from Sonnet CXXXIV by Petrarch:

Pace non trovo e non ho da far guerra;
E temo e spero, et ardo e sono un ghiaccio;
E volo sopra 'l cielo, e giaccio in terra;
E nulla stringo, e tutto 'l mondo abbraccio.
Tal m'ha in pregion, che non m'apre nè serra
Nè per suo mi ritien nè scioglie il laccio;
E non m'ancide Amor e non mi sferra,
Nè mi vuol vivo nè mi trae d'impaccio.
Veggio senz' occhi e non ho lingua e grido;
E bramo di perir e cheggio aita;
Et ho in odio me stesso et amo altrui.
Pascomi di dolor, piangendo rido;
Egualmente mi spiace morte e vita.
In questo stato son, donna, per vui.

I do not find peace and I cannot make war; I fear and I hope, I burn and I am ice; I fly over the heavens and I lie on earth; I hold nothing, and I embrace the whole world.

Love has so imprisoned me that he neither opens nor bars my way, nor holds me for his own nor unties the cord; and he neither kills me nor releases me, nor wants me alive nor frees me from obstruction.

I see without eyes, have no tongue and shout; I yearn to perish and I ask help; I hate myself and love another.

I feed upon sorrow, weeping I laugh; death and life displease me equally. I am in this state, lady, because of you.

Varchi comments that there are perhaps more contraries in this sonnet than in the works of all the Latin poets combined.[26] Indeed, antithesis is a figure that became common in the early Middle Ages; in Bruno it reassumes the Augustinian flavor of struggle against seductive evil.

Bruno's baroque amplification of this theme is illustrated in his sonnet by two exaggerated expressions and in the succeeding prose commentary by metaphysical observations. Where Petrarch said, "Non ho lingua e grido," Bruno trumpeted, "Son muto, e colmo il ciel de strida ardenti."

Where Petrarch said, "Piangendo rido," Bruno cried, "Chè a gli occhi ho Teti, ed ho Vulcan al core."

In the former instance, we have an example of Bruno's writing of heroic love exactly what in the Preface he had derided apropos of refined sensual love. In this sonnet the poet—albeit mute—"fills the sky with ardent cries"; in the Preface he mocked the *strida ch'assordiscon gli astri* ("Argument," 311) of suffering lovers. In the prose dialogue following the sonnet the *dolce-amaro* contrast of Petrarch is elevated to a philosophical doctrine.

. . . Nessuna cosa è pura e schetta. . . . Tutte le cose constano de contrarii, da onde avviene, che gli successi de li nostri affetti per la composizione ch'è nelle cose, non hanno mai delettazion alcuna senza qualch'amaro; anzi dico e noto di più, che se non fusse l'amaro nelle cose, non sarebbe la delettazione, atteso che la fatica fa che troviamo delettazione nel riposo; la separazione è causa che troviamo piacere nella congiunzione; e generalmente essaminando, si troverà sempre che un contrario è caggione che l'altro contrario sia bramato e piaccia (I, ii, 349).

. . . Nothing is pure and unalloyed. . . . All things consist of opposites, whence it happens that our affections, because of the mixture that is in things, never turn out to have pleasure without some bitterness; on the contrary I further say that if there were no bitterness in things, there would be no pleasure, since fatigue causes us to find

[26] Varchi, *Opere, Lezioni sulle tre canzoni degli occhi:* "E di questi contrari usa spessissime volte il Petrarca, e ne mise forse più in quel sonetto: *Pace non trovo . . . ,* che tutti i poeti latini in tutte le opere loro" (And Petrarch uses these opposites very often; he perhaps puts more of them in the sonnet *Pace non trovo . . . ,* than all the Latin poets in all their works).

pleasure in repose; separation is the cause of our finding pleasure in reunion; and examining things generally one will always find one contrary the occasion of the other contrary's being desirable and pleasing.

All things are composed of opposites. Not only is one contrary impossible without the existence of the other; but in the point of their conjunction is found virtue.

In the commentary on the sonnet succeeding the one which we have just examined, *Ahi qual condizion, natura, o sorte* (I, ii, 353), the passion of the hero is described as a "living death" or "dead life." Lyricists and theorists of love from Guinizelli and Cavalcanti and the *Stilnuovisti* through the commentators of "Platonic love" had described love as "death" either because of the consequent suspension of the body's normal functions or because of the soul's flight to the beloved. Both ideas were taken over by Bruno and incorporated into his conception of heroic love, the former in the Platonic *raptus,* the latter in the principle that the philosophic lover lives only in his exalted object.

Allora è in stato di virtude, quando si tiene al mezzo, declinando da l'uno e l'altro contrario . . . ; e là dove convegnono gli contrarii, consta la composizione e consiste la virtude. Ecco dunque come è morto vivente, o vivo moriente. . . . Non è morto, perchè vive ne l'oggetto; non è vivo, perchè è morto in se stesso; privo di morte, perchè parturisce pensieri in quello; privo di vita, perchè non vegeta o sente in se medesimo (I, ii, 353–54).

He is in a state of virtue when he holds to the middle, avoiding both opposites. . . . And where the two opposites coincide there is composition and there is virtue. See how he is dead while living or alive while dying. . . . He is not dead, because he lives in his object; he is not alive because he is dead in himself; he is deprived of death, because he brings forth thoughts in his object; deprived of life, because he does not flower or feel in himself.

The sweetness of this "death," which is painful only because it is a negation of the senses and a total dedication to the principle of intelligibility in nature, is constantly described in the *Eroici furori* in terms that may be considered an extension of the characteristic bittersweetness of Petrarchan love. This principle is exemplified in the sestet of a sonnet in the fifth dialogue of Part I, *Mai fia che de l'amor io mi lamente* (I, v, 400):

Al cor, al spirto, a l'alma
Non è piacer, o libertade, o vita,
Qual tanto arrida, giove e sia gradita,
    Qual più sia dolce, graziosa ed alma,
Ch'il stento, giogo e morte,
Ch'ho per natura, voluntade e sorte.

For the heart, the spirit, the soul, there is no pleasure or freedom or life so favorable, gratifying, or pleasing, which is sweeter, more gracious and vivifying than the labor, the yoke and death that I have by nature, will, and lot.

In the succeeding prose comments this experience becomes an ecstatic "vanishing" amidst "flames of amorous ardor." "Death" of the body accompanies "contemplation" of divine beauty (I, v, 400–401).

Pain, psychological rather than physical, is an inseparable accompaniment of exalted love—with the usual qualification, "in this state" or life. The contrary effects of pleasure and pain, again understood in a metaphysical sense, naturally and inevitably result from the dichotomy of man's soul, no matter how successfully he may develop his spiritual and intellectual propensities at the expense of the sensual (II, i, 435–36).

Even more contradictory at first glance than Bruno's Petrarchizing style is his appropriation in the first part of the *Eroici furori* of many of Luigi Tansillo's fine love sonnets, after his explicit denial in the Preface of any intent to allegorize upon "ordinary love" ("Argument," 315). It must be conceded, however, that the sonnets he selects from his compatriot's *Canzoniere* are strikingly applicable to the condition and character of the heroic lover. Moreover, the characters in the dialogue never comment on the sonnets of Tansillo, but rather, after merely reading them and noting their relevance, return to the exposition of Bruno's sonnets. The now resolved controversy about the attribution of some of Tansillo's sonnets to Bruno could have been avoided by taking at face value the words of the character Tansillo in the dialogues, for he invariably tells which are his own (i.e., the real Tansillo's) sonnets by some such phrase as *questo mio sonetto* (I, i, 341: this sonnet of mine), or *dissi* (I, iii, 363: I said), or *feci questo sonetto* (I, iii, 369: I made this sonnet).

Tansillo's sonnets are among the most refined and imaginative of the *Cinquecento*. Some of them depict the sublimity of his love and therefore lend themselves to Bruno's purposes. The sonnets selected by Bruno, only four in number, generally describe the condition of the lover, and are quite similar in tone and style to Bruno's sonnets, most of which exhibit less polish and grace than those of Tansillo. The first sonnet quoted from Tansillo, for example, *Cara, suave ed onorata piaga*, describes the sweet pain and languishing of the wounded and tormented lover (I, i, 341–42). The second, *O d'invidia ed amor figlia sì ria* (I, i, 342), is a description of Jealousy,

> Tisifone infernal, fetid'Arpia,
> Che l'altrui dolce rapi ed avvelene,

Infernal Tisiphone, fetid Harpy, who steals and poisons another's sweet.

equally applicable to vulgar and heroic love. It continues:

> Augel di duol, . . .
> Pena, . . .
>   Se si potesse a te chiuder l'entrata,
> Tant' il regno d'amor saria più vago,
> Quant'il mondo senz'odio e senza morte.

Bird of sorrow, . . . pain, . . . If the entrance could be closed to you, the realm of love would be as beautiful as a world without hate or death.

The third sonnet by Tansillo, *D'un sì bel fuoco e d'un sì nobil laccio* (I, iii, 363), and the fourth, *Poi che spiegat' ho l'ali al bel desio* (I, iii, 369), likewise mention favorite themes of Bruno. The former sonnet says:

> D'un sì bel fuoco e d'un sì nobil laccio
> Beltà m'accende, ed onestà m'annoda,
> Ch'in fiamm'e servitù convien ch'io goda[,]
> Fugga la libertade e tema il ghiaccio.
>   L'incendio è tal ch'io m'ardo e non mi sfaccio, . . .
> Ma tranquillo è l'ardor, dolce l'impaccio. . . .

Beauty kindles me with such fine fire, and honesty binds me with so noble a knot that I meetly enjoy flames and servitude, flee liberty, and fear ice.

The fire is such that I burn and am not dissolved. . . . But tranquil is the ardor, sweet the encumberment. . . .

The fourth sonnet, although written for a lady,[27] perfectly expresses the pride and exaltation of Bruno's heroic lover:

> E spreggio il mondo, e vers'il ciel m'invio. . . .
> Ch'i' cadrò morto a terra, ben m'accorgo;
> Ma qual vita pareggia al morir mio? . . . .
> Fendi sicur le nubi, e muor contento,
> S'il ciel sì illustre morte ne destina.
>   (I, iii, 369, ll. 4, 7–8, 13–14)

I despise the world and head toward heaven . . . I fully realize that I shall fall dead to earth. But what life can match my dying? . . . Fly surely through the clouds and die happy, if heaven destines such shining death.

Bruno's occasional borrowing of lines or phrases from Tansillo's poems, discovered by Spampanato and Fiorentino, are indicated by Gentile in his notes to the *Eroici furori* (pp. 362, 494, 495, 512, 514, 518). This fact is a further indication not only of Bruno's admiration and respect for Tansillo but also of the symbolic and linguistic affinity of the very different kinds of love poetry which they composed.

Despite the philosophic character of the *Eroici furori,* Bruno's sonnets and other poems are lyrical rather than philosophical or doctrinal. His verses are not philosophic in the didactic sense of the *Canzoni* of Cavalcanti and Benivieni; nor are they doctrinal in the manner of the third *canzone* of Dante's *Convivio* or of Bruno's Latin poems. This is not to deny, however, that the sonnets have a characteristic philosophic orientation, which is further developed by the prose commentary.

One of the sonnets which best evidence Bruno's lyrical expression of philosophical themes is the sonnet, *Bench'a tanti martir mi fai suggetto,* which we previously examined in regard to the duality of Bruno's philosophic object (pp. 187–89). The personification of Love and the description of the lover's sentiments vis-à-vis the god are more characteristic of lyric than of didactic poetry, as is the

---

[27] According to Fiorentino, as quoted by Gentile in his footnote to the sonnet, I, iii, 369–70, the sonnet was written either for the Marquess of Vasto, Maria d'Aragona, or for the Neapolitan Laura Monforte.

continual description of the emotions of the poet-lover in all their variation throughout the sonnets of the *Eroici furori*.

Bruno, as we have said, used Petrarchan language in his sonnets after attacking Petrarchan poetry in the Preface. There is a parallel to that paradox in his attitude toward the exaggerated imagery and expression which later became known as baroque poetry. Bruno recalls the endless repetition of motives from love lyrics: *quegli occhi, . . . quelle guance, . . . quel vermiglio, . . . quella lingua, . . . quel dente, . . . quel labbro* (those eyes . . . those cheeks . . . that ruby . . . that tongue . . . that tooth . . . that lip), etc., and ridicules it by Bernesque[28] extension to *quel martello, quel schifo, quel puzzo, quel sepolcro, quel cesso, quel mestruo, quella carogna* (that hammer, that nausea, that stench, that tomb, that toilet, those menses, that carrion), etc. (*Eroici furori*, "Argument," 311). In standardized and newly imported literary forms the Petrarchan theme was being worked to death:

Ecco vergato in carte, rinchiusi in libri . . . un rumore, un strepito, un fracasso d'insegne, d'imprese, de motti, d'epistole, de sonetti, d'epigrammi, de libri, de prolissi scartafazzi, de sudori estremi, de vite consumate, con strida ch'assordiscon gli astri, lamenti che fanno ribombar gli antri infernali, doglie che fanno stupefar l'anime viventi, suspiri da far exinanire e compatir gli dei . . . ("Argument," 310–11).

Here, written on paper, enclosed in books, are . . . a noise, an uproar, a tumult of emblems, standards, mottoes, epistles, sonnets, epigrams, books, verbose papers, dying perspirations, and of lives consumed, with cries which deafen the stars, laments that make the infernal caves resound, pains that stupefy the living souls, signs to reduce the gods to pity. . . .

With ever increasing exaggerations poets sought bolder images to replace trite metaphors. The extremism in poetic imagery and the search for effect which was the beginning of *seicentismo* were already discernible to Giordano Bruno in 1585. Indeed, like other motives which he attacks in the Preface as inappropriate to vulgar love, they reappear intensified in the dialogues of the *Eroici furori* to render homage to the Nolan's "divine object." With baroque

---

[28] Francesco Berni (1498–1535) was the author of mocking, grotesque, and occasionally anti-Petrarchan poetry.

boldness he calls his love not *amor divino*, but *eroici furori*. The dynamism of his linguistic expression infuses a vitalizing quality into the ten dialogues which is sorely lacking in most *trattati d'amore*.

Bruno's role in ushering in a new century of poetry has been altogether overlooked by his major critics. The *Eroici furori* is an important link between Petrarchan poetry of the sixteenth century and the baroque poetry of the *seicento*. Even the casual reader of Bruno's sonnets in the *Eroici furori* will notice that they exhibit the excesses of preciosity which characterize the poetry of the *seicento*. We have noted his exaggerations of Petrarch's antitheses in the sonnet, *Io che porto d'amor l'alto vessillo*. In that sonnet the heroic lover is subject to many of the same contraries which the author in the "Argument" (p. 309) attributes to the vulgar lover, whom he ridicules as *un uomo cogitabundo, afflitto, tormentato, triste, . . . or freddo, or caldo, or fervente, or tremante, or pallido, or rosso* (a pensive man, afflicted, tormented, sad . . . now cold, now hot, now fervent, now trembling, now pale, now red). Indeed, these contraries are exaggerated in the sonnet: "For in my eyes I have Thetys, and have Vulcan in my heart." [29]

The glossator will not call such effects a virtue, for virtue is the temperate mean between opposite extremes (I, ii, 351–52); rather, he says that such vicious effects are "more divinely" present in the *furor eroico* than in baser passions (I, ii, 352). This declaration is the nearest semblance of explanation of the poet's celebration of the same effects in heroic love that he despises in sensual love.

The most flagrant example of Bruno's high-flown and paradoxical diction occurs in the succeeding sonnet, *Ahi, qual condizion, natura, o sorte:*

"In viva morte morta vita vivo!" (I, ii, 353: In living death I live a dead life!).[30]

---

[29] Cf. the sonnets of dialogue between heart and eyes in II, iii.

[30] Cf. G. Marino, "Canzone dei Baci": "quel bacio, che mi priva / di vita, mi raviva; / ond'io c'ho nel morir vita ognor nova, / per ferito esser più, ferisco a prova" (that kiss that deprives me of life revives me; whence I, who find in death life ever new, in order to be more wounded, wound expressly), and Leone Ebreo, *Dialoghi d'amore*, p. 55: "L'amore fa che continuamente la vita muoia e viva la morte de l'amante" (Love continually causes life to die and the lover's death to live).

Arguzie (witticisms) and *concetti* (conceits), to be sure, are found in the earliest masters of Tuscan poetry, and even in Provençal verse. Dante celebrated Beatrice, who beatifies. In the thirteenth canto of the *Inferno* he wrote:

> Cred'io ch'ei credette ch'io credesse . . . (l. 25)

I believe that he believed that I believed . . .

Petrarch extolled Laura in puns such as *l'aura* (the air) and *lauro* (laurel), and his benefactor Cardinal Giovanni Colonna by making a metaphor of his name.

> Così LAUdare e REverire insegna
> La voce stessa.
> (*In vita di Madonna Laura, V*)

The word itself thus teaches to LAUd and REvere.

> Rotta è l'alta colonna e 'l verde lauro
> Che facean ombra al mio stanco pensero . . .
> (*In morte di Madonna Laura, CCLXIX*)

Broken is the high column and the green laurel which gave shade to my tired thought . . .

Petrarch and his imitators also delighted in the antitheses which Bruno and the *seicento* overworked.

Bruno's hyperbole in praising Queen Elizabeth—*specie soprumana . . . unica Diana;* (superhuman species . . . unique Diana);[31] his paradoxical mode of expression; and his consciously (*Eroici furori*, II, iii, 477) exaggerated artifices of the burning heart and the weeping eyes which fill the third dialogue of Part II—tears to fill an infinite ocean are held in check by the heart's infinite flame, *e un infinito l'altro non eccede* (II, iii, 480: and one infinity does not exceed the other)—all point toward the *seicento*.

The extreme of hyperbole is perhaps reached in Giambattista

---

[31] *Iscusazion del Nolano alle più virtuose e leggiadre dame*, p. 330, prefixed to the *Eroici furori*. Cf. *La cena de le ceneri*, in *Opere italiane*, I, 52, of Queen Elizabeth: "quel nume de la terra, . . . quella singolare e rarissima Dama, che . . . a tutto il terrestre globo rende sì chiaro lume: Elizabetta dico" (that goddess of the earth, . . . that singular and rarest Dame, who . . . renders such clear light to all the terrestrial globe: Elizabeth).

Marino's extravagant praise of Pope Paul V, whom he called *Migliore degli Ottimi, Maggiore dei Massimi, Colonna dell'universo, Miracolo del secolo, il cui Impero termina con le stelle* (Better than the Best, Greater than the Greatest, Column of the universe, Miracle of the century, whose Empire ends with the stars).[32]

Fortunately, there is a more important positive side to Bruno's contribution to Italian poetry of the seventeenth century. The philosophical orientation which led Giambattista Marino and his followers to search for daring metaphors is largely Bruno's and Campanella's. The cosmic enthusiasm of the Nolan is reflected in the stupendous metaphors sought by Marino in the "heroic" attempt to express the ineffable. In a universe—Bruno's—where all is in every minimal part, it is possible to extract from anything its contrary. Hence Marino can make the night a bearer of "ardor and light" (*La bella vedova*). Bruno's ultra-Copernican infinite universe in which there move innumerable shining and living stars is revealed in Marino's poem, *Le stelle*, where animated stars, which both love and enamor other beings, are described by such metaphors as *amorose faville / del primo foco ardente; vivi piropi accesi; danzatrici leggiadre; vaghe ninfe vezzose* (amorous sparks burning with the primal fire; living pyropes inflamed; graceful dancers; pretty, charming nymphs). As in Bruno, the stars bear witness to their Creator: they are

> luminose scintille
> del sommo Sol lucente,
> raggi del bel de l'increata mente, . . .
> bocche del ciel veraci,
> lingue di Dio lucenti.

luminous sparks shining with the highest Sun, rays of the beauty of the uncreated mind . . . truthful mouths of heaven, shining tongues of God.

"Astonishing" metaphors became the goal of Marino's poetry:

[32] Marino exhibits the opposite extreme in the unrestrained epithets which he hurls at Martin Luther: "Volpe malvagia . . . lupo fellon . . . immondo corvo . . . perfida iena . . . iniqua aragna . . . rana loquace . . . Piton . . . idra" (Wicked fox . . . cruel wolf . . . filthy raven . . . perfidious hyena . . . iniquitous spider . . . loquacious frog . . . Python . . . Hydra).

È del poeta il fin la meraviglia
(parlo dell'eccellente e non del goffo)
chi non sa far stupir, vada alla striglia!
(*Murtoleide, fischiata XXXIII*)

The aim of the poet is amazement (I speak of the excellent poet, not of the clumsy one). Let him who does not know how to create wonder go work in the stables.

The personification of inanimate things goes beyond previous poetic license. The night—*Quest' animata Notte*—is a "beautiful widow":

L'oriente ha nel riso, ha l'alba in fronte
il dì nel ciglio accolto,
e le stelle negli occhi e 'l sol nel volto.
(*La bella vedova*)

She has the orient in her laughter, the dawn in her forehead, the day gathered in her brow, and the stars in her eyes and the sun in her face.

In the occasional verses, *Per una donna uccisa dal suo amante,* not only does Nature cry for the lady taken away from her, but the dagger itself which killed her takes pity. Behind such verses is the philosophic concept of universal animism.

Non pur le pompe sue, che 'l Ciel le tolse,
pianse Natura, impoverita e vile,
ma 'l duro e crudo ferro oltre suo stile
intenerissi e, per pietà, si dolse.

Not only did Nature, impoverished and vile, weep for the pomp which Heaven took from her; but the hard and cruel dagger beyond its wont became tender and grieved for pity.

Bruno himself escapes the laughable excesses of *marinismo* because, being a philosopher, he is always more interested in substance than in effect: the word is never an end to itself. His consciousness of saying something important, the vitality and fervor of his thought, are reflected in the warm sincerity of his sonnets, even when his technique of expression falls short of expressing the inward message.

There is in the daring metaphors and rhetorical bravura of baroque poetry an ascensive or expansive quality spiritually akin to that expressed by Bruno in the *Eroici furori,* which will not tolerate the limitations of poetic rules. Bruno also blazed the trail for baroque poets in this field. Students of sixteenth-century literature know well the havoc wrought by the normative application of Aristotle's *Poetics,* which was more widely diffused in that century than formerly. The most famous controversy in this connection in Italian literature centers around the epic poem, *Gerusalemme Liberata,* of Bruno's illustrious contemporary, Torquato Tasso. Bruno's attitude, expressed in a digression in the first dialogue of the *Eroici furori* (I, i, 335–37), is strikingly modern. He was among the first to raise his voice in strong protest against the misapplication of Aristotle's analysis of Greek literature by *vere bestie* (true beasts) of pedants, who, armed with these "rules," "gnaw" away at the work of others. Poetry, says Bruno, is not born from rules; but rules derive from poems.

Sappi certo, fratel mio, che questi [regolisti di poesia] son vere bestie; perche' non considerano quelle regole principalmente servir per pittura dell'omerica poesia o altra simile in particolare, e son per mostrar tal volta un poeta eroico tal qual fu Omero, e non per instituir altri che potrebbero essere, con altre vene, arti e furori, equali, simili e maggiori, de diversi geni (I, i, 335).

Know for certain, my brother, that these [rule-makers of poetry] are true beasts; because they do not consider that those rules serve principally for the portrayal of Homeric or other such poetry in particular and are to illustrate, if anything, a heroic poet such as Homer, and not to instruct others who could in other veins, with other arts and passions, be equal, similar, and greater in different genres.

True poets can be known, says Bruno, *dal cantar de versi* (by the singing of their verses). He adds the Horatian proviso that poets should either delight or profit the reader, or both (I, i, 336).

CHAPTER IV

The Relation of the Eroici furori to the Other Philosophical Writings of Bruno

WE SHALL now examine briefly some of Bruno's other writings which have points of contact with the *Eroici furori*. The first of these is the *De umbris idearum* (1582), a sort of bridge between Bruno's Lullian and mnemonic works and his philosophical treatises. Bruno's mnemonic works are not as unrelated to his philosophical works as some critics (e.g., Olschki) have maintained. In *De umbris idearum,* he gives to the art of memory for which he was famous a theoretical basis in philosophy. By so doing he considerably supplements the epistemology of the *Eroici furori,* published four years later. In the *De umbris,* Bruno adopts elements of the logical system of Raymond Lully as symbols upon which to fix the concepts which one desires to remember.

The dialogue is permeated from its title onward by the Platonic metaphor of light. The human intellect is to ideas as the eye is to light. The first truth and goodness are hidden from rational search. Man's knowledge of ideas is always umbratile; hence the title *De umbris idearum.*

> Non enim est tanta haec nostra natura, ut pro sua capacitate ipsum veritatis campum incolat. . . . Sufficiens ergo est illi atque multum, ut sub umbra boni verique sedeat (*De umbris idearum, in Opere latine conscripta,* II, i, 20, Intentio A).

Our nature is not such that by its ability it can inhabit the very field of truth. . . . Thus it is sufficient and much for it to sit in the shade of the good and the true.

The divinity uses the umbrae to prepare the soul's eyes for light (p. 30, Intentio P). The umbra participates in both light and darkness (*tenebrae*); it is the vestige of light, *lux non plena* (p. 21, Intentio B), suitable to human knowledge because, like the rational soul which Bruno describes in the *Eroici furori*, it is characterized by duality, being located on the horizon of good and evil, of truth and falsity (p. 22, Intentio D).

The process by which one comes to know the ideas, repeated from Plotinus and Ficino, is a combination of ethical and gnoseological means reminiscent of the *Eroici furori*.

Septum gradibus (quibus duos addimus) constare intellexit Plotinus Schalam qua ascenditur ad principium. Quorum Primus est animi purgatio. Secundus attentio. Tertius intentio. Quartus ordinis contemplatio. Quintus proportionalis ex ordine collatio. Sextus negatio, seu separatio. Septimus, votum. Octauus transformatio sui in rem. Nonus transformatio rei in seipsum. Ita ab vmbris ad ideas patebit aditus, & accessus, & introitus (pp. 48–49, Conceptus T).

Plotinus understood that the ladder which leads to the origin consists of seven steps (to which we add two). The first of these is the cleansing of the soul; the second, attention; the third, intention; fourth, the contemplation of order; fifth, proportionate collection from order; sixth, negation or separation; seventh, the vow; eighth, transformation of oneself into the object; ninth, transformation of the object into oneself. Thus will the approach, entrance, and passage be open from shadows to ideas.

The *De umbris* is based like the *Eroici furori* on the hierarchical theory of being, in which the infinite multitude of things proceed from a single source, which is goodness and truth, and are the less true and good in proportion to their distance from their source (pp. 22–23, Intentio E). This order in the *De umbris* is compared to the natural progression of the four classical elements, fire into air into water into earth, and vice versa.

Cum veró in rebus omnibus ordo sit atque connexio, vt inferiora mediis & media superioribus succedant corporibus; Composita simplicibus, simplicia simplicioribus vniantur. Materialia spiritualibus spiritualia prorsus inmaterialibus adhaereant. Vt vnum sit vniversi entis corpus, vnus ordo, una gubernatio, vnum principium, vnus finis, vnum primum, vnum extraemum. Cumque (vt non ignorauerunt Platonicorum principes) demigratio detur continua á luce ad tenebras (cum mentium quaedam per conuersionem ad materiam, & auersionem ab actu; subeunt naturam, atque fatum) nihil impedit quominus ad sonum cytharae vniuersalis Apollinis ad superna gradatim reuocentur inferna: & inferiora per media, superiorum subeant naturam: quemadmodum & sensu constat terram in aquam, aquam in aerem, aerem in ignem rarefieri: sicut ignis in aerem, aer in aquam, aqua in terram densabatur (pp. 23–24, Intentio G).

As there is indeed such an order and connection in all things that lower things follow middle things and the middle follow the superior; so composite things are united to the simple, and the simple are joined to the more simple. Material things adhere to spiritual things and the spiritual to the utterly immaterial, so that the body of the universal being may be one, and one the order, one the government, one the beginning, one the end, one the first, one the last. And since (as the leading Platonists knew) there is a continual emigration from light to darkness (as certain minds by turning toward matter and away from act undergo matter's nature and fate), nothing prevents lower things being recalled by stages to the higher things to the sound of the lyre of the universal Apollo. And the inferior, through intermediate things, pass under the nature of superior things; just as it is evident to the senses that earth is rarified into water, water into air, air into fire; as fire condenses into air, air into water, water into earth.

At the apex of the hierarchy is absolute unity; at the base, number or matter. Both are infinite.

Unde sub infimo gradu schalae naturae est infinitus numerus, seu materia: in supraemo vero infinita vnitas, actusque purus (p. 49, Conceptus V).

Whence under the lowest rung of the ladder of nature is infinite number or matter; at the top indeed is infinite unity and pure act.

Since all things are interrelated and ultimately unified by the one governing principle of all being, it is possible to retrace the downward path of generation in the upward path of cognition. In other words, the interrelation of beings is the very order which makes knowledge possible.

Quoniam veró quod est simile simili; est etiam simile eidem similibus sive per ascensum, siue per descensum, siue per latitudinem: Hinc accidit vt (infra suos limites) natura facere possit omnia ex omnibus, & intellectus, seu ratio cognoscere omnia ex omnibus (pp. 25–26, Intentio I).

Since indeed that which is similar to its similar is also similar to the latter's similars whether by ascent or by descent or by latitudinal direction; hence it happens that (within its limits) nature can make all things from all things and the intellect or reason may know all things from all things.

Bruno is, in consequence, optimistic about the possibility of universal knowledge and unlimited action.

Ita cum de partibus & vniuersi speciebus, nil sit seorsum positum & exemptum ab ordine (qui simplicissimus, perfectissimus, & citra numerum est in prima mente) si alias aliis connectendo, & pro ratione vniendo concipimus: quid est quod non possimus intelligere memorari & agere? (p. 47, Conceptus P).

Thus since none of the parts and species of the universe is located apart and free from order (which is wholly simple, perfect, and without number in the first mind), if we conceive things in unity according to reason, connecting them with other things, what is there that we cannot understand, remember, and accomplish?

The umbrae are the objects of the two faculties, cognitive and appetitive, later given such prominence in the *Eroici furori*.

Vmbras eas in proposito maximé consideramus quae sunt appetituum & cognoscitiuae facultatis obiecta, sub specie veri bonique concepta, quae sensim ab vnitate illa supersubstantiali decedentia, per crescentem multitudinem, in infinitam multitudinem (vt Pythagoreorum more loquar) progrediuntur: quae quantum ab vnitate recedunt, tantum ab ipsa quoque veritate elongantur (pp. 22–23, Intentio E).

Let us consider principally here those *umbrae* which are the objects of the appetite and of the cognitive faculty, conceived under the species of the true and the good, which departing gradually from the supersubstantial unity proceed through a growing multitude into an infinite multitude (to speak in the Pythagorean manner). The further they recede from unity, the further are they withdrawn from truth itself as well.

Antiquity taught the dialectic (*discursus*) from the many to the one, although it did not teach the art of systematic memory (p. 25,

Intentio G). Where a natural connection between things is lacking, the understanding must substitute an artificial connection to make memory possible.

Man's capacity to act divinely in operations both of intellect and of will depends upon his ability to rise from the limitations of time and space into the realm of ideas.

Qui ergo in loco consistens atque tempore, á loco rationes idearum absoluet atque tempore: diuinis entibus in suis operibus conformabitur, siue ad intellectum pertineant, siue ad voluntates (p. 42, Conceptus C).

Therefore he who lives in space and time will free the reasons of ideas from space and time; he will conform to divine beings in his actions, whether they pertain to the intellect or to the will.

In the first mind there is one idea of all things (p. 46, Conceptus M). The ideas are not outside of God, who does not act for any end beyond himself (p. 51, conceptus XXV, E).[1] Bad things do not have their own ideas, but are known from other species (*in aliena specie*) (p. 33, Intentio X).[2]

Beauty is defined after Plato as proportion. The world itself is called *pulcherrima* (p. 27, Intentio M). This concept of beauty, as a result of Bruno's way of understanding metaphors concretely, is related to the imperfection of umbratile—i. e., human—knowledge.

In variorum ergo connexione, partium pulchritudo manifestatur: & in ipsa varietate totius pulchritudo consistit. Hinc rei vmbratilis visio est visionum imperfectissima: quia quod imago cum varietate demonstrat: vmbra quod est infra extrinsecae figurae terminos vt plurimum etiam ementitos, quasi sine varietate profert (p. 27, Intentio L).

In connection then with various things the beauty of parts is manifest, and beauty consists of the very variety of the whole. Hence the vision of an umbratile thing is the most imperfect kind of vision. This fact is demonstrated by a figure with variety: the shadow produces almost without variety that which is less than the limits of the extrinsic figure, already completely counterfeit.

The *Eroici furori* also has an intimate connection with the apparently dissimilar *De la causa, principio e uno* (1584) and *De*

---

[1] The nature of a final cause is here attributed to exemplary forms.
[2] Cf. p. 46, Conceptus M, "Deformium animalium formae formosae sunt in caelo."

l'infinito, universo e mondi (1584). The unifying factor in these three works is Bruno's concept of the infinite, which he also calls the object, the absolute, the One. In the *Causa* he analyzes it in the metaphysical terms of transcendent cause and immanent principle, of matter and form, of potency and act. In the *De l'infinito,* as in the *Cena de le ceneri* (1584), he examines the physical consequences of that transcendent creative entity in which will and intellect, potency and act, are undifferentiated. But even in cosmological and astronomical discussions, Bruno deduces the physical effects from metaphysical causes: an actual infinite universe is the necessary consequence of infinite divine creative power. In the *Eroici furori* Bruno, always the poet even in his more properly metaphysical treatises, gives combined verse and prose expression to his affective and intellectual reaction to the infinite in nature.

The trilogy of Latin verse and prose treatises which he published in 1591, while lacking the ethical motives of the *Eroici furori* and the *Spaccio,* repeats, revises, and supplements the *Causa* and the *De l'infinito.* However, the Italian dialogues have remained his most influential works; they have been read and discussed more widely than the Latin "revisions," perhaps because his original vernacular dialogues, which are a forceful statement of his position, are not radically altered by his subsequent modifications.

De l'infinito is a hymn to the glory of the objective universe; *De gli eroici furori* is its subjective counterpart, celebrating man's enthusiastic response to divinity in nature and in himself. *De l'infinito* and *De la causa* are repeated in the *De immenso* (1591) and *De minimo* (1591), respectively. A Latin recreation of the *Eroici furori* would have been not only superfluous but unthinkable, for its message is not the philosophical doctrine which it contains, but an emotional vitality that springs spontaneously from the breast of Bruno. Furthermore, the literary background of the *Eroici furori* was vernacular. The *Eroici furori* is a testimony of faith couched in the baroque style, then new, which today's reader finds precious and occasionally bombastic. He who questions the spontaneity of a work that treats with an elaboration of traditional forms a subject—Platonic love—which had been popular for over a century, misses the renewed if not new fervency and the prophetic sense of urgency which Bruno—never lukewarm or insincere in his writings—brings to this composition. The polemical and satirical intent of such works as the *Causa* and the *Cena* is absent from the *Eroici furori* because *trattati d'amore* traditionally had no such intent.

Bruno's philosophically minded predecessors in the genre of love treatises, from Marsilio Ficino and Leone Ebreo to Flaminio Nobili and Francesco de' Vieri, show a great respect for Aristotle. They frequently try to reconcile his thought with that of Plato or to minimize apparent disagreements between the two by showing that they were considering different aspects of the same problem or that underneath formal discrepancies there is basic agreement. Bruno's antagonism toward Aristotle was shared by others who wished to replace Aristotelian physics with unorthodox doctrines; but that interest is not shared by any of the other philosophers or humanists whose writings on love we have examined, although they were by and large Platonists.[3]

The *Cena* and *De l'infinito* seize upon the Copernican theory as corroborative evidence for Bruno's attack upon Aristotelian physics and astronomy. However, neither the sun nor any other heavenly body or place is the center of the universe; each body has equal claim to being the center in a cosmos without center or circumference. Copernicus, says Bruno in the *Cena*, had a keen and mature mind, but did not altogether abandon the vulgar—i. e., Aristotelian—philosophy; he was more of a mathematician than a student of nature (*Cena de le ceneri*, in *Opere italiane*, I, 22). In contrast, the Nolan (Bruno), in Teofilo's (Bruno's) words, speaks to divine and very wise men (p. 104).

Il Nolano . . . ha disciolto l'animo umano e la cognizione, che era rinchiusa ne l'artissimo carcere de l'aria turbolento; onde a pena, come per certi buchi, avea facultà de remirar le lontanissime stelle, e gli erano mozze l'ali, a fin che non volasse ad aprir il velame di queste nuvole e veder quello che veramente là su si ritrovasse. . . . Or ecco quello, ch' ha varcato l'aria, penetrato il cielo, discorse le stelle, trapassati gli margini del mondo, fatte svanir le fantastiche muraglia de le . . . sfere . . . ; cossì al cospetto d'ogni senso e raggione, co' la chiave

[3] Francesco Patrizzi was as anti-Aristotelian as Bruno.

di solertissima inquisizione aperti que' chiostri de la verità, che da noi aprir si posseano, nudata la ricoperta e velata natura, ha . . . illuminati i ciechi . . . (pp. 25–26).

The Nolan . . . has freed the human soul and cognition, which was in a very narrow prison of turbid air; whence it was barely able to look at the far distant stars as though through certain holes, and its wings were clipped, so that it might not fly to open these veiling clouds and see what was really to be found up there. . . . Now here is he who has traversed the air, penetrated the heavens, sped through the stars, passed through the bounds of the world, annihilated the fantastic barriers of the . . . spheres. . . . Thus with the key of diligent investigation has he opened to the sight of every sense and reason those recesses of truth which could be opened by us, laid bare that veiled and covered nature, and . . . given light to the blind. . . .

The *Cena* strongly emphasizes the immanence of God in all things. The stars reveal the excellence of their divine creator, whose infinite creative vigor is refound in the infinite universe. We are to seek God in nature, in ourselves, more intrinsic to us than we are to ourselves.

Cossì conoscemo tante stelle, tanti astri, tanti numi, che son quelle tante centenaia de migliaia, ch' assistono al ministerio e contemplazione del primo, universale, infinito ed eterno efficiente. . . . Cossì siamo promossi a scuoprire l'infinito effetto dell'infinita causa, il vero e vivo vestigio de l'infinito vigore; ed abbiamo dottrina di non cercar la divinità rimossa da noi, se l'abbiamo appresso, anzi di dentro, più che noi medesmi siamo dentro a noi . . . (p. 27).

Thus do we know so many stars, so many heavenly bodies and divine images, those countless hundreds of thousands, which attend the ministry and contemplation of the first efficient—universal, infinite, and eternal. . . . Thus are we stimulated to discover the infinite effect of the infinite cause, the true and living vestige of the infinite vigor. And we do not believe in seeking the divinity distant from us if we have it near, in fact within us more than we ourselves are within us. . . .

The *De l'infinito* goes on to deny the "vile fantasy of the spheres and the diversity of the skies" (*De l'infinito, universo e mondi,* in *Opere italiane,* I, 276). There is but one space, infinite, in which there are infinite worlds, all inhabited. Motion is relative (p. 317). Quintessence is "vanity" (p. 277); the earth has equal claim to beauty and nobility and animation with other planets and stars. No sense refutes infinity, and our reason confirms it (p. 272). The divine efficacy, itself infinite, cannot be idle (p. 274). The metaphysical basis of physical infinity is more explicitly stated than in the *Cena*.

> . . . Se la potenza infinita attiva attua l'esser corporale e dimensionale, questo deve necessariamente essere infinito; altrimente si deroga alla natura e dignitade di chi può fare e di chi può essere fatto (p. 273).

> . . . If the active infinite power actualizes material and dimensional being, the latter must necessarily be infinite. Otherwise one disparages the nature and worth of the maker and of that which can be made.

> Qual raggione vuole che vogliamo credere, che l'agente che può fare un buono infinito, lo fa finito? (p. 299).

> What reason would have us believe that the agent who can make an infinite good makes it finite?

In God will and action, liberty and necessity are the same. The distinction between potency and act applies only to changeable things (p. 300). Consequently, he who denies the infinite effect denies the infinite power (p. 301). However, the doctrine that divine necessity is consistent with human free will, taught (according to Bruno) by Plato and Aristotle alike, is not to be taught to the common people, but only to wise men who will understand it and continue to act justly (pp. 301–2). It is on the basis of this separation between unfettered philosophy for philosophers and religion for the instruction of rude people who need to be governed that philosophers and theologians can approve each other's endeavors (p. 302).[4]

The universe is an infinite corporeal simulacrum of the First Principle (p. 294), whose infinite excellence is therein "incomparably better" represented than by any finite means (p. 295). However, the infinity of God is different from that of the universe: the former is "complicated" and total infinity; the infinity of the universe is "explicated." Bruno clarifies these attributions when he explains his statement that the universe is "all infinite" but not, like God, "totally infinite": God alone is infinite in each of his attributes,

---

[4] Bruno's attitude toward philosophy and religion reappears to a considerable degree in the viewpoint of Giovanni Gentile.

whereas the physical universe is composed of innumerable finite worlds, in each of which God is totally present (p. 298).[5]

The innumerable worlds are in constant motion; the universe itself, however, is immobile, as the one divine substance is eternal and immutable. As all events are subject to the "optimum efficient" —providence—we must believe that everything is for the best (p. 282). The psychological result of such a belief is unqualified optimism.

Ecco la raggion della mutazion vicissitudinale del tutto, per cui cosa non è di male da cui non s'esca, cosa non è di buono a cui non s'incorra, mentre per l'infinito campo, per la perpetua mutazione, tutta la sustanza perserva medesima ed una (p. 281).

Here is the reason of the vicissitudinous mutation of everything, by which there is no evil from which one does not escape, and no good which one does not incur, while the whole substance through its infinite field and perpetual mutation remains one and the same.

Questa è quella filosofia che apre gli sensi, contenta il spirto, magnifica l'intelletto e riduce l'uomo alla vera beatitudine che può aver come uomo (pp. 281–82).

This is that philosophy which opens the senses, satisfies the spirit, magnifies the intellect, and leads man to the true beautitude that he can have as a man.

With Bruno's historic denial of celestial quintessence, the *scala naturae* which he himself upheld in the *De umbris* falls before his own ridicule.

. . . Quel bell'ordine e scala di natura è un gentil sogno ed una baia da vecchie ribambite (p. 277).

. . . That fine order and ladder of nature is a gentle dream and humbug for old ladies in their second childhood.

Ove è dunque quel bell'ordine, quella bella scala della natura, per cui si ascende dal corpo più denso e crasso, quale è la terra, al men crasso, quale è l'acqua, al suttile, quale è il vapore, al più suttile, quale è l'aria puro, al suttilissimo, quale è il fuoco, al divino, quale è il corpo celeste? dall' oscuro al men oscuro, al chiaro, al più chiaro, al chiarissimo? dal tenebroso al lucidissimo, dall'alterabile e corruttibile al libero d'ogni alterazione e corrozione? dal gravissimo al grave, da questo al

[5] This concept is derived from Nicholas of Cusa. See p. 256 of this book, footnote 19.

lieve, dal lieve al levissimo, indi a quel che non è nè grave nè lieve? dal mobile al mezzo, al mobile dal mezzo, indi al mobile circa il mezzo? (p. 351).

Where then is that fine order, that fine ladder of nature by which one climbs from the densest and grossest body (earth) to the less gross (water) to the subtle one (vapor) to the more subtle (pure air) to the most subtle (fire) to the divine (the celestial body)? from the dark to the less dark to the light to the lighter to the lightest? from the shadowy to the brightest, from the alterable and corruptible to that which is free of all alteration and corruption? from the heaviest to the heavy, from the latter to the light, from the light to the lightest, thence to that which is neither heavy nor light? from what is in movement toward the middle to that which moves from the middle, thence to that which moves around the middle?

The above paragraph is quoted in full because it shows that the object of Bruno's attack is the Aristotelian physics which attributed to each of the four elements a proper place, and the Aristotelian cosmology of a fixed earth and a revolving *primum mobile*. Bruno clearly does not intend by the phrase *scala della natura* the Neoplatonic ontological hierarchy which remains his basis for understanding existence in the *Eroici furori* and to which he makes reference in the *Causa*.[6] Moreover, even a sort of physical hierarchy is maintained in the *De l'infinito* in Bruno's statement that the universe must be infinite in order for the divinity to corporeally explicate innumerable degrees of incorporeal divine excellence (*De l'infinito*, p. 295).

The dialogue *De la causa, principio e uno* gives a logical and metaphysical basis for the distinction made also in the *Eroici furori* between the immanent and transcendent aspects of God. In the former aspect God is principle; in the latter, cause. The difference between principle and cause is that the latter is extrinsic, as the agent or the end, whereas the former, like matter and form, operates intrinsically and remains in the entity produced (*De la causa*, p. 178).

Relegating to the *Cena* and *De l'infinito* the description of the infinite universe, Bruno in the *Causa* analyzes the unchanging being which is both cause and principle of the phenomenological

[6] *De la causa, principio e uno, Opere italiane*, vol. I. E.g., p. 224 and p. 232.

world, with its change and diversity. Such being is the infinite, uncaused, self-sustaining external reality of which sensuous particulars and their proximate causes are but accidents. It is the universal unifying substance which imparts coherence and intelligibility to the infinitely varying phenomena of the universe. Ontologically it has no parts: it is the substance, one and indivisible. But logically two facets of the one being must be distinguished, form and matter. Each of these aspects of substance is infinite in its kind, as are also the attributes, in so far as they are predicable, of infinite being: beauty, goodness, and the like. The infinite substance is immutable: generation and dissolution, diversity and individualization are accidental or modal (p. 254).

. . . Questa unità è sola e stabile, e sempre rimane; questo uno è eterno; ogni volto, ogni faccia, ogni altra cosa è vanità, è come nulla, anzi è nulla tutto lo che è fuor di questo uno (p. 252).

. . . This unity is one and stable and always remains; this one is eternal; every aspect, every facet, everything else is vanity, is as nothing; indeed, everyhing which is outside of this one is nothing.

The knowledge of the First Principle is vestigial and indirect. As in the *Eroici furori*, it is stated that God is known in nature rather than in himself, and this knowledge is not achieved without a great effort of the will (p. 177).

Although Bruno makes little mention of Platonic ideas in the *Causa,* he maintains the dualistic relation between an ideal world and a participatory world which is its image. However, the ideas do not have the transcendent quality attributed to them in the *Eroici furori.* Like other Neoplatonists from the time of Plotinus he attributes to the world soul not only the principle of life but the power of creativity, thereby confusing it with Plato's demiurge (p. 138).[7] Thus the anima mundi, which prepossesses all forms, brings forth from matter the forms that are latent therein (pp. 179–80).[8] The end of this action is the perfection of the universe—a kind of symmetrical realization of divine potentialities (p. 182).

[7] See *Timaeus,* 30, where Plato states that the world soul was imparted to the universe at the time of creation by the demiurge.

[8] The notion that the forms are latent in matter is Arabic rather than Neoplatonic.

Matter in the *Causa* is not subordinated to forms as it is in the *Eroici furori*.[9] Material or accidental forms are themselves brought forth from matter, which is eternal and divine, by the operation of the world soul. Form and matter limit and complement each other; neither exists in nature separately from the other (*Causa*, p. 212). Soul animates everything that exists, and in everything there is potentially the all (pp. 187–88). As potency, matter is predicable not only of the sensuous world but of the intelligible world as well, for even in intelligible objects, being or act implies the power to be (p. 234).[10]

Contraries, such as matter and form, the one and the many, the end and the beginning, are the constituent principles in nature, which cannot be understood without the analysis of its elements. But since the universe is a continuum and all being is arranged in a sequence, opposites ultimately coincide, as Nicholas of Cusa said, and differences fade away. This key to the knowledge of the highest being Bruno cryptically formulates as follows:

> In conclusione, chi vuol sapere massimi secreti di natura, riguardi e contemple circa gli minimi e massimi de gli contrarii e oppositi (p. 264).

> In conclusion, let him who would know the greatest secrets of nature observe and contemplate the minimums and maximums of opposites and contraries.

Bruno seldom achieves in the sonnets of the *Eroici furori* the dynamism of expression and the electrifying pitch of emotion that he attains in this exalted prose passage of the *Causa*:

> . . . Son degnissimi di lode quelli che si forzano alla cognizione di questo principio e causa, per apprendere la sua grandezza quanto fia possibile discorrendo con gli occhi di regolati sentimenti circa questi magnifici astri e lampeggianti corpi, che son tanti abitati mondi e grandi animali ed eccellentissimi numi, che sembrano e sono innumerabili mondi non molto dissimili a questo che ne contiene; i quali, essendo impossibile ch' abbiano l'essere da per sè, atteso che sono composti e dissolubili (benchè non per questo siano degni d'esserno disciolti, come è stato ben detto nel *Timeo*), è necessario che conoscano principio e causa, e consequentemente con la grandezza del suo essere, vivere ed

---

[9] Compare *Causa*, p. 142, with *Eroici furori*, II, ii, 469–70.
[10] Plotinus and Avicebron also posited intelligible matter.

oprare: monstrano e predicano in uno spacio infinito, con voci innumerabili, la infinita eccellenza e maestà del suo primo principio e causa. Lasciando dunque, come voi dite, quella considerazione per quanto è superiore ad ogni senso e intelletto, consideriamo del principio e causa per quanto, in vestigio, o è la natura istessa o pur riluce ne l'ambito e grembo di quella (p. 177).

. . . They are most praiseworthy who force themselves to the knowledge of this principle and cause in order to comprehend its greatness as far as possible, scouting with the eyes of disciplined senses these magnificent stars and great animals and most excellent divinities, which seem and are innumerable worlds not very different from this which contains us. It being impossible for these worlds to derive their being from themselves, since they are compounded and dissolvable (although it does not follow that they are apt to be dissolved, as is well stated in the *Timaeus*), they necessarily know a principle and cause and consequently live and act with the greatness of their being: they demonstrate and preach in an infinite space with innumerable voices the infinite excellence and majesty of their first principle and cause. Leaving aside then, as you say, that consideration by which it is superior to every sense and intellect, let us consider the principle and cause in that regard wherein vestigially it either is nature itself or shines in the periphery and bosom of nature.

This passage has a fervor and immediacy of expression that are frequently lacking in the strained and recherché devices of the *Eroici furori*. Yet through the ingenious but cumbersome formal apparatus there shines the same cosmic enthusiasm. Perhaps the tonal and stylistic difference of the verse and prose of the *Eroici furori* from the passage quoted above was almost inevitable in Bruno's age when the author turned to introspection. Western culture had barely reached the stage where, to use Dante's words, it was licit to speak of oneself. Neither Montaigne's avowed, nor Cellini's naive, egocentricism had as yet established a literary pattern in Italy. The intimacy of Petrarch's sonnets had long since become a matter of form, a pose. Bruno's "heroic passion" was presented in the third person through the commentary of two impersonal interlocutors who examine a maze of emblems, mottos and heavily metaphorical verses.

The *Spaccio della bestia trionfante* (*Expulsion of the triumphant beast*, 1584) more properly than the *Eroici furori* may be called a dialogue on morality. Its subject is the reform of the skies—an allegory of the soul's purgation of error and vice and its assumption of virtue. Despite the similarity of its theme to that of the *Eroici furori*, the differences are many. Bruno's typical fondness for satire and sense of the bizarre are manifest in the *Spaccio*. The *furor divino* is given only cursory attention and is relegated to a relatively unimportant place in the heavens *Spaccio della bestia trionfante*, in *Opere italiane*, II, 169. The asceticism of the *Eroici furori* is absent; the morality of the *Spaccio* is that nature is divine, and consequently the natural is good. Hence sensual desires are to be regulated rather than denied. There are indeed in the *Eroici furori* hints of the more practical and mundane ethics of the *Spaccio*;[11] however, there the austere concept of heroic love is dominant. In the *Spaccio* the body is not the prison of the soul, but its vessel. The soul's reform in the *Spaccio* may be viewed as a prelude to its soaring flight in the *Eroici furori*.

Divine providence oversees all events, even the smallest. Hence evil is only apparent, and nothing is without a beneficent end (*Spaccio*, p. 81, *Eroici furori*, I, iii, 372). Prudence is the human counterpart of providence. Virtue is in positive action; it goes far beyond "not being vicious" (*Spaccio*, p. 154). Actions, not intentions, are what counts: the tree is judged by its fruit p. 91–92. The poor man is not he who has little, but he who desires much (p. 108). All things are derived from their contraries: without pain there would be no pleasure; without transgression, no justice. The worthiest of the Nine Muses is Ethics (p. 128).[12]

The moral tone of the *Spaccio* is frequently reminiscent of the *Dialoghi d'amore* of Leone Ebreo: here as there virtue consists in good works; continence is praised as a great virtue between two

---

[11] E.g., *Eroici furori*, I, iv, 386: "Pascasi dunque il senso secondo la sua legge de cose sensibili, la carne serva alla legge de la carne, il spirito alla legge del spirito, la raggione a la legge de la raggione: non si confandano, non si conturbino. Basta che uno non guaste o pregiudiche alla legge de l'altro . . ." (Let sense be nourished according to its law of sensible things; let the flesh observe the law of flesh; the spirit, the law of spirit; reason, the law of reason. Let them not be confused or upset. It is sufficient that one not spoil or prejudice the law of the other . . .).

[12] In the *Spaccio* (p. 15 and p. 127), Bruno lists the Nine Muses as Arithmetic, Geometry, Music, Logic, Poetry, Astrology, Physics, Metaphysics, and Ethics.

extremes; the truly rich man is he who is happy with what he has (Leone, *Dialoghi d'amore,* p. 14); morals depend upon wisdom, and knowledge is difficult of attainment (*ibid.,* p. 273). The ethical process, for both authors, is the soul's return to God, who is the world's efficient, formal, and final cause. Pleasure depends upon pain, of which it is the remedy. Like Bruno in both the *Spaccio* and the *Eroici furori,* Leone in his *Dialogues on Love* frequently refers to his allegiance to both reason and faith, the latter in his case referring to the Mosaic law. Heavenly bodies are "the most perfect of animals" (pp. 97, 158). His attitude toward Aristotle, while much more favorable than that of Bruno, is similar in that he greatly respects Aristotle's logical works (p. 338), but opines that he fell short of Plato in failing to see the hidden principles of being known to ancient theologians (p. 351). Furthermore the Neoplatonic notion that different ideas are identical in the divine mind is stated by Leone in a way that reminds one of the coincidence of contraries—a doctrine which Bruno took from Cusanus.

Ivi l'un contrario non è diviso in luogo de l'altro, nè diverso in essenzia opponente; ma insieme in la idea del fuoco è quella de l'acqua; e in quella del semplice è quella del composto, e in quella d'ogni parte è quella de l'universo tutto, e in quella del tutto quella di ciascuna de le parti: di sorte che la multitudine ne l'intelletto del primo opifice è la pura unità, e la diversità è la vera identità, in tal maniera che più presto questa cosa l'uomo la può comprendere con mente astratta che dir con lingua corporea . . . (p. 342).

There one contrary is neither separate in location from another nor different and opposite in essence. In the idea of fire is that of water; in that of the simple is that of the compounded; in that of every part is the idea of the whole universe, and in that of the all, that of each of its parts. The result is that multitude in the intellect of the first creator is pure unity, and diversity is true identity, in such manner that one may more quickly comprehend this thing with abstract mind than say it with corporeal tongue. . . .

In this important passage we find not only the coincidence of contraries and the Neoplatonic belief adopted also by Bruno that the idea of the whole universe is in each part of it: there is also in the last sentence the suggestion of ineffable reverence toward the divinity latent in nature and self-existent above nature.

Bruno's attitude toward the society in which he lived is probably nowhere (except in the *Candelaio*) more manifest than in the brief and pungent dialogue *L'asino cilenico,* published as an addendum to the *Cabala del cavallo pegaseo* (1585). Authority in general is ridiculed as the mask of ignorance; institutions of learning as well as the church itself are recognizable as particular objects of satire.

The Platonic idealism, negative theology, and Socratic ignorance which have their place in the *Eroici furori* come in for severe, if incidental, criticism in the *Cabala del Cavallo Pegaseo*—"incidental" because the real object of attack, under guise of the "ideal ass," is Christianity itself, the churches, and the priesthood. Probably for this reason in his testimony before the Venetian Inquisition Bruno disapproved the work. The teaching of the church is reduced to a prayer that one may become an ass, for ignorance, according to St. Augustine, is a better guide to God than knowledge (*scienza*), which may lead to perdition.[13] The ideal ass thus becomes the prototype of man himself. Rabbis transmitted asininity to Christian priests; but the "greatest asses in the world" are the reformers of the corrupt faith (*Spaccio*, p. 247).

Many critics have pointed out that Neoplatonism plays a diminished role in the three philosophical Latin works published as a trilogy with a common introduction in 1591: *De triplice minimo et mensura, De monade,* and *De immenso et innumerabilibus.* Instead of the transcendentalism of the *Eroici furori,* we find (as earlier in the *Causa*) nature, or God, working from within matter. The separate realm of Platonic ideas, as well as the Platonic cosmic year, is repudiated in the *De immenso.* The explanatory principle of existence is the atom or monad. However, despite his abandonment of some Neoplatonic doctrines for a more materialistic explanation of reality, Bruno maintains in all his works, even side-by-side with the atomic theory, the Neoplatonic concept of the world soul, as well as the doctrine of universal animism. The *De monade* is replete with Platonic doctrines: ideas *ante rem, in re* and *post rem;* the emanation of the world of soul from the world of mind, and of the corporeal realm of matter in turn from that of the soul;

[13] *Cabala del Cavallo Pegaseo,* in *Opere italiane,* II, 269–70.

the four kinds of being—intelligible, cogitable, sensuous, and shadowy—according to Plato's metaphor of the broken line in the *Republic;* the four divine furors; the five supreme species attributed to Plato and others—mind, the world soul, the human soul, the vital principle, and corporeal mass. Marsilio Ficino is called *unus e principibus Platonicis.*[14] In the *De immenso,* as in the *De l'infinito,* the infinite universe is the simulacrum of God. Here the extension of Copernican doctrines is bolder and more explicit, the refutation of Aristotelian astronomy more systematic. There is no sphere of fixed stars; there is no one "center" in the universe; the Aristotelian arguments for quintessence are rejected one by one, and the difference between earth and heavens repudiated.

There are many points of contact between *De vinculis in genere* and *De gli eroici furori.* There are as many kinds of *vincula* as there are varieties of beauty and of good (*De vinculis in genere,* in *Opere latine conscripta,* III, 645). The tone of this work is somewhat like that of treatises on human love; the heroic plane of the *Eroici furori* is absent. Philosophical theories of beauty, goodness, and love are interspersed with observations on the psychological processes of attraction and response. Bruno more than once repeats the Neoplatonic concept of beauty radiating from goodness through the four realms of beings, creating in mind the order of ideas, in the soul the series of reasons, in nature seeds, and in matter forms.

Vinculum pulchritudinis dicitur actus seu radius boni, primo diffusus in mentem, secundo in animam, tertio in naturam, quarto in materiam. Hoc mentem rationum ordine decorat, animam rationum serie complet, naturam seminibus fulcit, materiam formis exornat (ibid., p. 639).[15]

The bond of beauty is called the act or ray of the good, diffused first in mind, second in soul, third in nature, fourth in matter. It adorns the mind with the order of reasons, fills the soul with the series of reasons, strengthens nature with seeds, provides matter with forms.

He also repeats the Plotinian objection to Plato's conception of beauty as proportion of parts, and like Ficino and some other

[14] *De monade,* in *Opera latine conscripta,* I, ii, 408.
[15] Bruno repeats himself later in the same treatise, pp. 642–43, and again, pp. 684–85, where he adds that the ray is clearest in mind, clear in the soul, obscure in nature, and very obscure in the subject of natural things (matter).

writers wavers in his adherence now to one, now to the other. However, the role of beauty in love is conceived in an entirely new way.

Platonicorum quidam vinculum a certa membrorum proportione proficisci definiunt cum colorum quadam suavitate concurrente. Ad plura vero respicientibus, saltem ad hoc quod non solum res compositae et membrorum varietate consistentes vinciunt, sed interdum purus color, pura vox; nihil item citius labitur et senescit quam pulchritudo, nihil vero tardius alteratur quam figura et forma quae ex membrorum compositione exterius enitescit; vinculum igitur pulchritudinis in alio respiciendum esse videtur, quam in figura et membrorum proportione, quinimo eadem pulchritudine permanente etiam atque figura, interdum post rei amatae fruitionem praeterit amor. Quocirca praesertim in quadam rapientis et rapti condispositione vinculi ratio consistit (pp. 685–86).

Some Platonists declare that the bond [of beauty] arises from a certain proportion of members together with a certain agreeableness of colors. Those, however, who consider further—particularly, that not only do compound things having variety of members fetter one, but also at times pure color, pure voice; and likewise, nothing wanes and passes away faster than beauty, while nothing changes slower than the figure and form which shines outwardly from the composition of the members—those persons are of the opinion that the bond of beauty is to be found in something else than in figure and in proportion of members. For although beauty and figure remain the same, sometimes after the enjoyment of the beloved object, love passes. Therefore the reason of the bond consists in a certain affinity between the ravisher and the enraptured.

The bond of lovers is a certain *condispositio*.[16] Beauty itself is conceived in the *De vinculis in genere* no longer in the dualistic terms of ideal beauty and participatory material beauty, but in the relative terms of the individual's subjective reaction to whatever attracts him.

Nihil absolute pulchrum quod vinciat, sed ad aliquid pulchrum; alioqui asini amarent pulchras mulieres, simiae abolerent filios (p. 637).

Nothing which binds is absolutely beautiful, but is beautiful to someone; otherwise asses would love beautiful women and monkeys would destroy their offspring.

[16] The notion of this *condispositio*, though not the term itself, is found also in Ficino, who emphasizes affinity as a basis for love.

Cum nullum particulare sit simpliciter pulchrum, nil simpliciter vincire potest. Est tamen appetitus simpliciter pulchri in omnibus; omnia enim appetunt esse absolute et ex omni parte pulchra, non simpliciter, quod hoc est impossibile particularibus; alia enim est pulchritudo unius speciei, alia alterius, alia unius generis, alia alius (p. 638).

As no particular is beautiful simply, nothing can bind simply. Nevertheless, there exists simply in everything the appetite of the beautiful; all things desire to be absolutely beautiful in every part—not simply, for that is impossible in particulars; because the beauty of one species is different from that of another; and the beauty of one genus, different from that of another.

A contrariis dispositionibus evenit ut hic vinciatur amore, alius omnino solvatur et fastidiat illud idem. Unde patet non idem esse pulchrum et in eadem specie; simpatiam enim habet hic qua caret ille; ideo pulchrum est huic quod illi deforme; ideo qui vincire cupit videat quos possit et quomodo possit. Non ignoret autem causam huius esse satis occultam, item effectus esse inconstantes, quia hodie consonat quod cras dissonabit, imo et eadem hora (p. 646).

Because of contrary dispositions, it happens that one person is fettered by love while another is completely unbound and indeed loathes that which the other loves. Hence it is clear that beauty is not identical in the same species; for one has the sympathy which the other lacks. Likewise, what is beautiful to one is ugly to the other. So let him who would bind see whom he may bind and how he may do it. Let him not be unaware, however, that the cause of this condition is quite hidden and that the effects are inconstant, because what harmonizes today will be dissonant tomorrow—nay, at the same time.

In short, Bruno in this treatise adopts a quite modern approach to beauty and love. Generally in the love treatises of the Renaissance the Platonic doctrine that beauty is eternal is reflected in the maxim that if one person truly loves another, he will love that person always. In the *De vinculis* the permanent quality of both beauty and love is replaced by an attitude of relativity. However, Bruno in no way applies these concepts to the *Eroici furori* (pp. 658–59).[17]

The *Summa terminorum metaphysicorum,* as was mentioned in

[17] Bruno quotes the first eight lines of the opening sonnet of the second dialogue, part I, of the *Eroici furori, Io che porto d'amor l'alto vessillo,* to illustrate the lover's confusion when he is assailed by contrary *vincula.*

the Introduction, returns to Neoplatonic themes prominent in the *Eroici furori* and supposedly abandoned, according to the "development" thesis about Bruno, in the Latin trilogy published in Frankfurt in 1591. The titles of the three sections of the second, constructive part—following the definitions of the first part—are hardly those of a writer who has forsaken Platonism: *De Deo seu mente, Intellectus seu Idea*, and the third, unwritten, *Amor seu anima mundi*. Bruno posits not only "pure" (*Summa terminorum metaphysicorum*, in *Opere latine conscripta*, I, iv, pp. 63, 92) forms apart from matter, but a God transcending all being, incomprehensible, the "inaccessible" object of negative theology.

Ipse est lux, tum omnia videns, tum omnia videre faciens, quem nihil latet; . . . mens omnem intellectum, rationem atque sensum antecedens et superastans, lux inaccessibilis omnem lucem terminans a nullo terminata (p. 78).

This is the light, now seeing all, now making everything see, which nothing conceals; . . . the mind which precedes and stands above every intellect, reason, and sense, the inaccessible light terminating every light, but terminated by nothing.

Deus igitur aut nullo nomine aut omnibus nominibus erit significandus. Est enim in omnibus, quia dat esse omnibus; et est nullum omnium, quia est super omnia, singula et universa essentia et nobilitate et virtute praetergrediens. Ut autem omne esse supereminet, continet, effundit atque conservat, ita omnia, quatenus sunt extra ipsum vel aliud ab ipso, sunt vanitas, nihil, non ens; relinquitur ut ipse sit solum ens, et hoc est nomen quod ipsius maxime possumus efferre et quod auditum et revelatum accepimus, ut appelletur 'qui est' vel 'quod est' (p. 86).

God then will be signified either by no name or by all names. For he is in all things, since he gives being to all; and he is nothing of everything, because he is above everything—a single and universal essence, transcendent in nobility and virtue. Since, moreover, he surpasses, contains, gives forth, and conserves all being, thus all things in so far as they are beyond him or other than he, are vanity, nothing, non-being. It remains that he is the only being, and the name which we can best utter of him and which we accept as heard and revealed is "He who is" or "that which is."

As in the *Eroici furori*, God is both transcendent and immanent, *supra res et in rebus*; intelligence and love and beauty are likewise twofold.

Ita in divinae substantiae simplicitate haec tria possumus contemplari secundum similitudinem, ut in ea sit substantia, nempe mens prima quae producit externas omneis substantias, ut divinam substantiam intelligamus et supra res et in rebus; comparata luci est intelligentia, quae et supra res una est et in rebus omnibus una; est et amor seu pulchritudo, alia idealis supersubstantialiter supra res, alia in rebus omnibus (p. 102).

Thus in the simplicity of divine substance we can contemplate these three things by comparison, whereby substance is present, namely, the first mind, which produces all external substances, as we understand the divine substance to be both above things and in things; intelligence is compared to light, which also is one entity above things and one entity in all things; and love or beauty likewise is both superstantially ideal, above things, and otherwise in all things.

If further evidence be needed that Bruno did not, as some critics have maintained, repudiate transcendental concepts, we have his clear and explicit statement before the Venetian Inquisition, which reveals that Bruno to the last maintained that God has two aspects, transcendent and immanent.

Di più, in questo universo metto una providenza universal, in virtù della quale ogni cosa vive, vegeta e si move e sta nella sua perfezione; e la intendo in due maniere, l'una nel modo con cui presente è l'anima nel corpo, tutta in tutto e tutta in qual si voglia parte, e questo chiamo natura, ombra e vestigio della divinità; l'altra nel modo ineffabile col quale Iddio per essenza, presenzia, e potenzia è in tutto e sopra tutto, non come parte, non come anima, ma in modo inesplicabile.

Doppoi, nella divinità intendo tutti li attributi esser una medesma cosa insieme con teologi e più grandi filosofi; capisco tre attributi, potenzia, sapienza e bontà, overamente mente, intelletto ed amore, col quale le cose hanno prima l'essere, raggion della mente, doppoi l'ordinato essere e distinto per raggione dell'intelletto, terzo la concordia e simitria per raggione dell'amore. Questo intendo essere in tutto e sopra tutto: come nessuna cosa è senza participazione dell'essere e l'essere non è senza l'essenzia, come nessuna cosa è bella senza la beltà presente, cusì dalla divina presenzia niuna cosa può esser esenta; ed in questo modo per via di raggione e non per via di substanziale verità intendo distinzione nella divinità.[18]

[18] From testimony before the Venetian inquisition, as quoted by Vincenzo Spampanato, *Vita di Giordano Bruno*, pp. 709–710.

Moreover, in this universe I place a universal providence, in virtue of which everything lives, vegetates and moves and remains in its perfection. And I understand it in two ways: one, in the mode in which the soul is present in the body, entire in the whole and entire in whatsoever part, and this I call nature, shade and vestige of the divinity; the other, in the ineffable mode in which by essence, presence, and potency God is in all and above all, not as part, not as soul, but in an inexplicable way.

Then, in the divinity I understand all the attributes to be the same thing as with theologians and the greatest philosophers. I understand three attributes, power, wisdom, and goodness, or in fact mind, intellect, and love, whereby things have first their being, because of the mind, then being ordered and distinct by reason of the intellect, and third, concord and symmetry by reason of love. This I understand to be in all and above all: since nothing is without the participation of being, and being is not without essence, as nothing is beautiful without beauty present, so nothing can be exempt from the divine presence; and in this manner by way of reason and not by way of substantial truth I understand distinction within the divinity.

The basis of Bruno's philosophy is not contradiction, but duality and co-existence. There is one substance, the subject of modal and gnoseological dichotomy. Ontologically, there are the transcendent and the immanent; the two modes of matter and form, potency and act; conceptually, there are the knowable and the unknowable; hence, both a positive and a negative religion.[19]

[19] In the comparison of Bruno's *Eroici furori* to previous Platonic love treatises it has happened that one of his most important Renaissance Platonic sources, Nicholas of Cusa, has been omitted. This philosopher-theologian, frequently cited by Bruno himself, although a contemporary of Marsilio Ficino, had no direct link with the Florentine tradition of Platonism. His influence on Bruno is direct and important in such doctrines as the coincidence of contraries, the differing infinities of God and of the universe respectively, the plurality of worlds, and the motion of the earth. Like Bruno he drew physical consequences from metaphysical premises. However, it does not seem appropriate to study his influence at length in this work, not only for the formal reasons, (1) that his influence was felt much more in the *Causa* and *De l'infinito* than in the *Eroici furori* and (2) that he wrote no treatise on love; but also because Felice Tocco, while failing fully to recognize the influence of Ficino on Bruno, devotes many pages of *Le fonti più recenti della filosofia del Bruno* to the influence of Nicholas of Cusa on Bruno, after the example of F. J. Clemens' *Giordano Bruno und Nicolaus von Cusa.*

CHAPTER V

Conclusion

THE *Eroici furori* is the culmination, in Italy, of a literary tradition with a history in that country of well over a century and in the world at large of almost two thousand years. In Bruno's dialogue the genre of Platonic love treatises seems to reach a climax which exhausts its possibilities. After him no important figure in Italy chose the Platonizing dialogue of love as the vehicle for expounding his philosophy. Ficino's *Commentary* on the *Symposium* proved definitive until the late eighteenth century. The courtly tradition of superficially learned Platonizing comment upon love, deriving from Pietro Bembo, had become hackneyed before Bruno undertook to revivify the genre of love treatises. The problems of the succeeding century were very different from those of the century which ended with Bruno's demise: in science and philosophy there was the formulation of mathematical and experimental methods by Galileo, Bacon, and Descartes; in Italian literature, a new approach based on the baroque concept of the metaphor. It is to Bruno's enduring credit that on the one hand he was able to create from his by then stereotyped models a dialogue deeply imbued with his own personality and pointing the way toward the literature of his successors; and on the other hand that by his rejection of authority in his metaphysical and cosmological dialogues he helped prepare the way for his great compatriot Galileo.

The modern mind finds it difficult to understand the keen interest of the *trattatisti d'amore* and their readers in a subject matter which on the surface appears dull and lifeless, and which today has at best the appeal of an interesting museum exhibit. On the other hand, one may nevertheless appreciate their striving for intellectual and moral elevation. To understand the sentiment aroused by such a passionless body of love literature one must remember that even in the sixteenth century the "rediscovered" doctrines of Plato (combined and confused with those of Plotinus and other Neo-platonists) were new enough for their divulgence to be surrounded by an esoteric aura. Plato was still a new savant challenging the reign of Aristotle; a pre-Christian voice, expert in ancient pagan mysteries, which almost prophetically professed a philosophy of love consonant with the Christian revelation. When Plato in his dialogues met with a difficulty in epistemology or doctrine, he told a story. Renaissance scholars, following the lead of late classical philosophers, assumed that under his myths he must have wished to preserve secret doctrines; hence the popularity of interpretations of Plato. Medieval theologians had anticipated the spirit of early humanism in supplementing divine revelation with human authority. The Renaissance then reached a point at which the authority of Plato was raised to challenge that of Aristotle. Bruno was a pioneer who helped to usher in its final stage, when authority itself was judged and abandoned for the direct interrogation of nature. In this broad sense only were Telesio and Bruno and Campanella the predecessors of Galileo and Bacon. The scientific method for that interrogation was totally unknown to the generation which immediately preceded the birth of modern science. Bruno stands barely at the threshold of the modern age; the remnants of medievalism are heavy in his thought. In his mighty will, mankind seems to struggle titanically and to feel the old earth trembling under foot as it steps haltingly toward the gateway of a new world. It is from this hard-earned vantage point that man soon after strides confidently forward into the modern era in the figures of Galileo, Descartes, and Newton. The Renaissance proper does not yet represent the modern mind; but it is preeminently an age of transition, characterized by the myriad of forays and trials, contradictions and triumphs that a transitional stage entails. Bruno felt that his inquiry into nature repeated the speculation of pre-socratic philosophers. His mode of thinking is in large degree speculative; it is far removed from the way of Galileo and mathematical, experimental science. The universe is infinite because an infinite God would not make it finite. Nevertheless, Bruno's part in shattering the wall that separated man from the universe must not be underestimated because of the medieval elements which condition his thinking.

Retractions in the literature of the late Middle Ages and early Renaissance are a familiar phenomenon. The *De Reprobatione* of Andreas Capellanus, Boccaccio's wish to burn the Decameron, Chaucer's palinode to *Troilus and Cressida*, the religious qualms expressed in Petrarch's verse and prose, Iacopone da Todi's songs to divine love, Girolamo Benivieni's allegorical commentaries on his love lyrics—to cite but a few examples—are all cut from the same cloth. In them Christian conscience reacts to a code of morals —ultimately based on a naturalistic and rationalistic concept of man—that is in flagrant contrast with Christian authority. The Platonic concept of love is neither naturalistic nor Christian. Hence its history in the Renaissance follows a wavering line in relation to those two theories. In Castiglione, for example, as in Bembo and other authors who saw it in an aura of Christian sanctity, Platonic love appears to be the antithesis of courtly and mundane love. Authors such as Ficino, Benivieni, and Pico—more sensitive than the above mentioned Platonists to philosophical values—are sufficiently aware of basic antagonisms between Platonic and Christian love to see their reconciliation as a major problem. Ficino's chief philosophical work, as is well known, is the reconciliation of Platonism with Christian theology. Benivieni and Pico see Platonic love as a doctrine whose reconcilability with Christianity is difficult if not impossible; hence Benivieni's ode to Platonic love—conversely to the Platonism of Castiglione and Bembo—itself demands a retraction. The chronological fact also is significant: since in Ficino and his school Platonism had undergone a process of Christianization, sixteenth-century Platonists could see in Platonic love a religious and other-worldly corrective for mundane and sensual preoccupations.

To say that the Renaissance was an age of antitheses is not a mere platitude: it is in terms of thesis and antithesis that this dramatic period in western civilization may best be studied. Perhaps in no other age is there a more brilliant contrast and admixture of beauty and deformity, sense and spirit, freedom and restriction, conservatism and innovation. What at first appears incongruous to the researcher of today is the coexistence of these seemingly incompatible motives in the same individual, not only in succession, but simultaneously. In this respect Giordano Bruno is a typical Renaissance figure.

It is evident from Marsilio Ficino's letters that he tried to make Platonic love the actual basis of personal relationships in his Platonic Academy. On the other hand Sperone Speroni, Flaminio Nobili, and Torquato Tasso specifically, and some others implicitly, criticized the validity and practicability of the Platonic concept of love as an ethical and social norm. Leone Ebreo saw Platonic love as a philosophical principle around which he wove an entire system of doctrine. That he intended the concept as a guide to everyday morals is at least thrown into doubt by the lively contrast which the flirtatious banter of Filone and Sofia provides to his rigorous doctrine. With Bembo and Castiglione, there is a change both in the concept of Platonic love and in the attitude toward the concept. Both authors are conscious of writing for court audiences and both infuse courtly atmosphere and attitudes into their dialogues. The artistic and scholarly integrity of men who worked under Medici patronage is no longer discernible. The vestige of homosexuality inherited from the Platonic dialogues is banished. It is the *gentil donna,* someone not unlike Petrarch's Laura, who now excites love. Love of such a lady will be virtuous if restricted to conversation and desirous glances; it may even encompass the kiss. The sign of its virtue is the courtly achievements to which it inspires the lover. There is now only the pretense that a sensual love can provide the dynamic for a spiritual ascent to the realm of ideas. Castiglione and many later writers can picture the Platonic lover only as an old man in whom the fires of youth are spent. Divine love is cut off from human love and identified with an otherworldly *caritas.* In Bembo the Platonic lover is a Christian saint who is as separate from society as the saintly hermit who instructs Lavinello. The Platonic element of intellectuality maintained by Ficino, Diacceto, and Leone Ebreo is de-emphasized. Platonic love is no longer seen as being within the realm of human possibilities. The cleavage between the first and second kinds of Platonic love in Ficino's classification is complete and irrevocable. The Platonic *raptus* is relegated to a realm outside of ethics; its gnoseological implications are disregarded. What is still achievable is a mockingly pale reflection of Platonic divine love, a sort of vulgar imitation of it by gentlemen who are so old as to appear ridiculous if they love with the sensual ardor of their youth. The ideal itself becomes merely a topic for polite conversation; and one wonders whether it means much more to its proponents than to the scoffers, such as Signor Morello, who also participate in the discussions.

Nobili and Tasso voice a justified criticism of the artificiality of such treatises on love. Nobili clings to the formal outlines of Platonic love doctrines, but does not believe in them even as a system of theory. Tasso is much more explicit in his criticism of Platonizing writers on love.

The cycle seems almost to have run its course when Giordano Bruno brings the Platonic love doctrines back to their original area of importance in epistemology and ontology, which they enjoyed in Leone Ebreo. The *Eroici furori* is in part a personal allegory of Bruno's life. It is certainly not intended as an ethical guide for courtly audiences; nor is it a universal ethics. The latter is provided by his *Spaccio della Bestia Trionfante,* which one can imagine is not very unlike the ethical system which Leone Ebreo would have formulated if he had undertaken such a task. Parallel to the personal asceticism of the *Eroici furori* is the more human and natural system of morals to which Bruno occasionally alludes in the *Eroici furori* and which he had elaborated in the *Spaccio.* The importance of the love doctrine of the *Eroici furori* is both gnoseological and ethical, but the ethics are consequent upon the intellectual love of God. They are not regulative norms for nonphilosophers.

The characteristic verve of Bruno's philosophy, which sets him apart from the preceding and contemporary humanist and philosophical writers on love, whose motives he repeats in the *Eroici furori,* consists in his vision of the infinite reflecting and repeating itself in the physical universe. The *Eroici furori* is illuminated by this cosmic fire; the divinity is immanent in the physical universe and infinitely creative therein. Only in this light is the *padre oceano* of the last dialogue understandable.

Many of Bruno's deep philosophical problems are not so much those suggested by the tradition of love treatises as they are a heritage from medieval theology: the relation of intellect to will; transcendence and immanence; the concept of infinity; the nature of the soul. One must not forget that Bruno was educated and ordained as a Dominican priest.

The *Eroici furori* is by all odds the most thoroughly Neoplatonic of Bruno's Italian dialogues. Both the downward path of creative generation and the upward path of knowledge to the ultimate principle of intelligibility are clearly in evidence. It was altogether natural for an eclectic like Bruno to adhere most closely to the Neoplatonic scheme when writing about the love of supernal beauty, a theme long since given its fullest philosophical expression by Plotinus and recently taken up with renewed enthusiasm by Marsilio Ficino, Leone Ebreo, and their disciples. To supplement this philosophical framework, Bruno found ready-made a stylistic framework in vernacular love treatises, sonnets, and commentaries.

The Neoplatonism of his earliest philosophical treatises, notably the *De umbris idearum,* is modified by the materialism of the *Causa* and the ethical naturalism of the *Spaccio.* An important factor in the "return" to Neoplatonism in the *Eroici furori* is the tradition of Platonic love treatises of the preceding 116 years, which could not but influence Bruno in a work belonging to that genre. However, it is absurd to look upon the *Eroici furori* as a mere contrasting episode in Bruno's alleged progressive abandonment of Platonism. Surely there are changes in Bruno's philosophy in the direction of naturalism and sensationalism. Yet the original Neoplatonic intuition of the universe, which for Bruno is a dualistic conception because of his emphasis upon the transcendent-immanent distinction, recurs throughout his works from beginning to end. There is no "final" rejection by Bruno of either Platonism or transcendentalism. Even more conclusive in this regard than the *Summa terminorum metaphysicorum* is Bruno's testimony before the Venetian inquisition. Of all the many philosophic traditions which Bruno studied and from which he drew, the decisive one is the Platonic. It is for this reason that the *Eroici furori* is indispensable for the understanding of Bruno's philosophy.

Much of the literary value of the *Eroici furori* is a result of the grace with which Bruno fused and renovated traditional forms and motives. The *Eroici furori* is the only work in Italian literature which combines the dialogue form of Leone Ebreo and other authors of Platonic love treatises with the older tradition of prose commentary upon verses.

The chief ethical and gnoseological message of Bruno's philosophy, explicit in the *Eroici furori* and implied in the *De la causa* and the *De l'infinito,* is that man can progress, at first discursively from the knowledge of particulars to the knowledge of the infinite in nature, and finally, in a suprarational intensification of the will, to a unity with the ultimate source of all, infinite self-existent substance. In so doing the soul returns to its celestial origin. Knowledge is not the assimilation of doctrine, but intuition, fantasy, rapture. And he who intuits God in the universe is beyond pain and death, fearless of whatever eventuality, conscious of his own divinity. The same God who dwells within man's soul animates everything in the entire universe; hence the human consciousness need but call upon its own resources to discover the divine truth latent in the universe, which reflects God not in the way of medieval trinitarian symbolism, but in the way of natural inhering causality. Man belongs to the cosmos; his spirit is united with the absolute.

This knowledge of the essential unity was a possession of ancient sages, a secret heritage revealed only to initiates, yet forever rediscoverable in the interior recesses of nature and the human soul. There is for Bruno a practical reason for adhering to the esoteric idea, in his attitude toward the relation of philosophy and religion. He believes his philosophy to transcend the Christian religion of the people. There is no conflict between them, to his mind, so long as they are kept separate. It thus becomes essential to exclude the vulgar and the ignorant from scientific teachings which they cannot understand.

Bruno was led by his philosophic enthusiasm and synthetic approach to follow now one, now another doctrinal lead. What he did in the *Eroici furori* was to elaborate variations on the theme of divine love offered him by humanistic love treatises. He found other appealing leads in the quite dissimilar writings of Raymond Lully, the geometrician Fabrizio Mordente, Nicholas of Cusa, Copernicus, and Lucretius, and in the thesis common to many humanists, both Byzantine and Italian, of Plato's superiority to Aristotle. Inevitably, he was unable to organize such widely divergent material into a unified philosophy. More serious is his apparent unawareness of the direct contradictions, metaphysical and moral, which remain in his writings. Some of the differences between the Neoplatonic *Eroici furori* and the more materialistic *Causa*[1] and *De immenso*—the ontological value of matter, for example—cannot be reconciled. The heritage of love treatises upon which Bruno drew in the *Eroici furori* is responsible not only for the comparatively more dualistic, ascetic, and generally Platonic tone of that dialogue, but also for its esthetic and moral dignity in contrast to the derisive tone of the *Cena,* the sarcasm of the *Cabala,* and the scurrility of the *Candelaio.* In one sense, however, Bruno's work was the opposite of Ficino's and of Ficino's disciples: he wished to completely separate his philosophy, still based on the Neoplatonic conception, from the dogmas of Christianity. Unlike Ficino, Bruno put contemplation and free philosophical inquiry above revelation. His attitude toward classical, as well as ecclesiastical, authority is much more critical than that of Ficino, Pico, and the humanist authors who preceded him. He is fully conscious of his own speculative strength. He relies more than they upon the intuitive testimony of his own consciousness: he will listen to the "God within him."

Although to the Christian mind finiteness is limitation, imperfection, to the Greek mind infinity argues imperfection, for its existence is limited to the realm of the potential. Hence the Greek God, in so far as Greek philosophers speak in monotheistic terms, is finite, and the Greek universe is finite. Christian theologians had

---

[1] The *Causa* has, however, strong elements of Neoplatonism, as I have said in Chapter IV.

long since established the infinity of God when Bruno sought to equalize man's concept of the universe with the Christian conception of God. It is for this reason that he is able plausibly to argue in defense of his cosmology that his philosophy more than any other favors religion, by certain of its tenets: an infinite universe caused by infinite divine power, the incorruptibility of substance, innumerable intelligences, eternal soul, and an immutable divine justice above human actions (*Cena*, p. 96).

Bruno saw himself as a prophet, as a hero of the intellect destined to set free his own and future generations from the dead weight of sterile doctrines, in particular the Aristotelian concept of the universe, and to enlighten men who would listen in the face of the institutionalized "ignorance" and mediocrity of schools and church. There is almost a presage of romanticism in Bruno's dramatic sense of life, his internal seething, his passion for rebellion and spiritual freedom and his feeling for the grandiose and unlimited. His ideal —of great historical importance—was to seek the truth for oneself. The persistence with which he adhered to this principle through seven years of trial and imprisonment is a story that has been told and retold within the limitations prescribed by the available documents. He wished to persuade the hierarchy, on the basis of his avowed adherence to the Catholic faith, to let him pursue unfettered his philosophic investigations. His condemnation as a heretic was consistent with the tenets and discipline of the Roman Catholic Church, notwithstanding his attempt to separate his philosophic speculations from the theological dogmas with which they frequently conflicted. His heroic death in defiance of that authority, inevitably reminiscent of the demise of Socrates, is one of the salient glories of the human spirit. His awareness of playing a historic and prophetic role is unmistakable in the defiant words which he hurled at his judges: "You perhaps tremble more in pronouncing the sentence than I in receiving it." There is an unconscious presage of these words in the *Eroici furori*: *Certo che meglio è una degna ed eroica morte, che un indegno e vil trionfo* (*Eroici furori*, I, iii, 369: Certainly a worthy and heroic death is better than an unworthy and cowardly triumph). His death reaffirmed the great sincerity of his writings and dramatized his message to his own and future generations with the uttermost intensity.

> Bench' a tanti martir mi fai suggetto,
> Pur ti ringrazio, e assai ti deggio, Amore,
> Che con sì nobil piaga apriste il petto,
> E tal impadroniste del mio core,
>   Per cui fia ver, ch' un divo e viv' oggetto,
> De Dio più bella imago 'n terra adore;
> Pensi chi vuol ch' il mio destino sia rio,
> Ch' uccid' in speme e fa viv' in desio.
>   Pascomi in alta impresa;
> E bench' il fin bramato non consegua,
> E 'n tanto studio l'alma si dilegua;
>   Basta che sia sì nobilment' accesa;
> Basta ch' alto mi tolsi,
> E da l'ignobil numero mi sciolsi.[2]

[2] This sonnet is translated on p. 188.

Appendix

THE AUTHORSHIP OF THE COMMENTARY, ATTRIBUTED TO EGIDIO COLONNA, ON GUIDO CAVALCANTI'S *CANZONE,* "DONNA MI PREGA"

Gerardo Bruni in his *Catalogo critico delle opere di Egidio Colonna*[1] refers to this work by the title *Sopra la canzone di Guido Cavalcanti: "Donna mi priega,"* and lists it[2] among the "doubtful works" of Egidio Colonna. Bruni lists seven manuscripts of the commentary, two of which are fourteenth-century:

Barb. misc. XLV, 47, c. 105, sec. XIV (Now Vaticano Barberiniano Latino 3953).
Firenze, Laurenz. Plut. 41, cod. 20, sec. XV–XVI.
Firenze, Laurenz. Plut. 90 Sup. cod. 135, sec. XV.
Firenze, Riccard. 1651, sec. XIV.
Firenze, Magl. cl. viii, cod. 36, sec. XVI–XVII.
Firenze, Magl. cl. vii, 1108 (Strozziano, cod. 336), sec. XVII.
Firenze, Magl. cl. vii, 1023 (Strozziano, cod. 950).

He adds:

Da notare che i codici più antichi, e cioè il barberiniano e il riccardiano, ambedue del sec. XIV, sono anonimi . . . Gli altri manoscritti a cominciare da quelli del sec. XV, recano il nome di Egidio.

It is to be noted that the oldest manuscripts, both of the fourteenth century, are anonymous. . . . The other manuscripts, beginning with those of the fifteenth century, bear the name of Egidio.

[1] Florence, 1936.
[2] Number 115, p. 169.

In the fourteenth century Benvenuto da Imola and Filippo Villani mention Egidio Colonna as the author of a commentary on Guido Cavalcanti's *Canzone*. Benvenuto da Imola (d. 1390) in his *Comentum super Dantis Aldigherij Comoediam*,[3] says (I, 342):

. . . Et tangit curialiter illum Guidonem dicens: *forse cui Guido vostro ebbe a disdegno*. Et hic nota quod iste Guido non est delectatus in poeticis, licet fuerit acutus philosophus et subtilis inventor, qui fecit inter alia unam cantionem de amore ita profunde quod Aegidius romanus non erubuit facere comentum super eam; et Dinus florentinus magnus physicus similiter glosam fecit.

. . . And he mentions that Guido elegantly as saying, "Whom perhaps your Guido held in disdain." And note here that this Guido did not take delight in poetry, although he was an acute philosopher and subtle inventor, who wrote among other things a *canzone* about love so profound that Egidio Romano was not ashamed to write a commentary about it; and the great Florentine physician Dino similarly wrote a gloss.

Filippo Villani in his *Liber de civitatis Florentiae famosis civibus*[4] writes as follows:

Hic [Guido de Cavalcantibus] de amore qui in sensualitate potius, quam in ratione versatur, eiusque natura, moribus et affectu subtilissime disputando, elegantissimam et mirabilem edidit cantilenam, in qua physicae inaudita hactenus, ingeniosissime et copiose tractavit; cujus mirabilem intellectum mirati Dinus de Garbo physicus, de quo supra habui mentionem, et Aegidius Romanus, insignis physicus, commentare dignati sunt.

He [Guido Cavalcanti] published a very elegant and remarkable *canzone* which very subtly discusses love, which consists of sensuality rather than reason, and its nature, qualities, and affection. In this *canzone* he treated most ingeniously and abundantly matters of natural science previously unheard of. The natural philosopher Dino del Garbo, whom I mentioned above, and Egidio Romano, the renowned natural philosopher, having admired its remarkable understanding, deigned to comment it.

Nicola Mattioli in his *Studio critico sopra Egidio Romano Colonna*[5] rejects the authorship of Egidio Colonna on the somewhat

[3] Five vols., Florence, 1887.
[4] Florence, 1847, ed. Gustavo Camillo Galletti, p. 33.
[5] *Antologia agostiniana*, vol. 1 (Rome, 1896), pp. 195–221.

dubious grounds that the commentary is unworthy of Colonna, who would have had a more moral and Christian approach to the *Canzone*, and because Mattioli doubts that the life of Guido Cavalcanti attributed to Filippo Villani, which attributes a commentary on Guido Cavalcanti's Canzone to Egidio Colonna, was written by Filippo Villani. Even if the authenticity of this biography were disproved—it is accepted by G. C. Galletti, Filippo Villani's editor—there remains the reference to Egidio Colonna by Benvenuto da Imola, which Mattioli does not mention.

Bruno Nardi in *Dante e la cultura medievale*[6] and James Eustace Shaw in *Guido Cavalcanti's theory of love*,[7] though differing in their interpretations of Cavalcanti's *Canzone*, agree with Mattioli that Colonna is not the author of the commentary attributed to him. Shaw declares that the philosopher Colonna could not be the author of a commentary which shows a lack of understanding of philosophic terms and philosophic thinking.

The manuscript Vaticano Barberiniano 3953, containing Cavalcanti's poem and the commentary, was published in a printed edition, edited by Gino Lega.[8] Lega dates the manuscript from both internal and external evidence as having been written between 1325 and 1335. The manuscript contains mainly Italian verse and includes such well known poets as Guinizelli, Guittone d'Arezzo, Dante, and Cino da Pistoia, in addition to poems and a commentary by Niccolò de' Rossi, under whose direction, apparently, the manuscript was made.

The commentary attributed to Colonna is in Italian, and if written prior—perhaps well prior—to 1325, as seems certain, is among the earlier documents of Italian prose. For that reason it seems highly unlikely that it could have been written by a non-Tuscan. Egidio Colonna was a Roman. Furthermore, of the 213 works written by or attributed to Egidio Colonna, all the others are in Latin. The available evidence strongly indicates that the commentary attributed to Egidio Colonna actually was not written by him. There is no link between the early manuscripts of this commentary and

[6] Bari, 1949.
[7] Toronto, 1949.
[8] Bologna, 1905.

the attribution of *a* commentary to Egidio Colonna by Benvenuto da Imola and Filippo Villani. In the absence of further information the work must be considered anonymous.

It is interesting to note that the colophon of our manuscript immediately following the commentary concludes with the words *Minatii est.* Lega's footnote[9] states that these words are written in red by the hand of the amanuensis who copied the commentary. Can the author have been a Minatius?

[9] *Il Canzoniere* . . . , p. 126.

Bibliography

PRIMARY SOURCES

Barba, Pompeo della. Spositione d'un sonetto platonico, fatto sopra il Primo effecto d'Amore, che è il separare l'anima dal corpo de l'Amante, dove si tratta de la immortalità de l'anima secondo Aristotile, e secondo Platone. Florence, 1554.

Bembo, Pietro. Gli Asolani e le Rime. Turin, 1932.

Benivieni, Girolamo. Opere di Girolamo Benivieni Fi[o]rentino. Novissimamente rivedute et da molti errori espurgate con una Canzona dello Amor celeste & divino, col Commento dello Ill. S. Conte Giovanni Pico Mirandolano distinto in Libbri III. Et altre Frottole de diversi Auttori. Venice, 1522.

Betussi, Giuseppe. Il Raverta, dialogo di Messer Giuseppe Betussi nel quale si ragiona d'Amore e degli effetti suoi, in Trattati d'amore del Cinquecento, ed. by Zonta.

———La Leonora. Ragionamento sopra la vera bellezza di Messer Giuseppe Betussi, in Trattati d'amore del Cinquecento, ed. by Zonta.

Bruno, Giordano. Opere italiane, ed. G. Gentile and V. Spampanato. 3 vols. Bari (2d ed.), 1925–27.

———Opera latine conscripta, ed. F. Fiorentino, F. Tocco, H. Vitelli, V. Imbriani, and C. M. Tallarigo. 3 vols. in 8. Naples and Florence, 1879–91.

———Due dialoghi sconosciuti e due dialoghi noti, ed. Giovanni Aquilecchia. Rome, 1957.

Castiglione, Baldassare. Il libro del Cortegiano, ed. Vittorio Cian. Florence (4th ed.), 1947.

Dante Alighieri. Le opere di Dante. Testo critico della Società Dantesca Italiana. Florence, 1921.

———Il convivio, ed. G. Busnelli and G. Vandelli. Florence, 1934.

———La vita nova, ed. M. Barbi. Florence, 1932.

Diacceto, Francesco Cattani da. Opera omnia. Basel, 1563.

———Panegirico allo amore. Rome, 1526.

———I Tre libri d'amore . . . con un Panegirico all'amore. Venice, 1561.

Equicola, Mario. Libro di natura d'amore, novamente stampato et con somma diligentia corretto. Venice, 1536.

Ficino, Marsilio. Opera omnia. 2 vols. Basel, 1561.

———Sopra lo amore o ver' Convito di Platone. Florence, 1544.

———Supplementum Ficianum, ed. Paul Oskar Kristeller. 2 vols. Florence, 1937.

Garbo, Dino del. "La glossa latina di Dino del Garbo a 'Donna me prega' del Cavalcanti," ed. G. Favati, *in* Annali della Scuola Normale Superiore di Pisa, Serie II, XXI (1952), Fasc. I–II, 70–103.

Gottifredi, Bartolomeo. Specchio d'amore, dialogo di messer Bartolomeo Gottifredi nel quale alle giovani s'insegna innamorarsi, *in* Trattati d'amore del Cinquecento, ed. by Zonta.

Lega, Gino, ed. Il Canzoniere Vaticano Barberino Latino 3953 (già Barb. XLV. 47). Bologna, 1905.

Leone Ebreo. Dialoghi d'amore, ed. Santino Caramella. Bari, 1929.

Marino, Giovanni Battista. Poesie varie, ed. Benedetto Croce. Bari, 1913.

Medici, Lorenzo de'. Comento sopra alcuni de' suoi sonetti, *in* Opere, I, 1–141. Bari, 1913.

Nobili, Flaminio. Trattato dell'Amore Humano. Lucca, 1567, as republished Rome, 1895.

Petrarch, Francesco. Le rime sparse e i trionfi, ed. Ezio Chiorboli. Bari, 1930.

Pico della Mirandola, Giovanni. De hominis dignitate, Heptaplus, De ente et uno, e scritti vari, ed. Eugenio Garin. Florence, 1942.

———Opere omnia. Basel, 1572.

Plato. Omnia D. Platonis opera tralatione Marsilij Ficini. . . . Venice, 1571.

Plotinus. Enneades cum Marsilii Ficini interpretatione . . . , ed. F. Creuzer and G. H. Moser. Paris, 1896.

Romei, Annibale. I discorsi, *in* Angelo Solerti, Ferrara e la corte estense nella seconda metà del secolo decimosesto. Città di Castello, 1899.

Rosso, F. Paolo del. Comento sopra la Canzone di Guido Cavalcanti. Florence, 1568.

Sansovino, Francesco. Ragionamento di Messer Francesco Sansovino nel quale brevemente s'insegna a' giovani uomini la bella arte d'amore, *in* Trattati d'amore del Cinquecento, ed. by Zonta.

Speroni degli Alvarotti, Sperone. Dialogo di amore, *in* Opere di M. Sperone Speroni degli Alvarotti tratte da' Mss. originali (5 vols., Venice, 1740), I, 1–45.

Tasso, Torquato. I dialoghi amorosi. Lanciano, 1914.

Tullia d'Aragona. Della infinità di amore, *in* Trattati d'amore del Cinquecento, ed. by Zonta.

Varchi, Benedetto. Opere. 2 vols. Trieste, 1858–59.

Vieri, Francesco de'. Lezzione di M. Francesco de' Vieri fiorentino, detto il Verino Secondo. Per recitarla nell' Accademia Fiorentina, . . . l'Anno 1580. Dove si ragiona delle idee, et delle bellezze. Florence, 1581.

Zonta, Giuseppe, ed. Trattati d'amore del Cinquecento. Bari, 1912.

SECONDARY SOURCES

Bartholmess, C. Jordano Bruno. 2 vols. Paris, 1847.

Berti, Domenico. Vita di Giordano Bruno da Nola. Florence, 1868.

Cicuttini, Luigi. Giordano Bruno. Milan, 1950.

Clemens, Friedrich Jakob. Giordano Bruno und Nicolaus von Cusa. Bonn, 1847.

Corsano, Antonio. Il pensiero di Giordano Bruno nel suo svolgimento storico. Florence, 1940.

Denomy, Alexander J. The Heresy of Courtly Love. New York, 1947.

Firpo, Luigi. Il processo di Giordano Bruno. Naples, 1949.

Gentile, Giovanni. Il pensiero italiano del rinascimento. Florence, 1940.

Greenberg, Sidney. The Infinite in Giordano Bruno. New York, 1950.

Guzzo, Augusto. I dialoghi del Bruno. Turin, 1932.

Hunt, Richard William. "The introductions to the 'Artes' in the twelfth century," in *Studia Mediaevalia in honorem admodum reverendi patris Raymundi Josephi Martin.* Brussels, Flanders, 1943, pp. 85–112.

Kristeller, Paul Oskar. The Philosophy of Marsilio Ficino. New York, 1943.

——"A philosophical treatise from Bologna dedicated to Guido Cavalcanti: Magister Jacobus de Pistorio and his 'Quaestio de felicitate'" in *Medioevo e Rinascimento: studi in onore di Bruno Nardi* (Florence, 1955), I: 425–463.

——"Francesco da Diacceto and Florentine Platonism in the Sixteenth Century," in *Biblioteca Vaticana* Studi e Testi, vol. 124, *Miscellanea Giovanni Mercati* (Vatican, 1946), pp. 260–304.

——Studies in Renaissance thought and letters. Rome, 1956.

Lippari, Angelo. The Dolce Stil Nuovo according to Lorenzo de' Medici. New Haven, 1936.

Lorenzetti, Paolo. La bellezza e l'amore nei trattati del Cinquecento. Pisa, 1917.

McIntyre, James Lewis. Giordano Bruno. London, 1903.

Mercati, Angelo. Il sommario del processo di Giordano Bruno. *Biblioteca Vaticana Studi e Testi,* vol. 101. Vatican, 1942.

Michel, Paul-Henri, ed. and trans. Giordano Bruno, *Des fureurs héroïques.* Paris, 1954.

Mondolfo, Rodolfo. "La filosofia di Giordano Bruno e la interpretazione di Felice Tocco," in *La cultura filosofica,* V (1911), 450–82.

Nardi, Bruno. Dante e la cultura medievale. Bari (2d ed.), 1949.

Olschki, Leonardo. Giordano Bruno. Bari, 1927.

Pflaum, Heinz. Die Idee der Liebe. Leone Ebreo; zwei Abhandlungen zur Geschichte der Philosophie in der Renaissance. Tübingen, 1926.

Quain, Edwin A., "The medieval accessus ad auctores," in *Traditio,* III (New York, 1945), 215–64.

Robb, Nesca A. Neoplatonism of the Italian Renaissance. London, 1935.

Rosi, Michele. Saggio sui trattati d'amore del cinquecento; contributo alla storia dei costumi italiani nel secolo XVI. Recanati, 1889.

Saracista, Maria. La filosofia di Giordano Bruno, nei suoi motivi plotiniani. Florence, 1935.

Salvestrini, Virgilio. Bibliografia delle opere di Giordano Bruno e degli scritti ad esso attinenti. Pisa, 1926.

Sarauw, Julie. Der Einfluss Plotins auf Giordano Brunos Degli Eroici Furori. Leipzig, 1916.

Shaw, James Eustace. Guido Cavalcanti's Theory of Love. Toronto, 1949.

Singer, Dorothea Waley. Giordano Bruno, His Life and Thought. With annotated translation of his work *On the Infinite Universe and Worlds.* New York, 1950.

Singleton, Charles Southward. An Essay on the *Vita Nuova.* Cambridge, Mass., 1949.

Spampanato, Vincenzo. Vita di Giordano Bruno. Messina, 1921.

———L'antipetrarchismo di Giordano Bruno. Milan, 1933.

———Documenti della vita di Giordano Bruno. Florence, 1933.

———Bruno e Nola. Castrovillari, 1899.

Spaventa, Bertrando. "La dottrina della conoscenza di Giordano Bruno," in *Saggi di critica.* Naples, 1867.

Tocco, Felice. Le opere latine di Giordano Bruno esposte e confrontate con le italiane. Florence, 1889.

———Le opere inedite di Giordano Bruno. Naples, 1891.

———Le fonti più recenti della filosofia del Bruno. In: *Rendiconti della Reale Accademia dei Lincei,* Classe di Scienze Morali, Storiche e Filologiche. Serie Quinta (Rome, 1892), I, 503–38; 585–622.

Tonelli, Luigi. L'amore nella poesia e nel pensiero del Rinascimento. Florence, 1933.

Troilo, Erminio. La filosofia di Giordano Bruno. Turin, 1907.

Index